¡Órale! lowrider

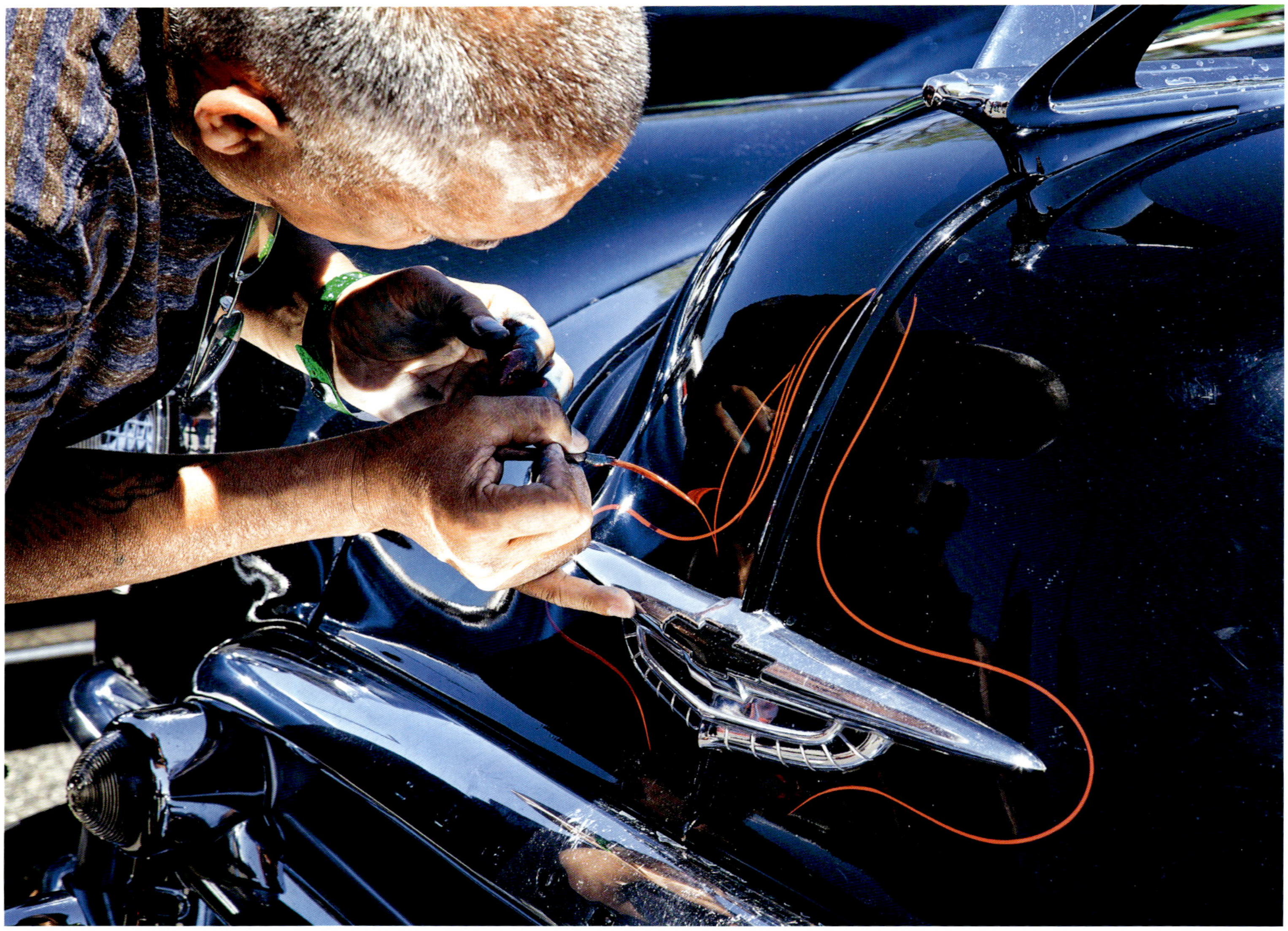

¡Órale! lowrider

CUSTOM MADE IN NEW MEXICO

Essay by Don J. Usner
Interview by Katherine Ware

Photography selections
by Daniel Kosharek and Katherine Ware

Museum of New Mexico Press
Santa Fe

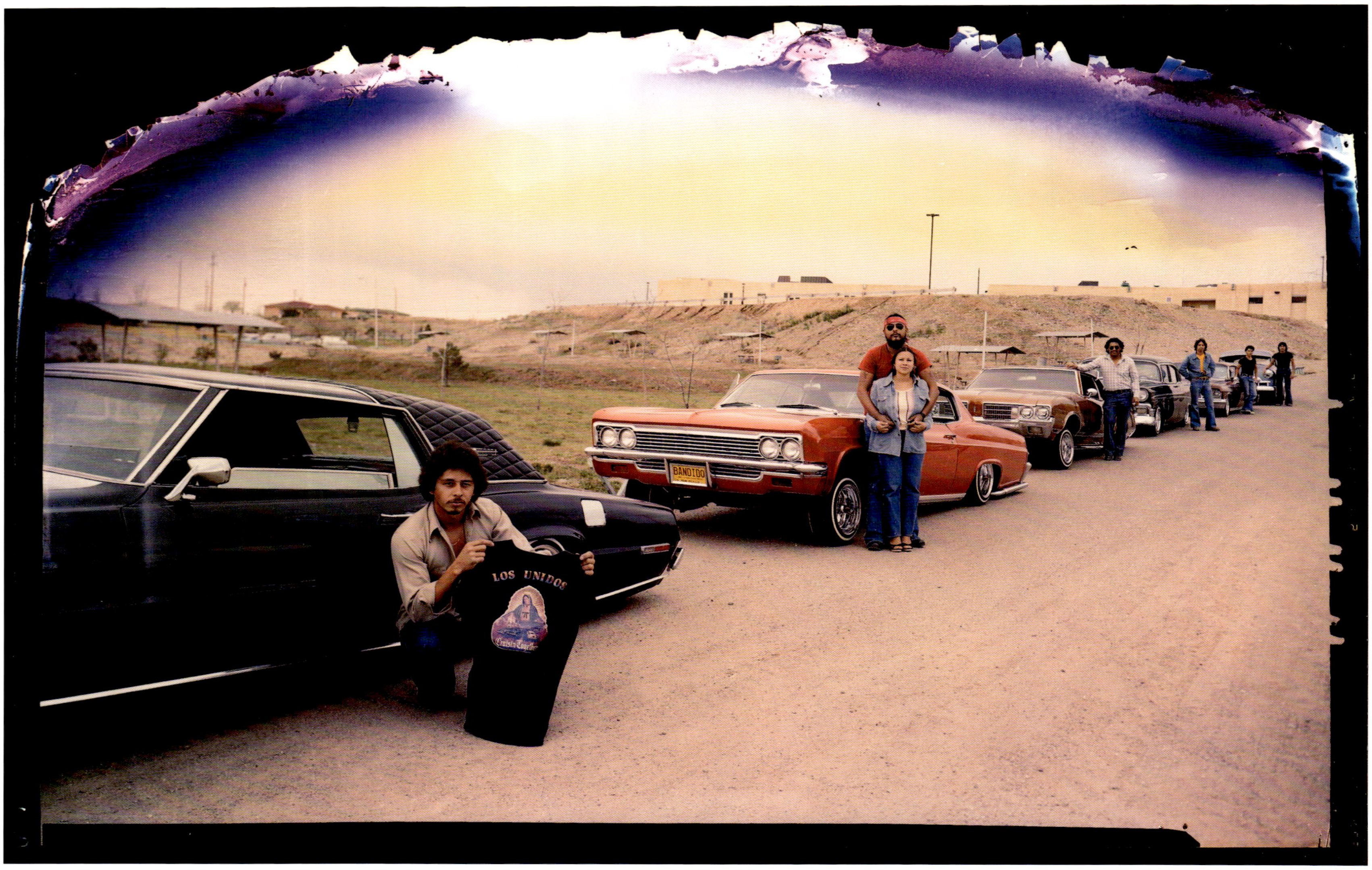
LOS UNIDOS
BANDIDO

contents

Cruising in the Heart
of the Lowrider World 9
DON J. USNER

The Art of the Lowrider:
Interview with Meridel Rubenstein 41
KATHERINE WARE

Wheels 61
LEVI ROMERO

Plates 59

Acknowledgments 176

About This Book 178

About the Exhibitions 179

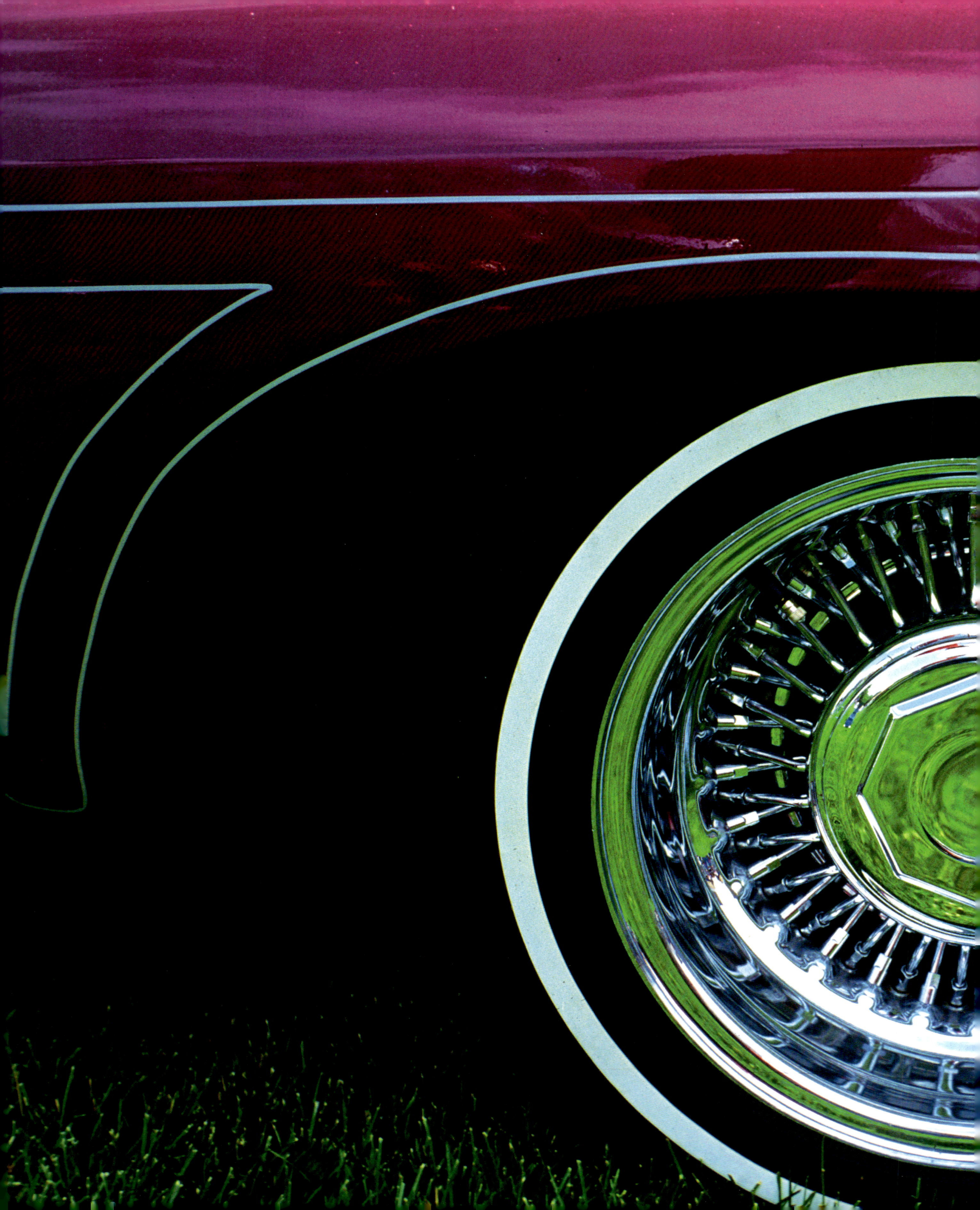

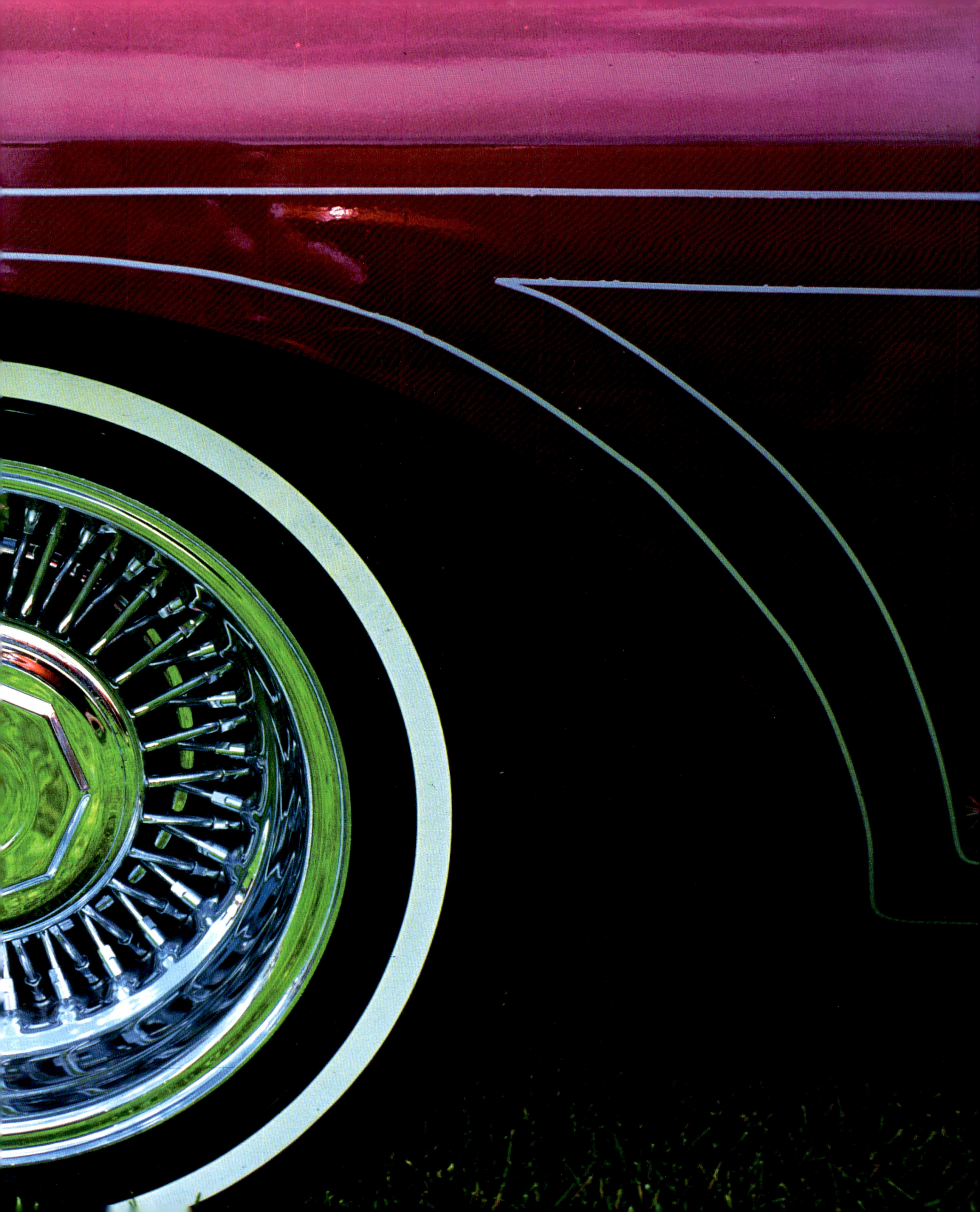

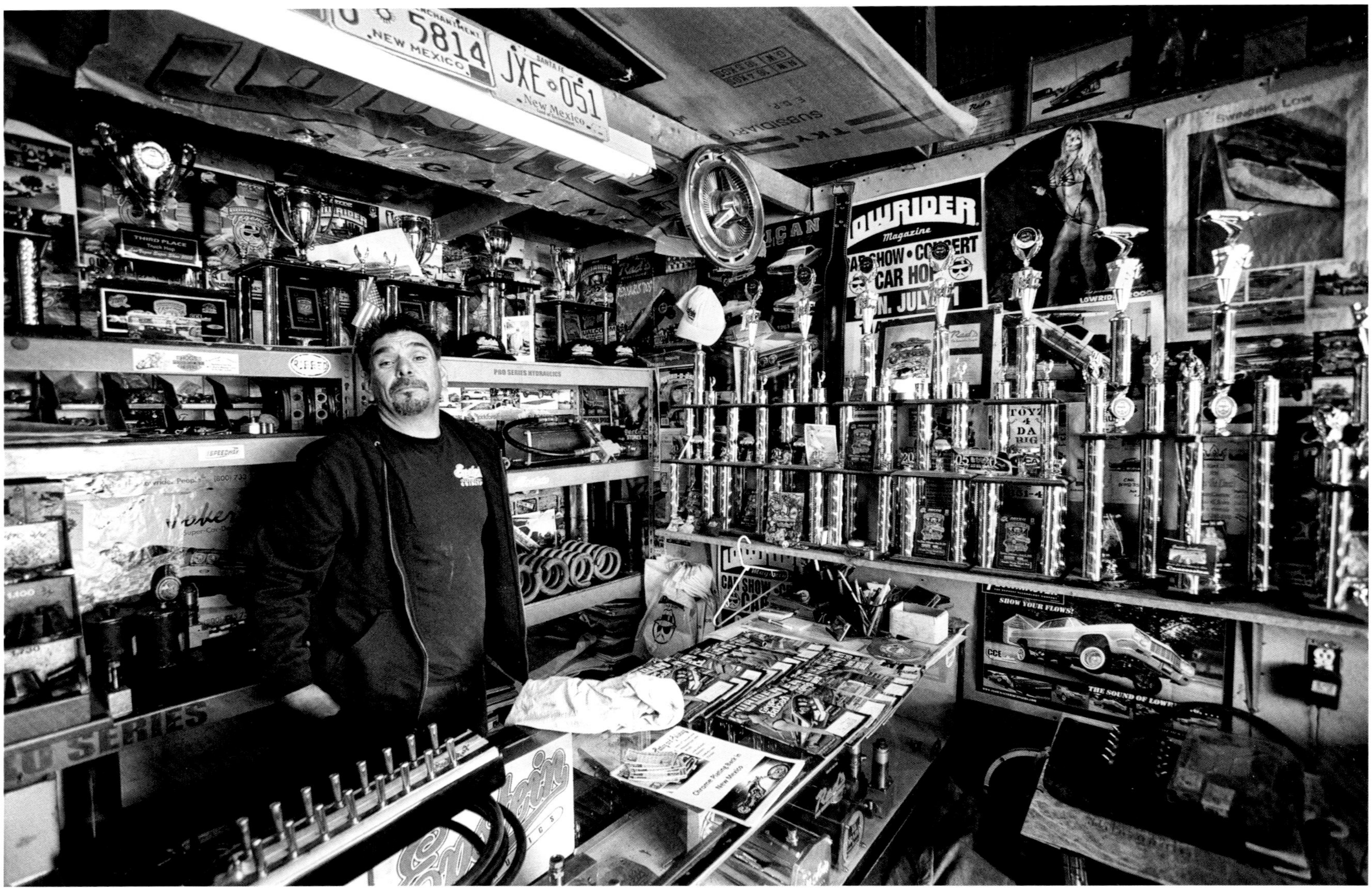
5814
NEW MEXICO
JXE 051
New Mexico
Magazine
THIRD PLACE
SHOW YOUR FLOWS!

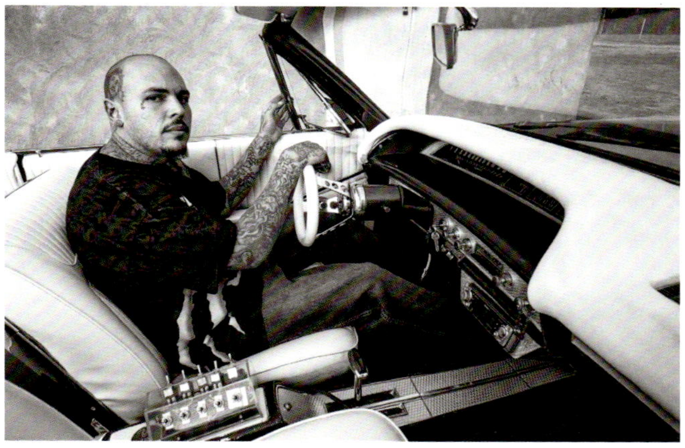

cruising in the heart of the lowrider world

TEXT AND PHOTOGRAPHS BY DON J. USNER

It's just a few days before Good Friday as I drive slowly down a narrow road that leads to La Cuchilla Plaza in Chimayó. Not far from the plaza's adobe *capilla*, I find my way to Ray's Hydraulics, a two-bay garage in the shade of gnarled old cottonwood trees that frame the still-snowcapped peaks of the Sangre de Cristo Mountains.

As I pull into the yard filled with an assortment of vehicles awaiting repair, I notice a mural on the garage's exterior wall. In bright colors and rough brushstrokes it depicts two 1964 Chevy Impalas in front of the Santuario de Chimayó, a two-hundred-year-old church situated just a couple of miles down the road and long revered as a holy site. Both cars are classic "lowriders," their suspensions altered so that they can ride just inches off the road surface.

"That's part of who we are," a voice declares as I study the painting, and I turn to see two men emerging from the darkness of the garage to greet me. They introduce themselves as Epimenio "Eppie" Martínez and Ernie López. Eppie continues, "How could it not be? Look where we are, man—we're in the Holy Land!"

Eppie's father, Ray, has been running this business for decades, and Eppie has worked here long hours, too, since he was a kid. But today he and friends are getting their lowriders ready to take a cruise—and not to the Caribbean in a big boat. This will be a slow drive to the Santuario on Good Friday. They'll meet up with other lowriders from around the valley, as they do every year, to make a pilgrimage of sorts, on wheels. The belly-dragging cars will merge with the throngs of thousands of visitors making their way to the shrine more piously, on foot, as is the annual Holy Week ritual in Chimayó. It will be a leisurely ride, *bajito y suavecito*, low and slow,

opposite
Eppie Martínez and His Trophies, Chimayó, 2012

above
Elmo Sánchez, Chimayó, 2015

at about the same pace as the foot travelers. But that's how it should be for such a journey—and with this kind of car.

As Eppie shows me around the shop, he radiates his love for this place and his enthusiasm for transforming ordinary automobiles into cars that ride outrageously close to the road and can hop up on end, like one of the lowriders in the mural. Eppie has been building lowriders for a long time, but his specialty is fashioning these lowrider "hoppers." Trophies won at car shows line the walls, a testament to his dedication and skill, but Eppie deflects all credit for his success. "I owe it all to my dad. When I was twelve, he gave me my first car, that one right there," he says, pointing to an emerald green 1953 Chevy Bel Air with a white top, hood open. "My dad was more into racing, and he raced that '53, but I used to tell him, 'I want that car.' So he let me have that car to fix up before I could even drive, and then later I drove it to high school—and then one day I lowered it."

Eppie is more than happy to oblige when I ask to see one of his hoppers in action. Before I know it, the yard is cleared and he is maneuvering a blue hardtop Impala into place. This is no ordinary lowrider; it's been beefed up with extra-powerful hydraulics and a reinforced frame to take the punishment of banging down onto the ground. The workers come out of the garage to watch as Eppie flicks switches on a remote control and begins "clowning" with the hopper—making it bounce, front wheels in the air, higher with each jolt from the hydraulic pumps and cylinders. Grins spread all around—none brighter than Eppie's—as he concentrates, hitting the switch at just the right time, until the car stands dizzyingly close to vertical, pounding the earth

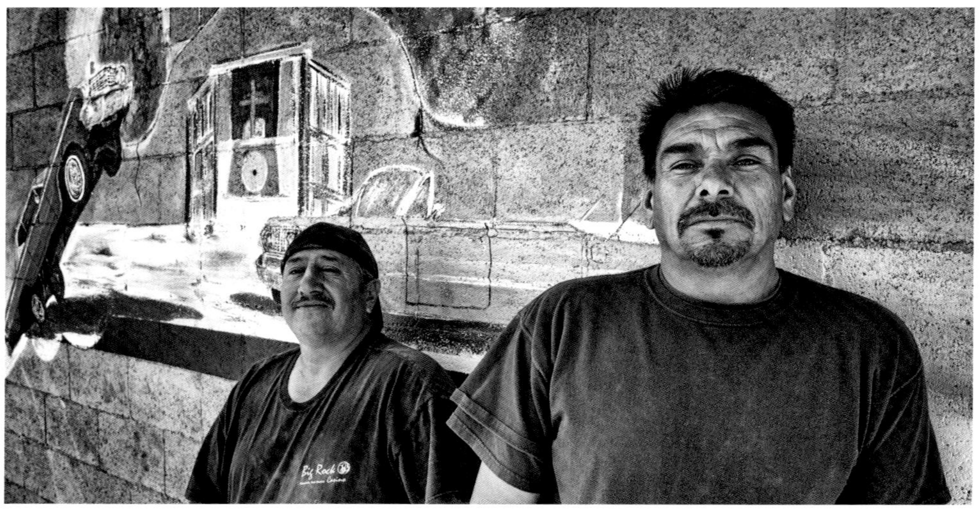

Ernie López and Eppie Martínez with Lowrider Mural, Chimayó, 2012

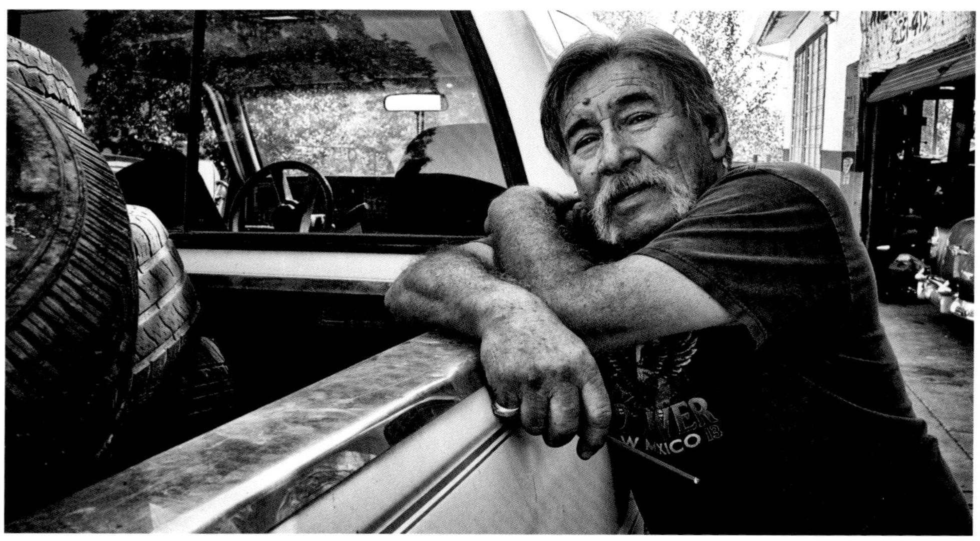

Ray Martínez, Chimayó, 2015

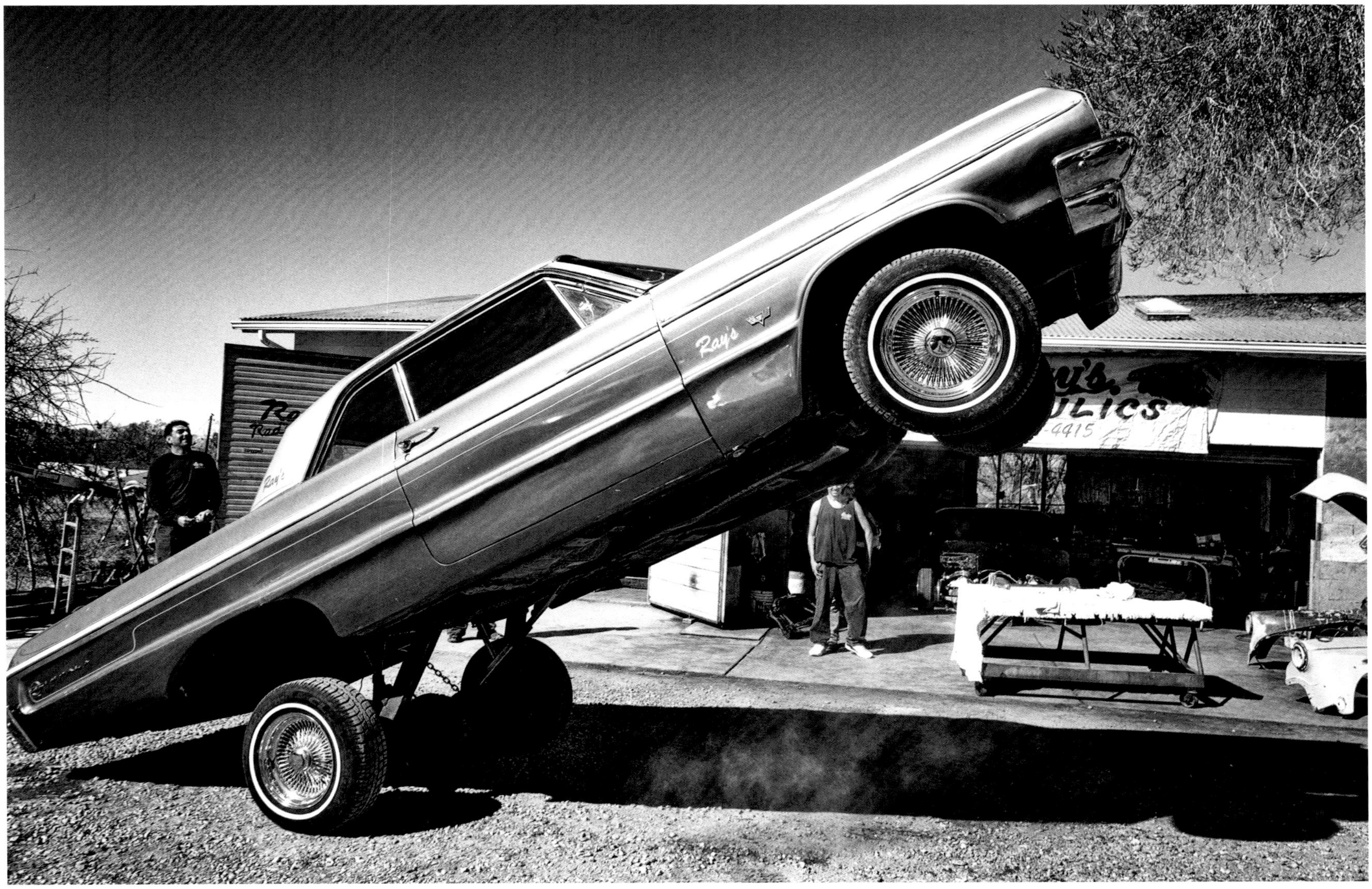

Eppie Clowning with His '64 Impala, Chimayó, 2012

and stirring up a cloud of dust. It's astonishing that the car can take the battering, and no wonder that Eppie holds several records for his hopping prowess.

After the Impala, Eppie takes out another hopper, a mid-'80s Ford Ranger pickup, and repeats his clowning performance, with even more impressive results. But it's a momentary diversion from the work at hand, and soon all the mechanics are back to prepping their cars for the cruise to the Santuario.

A few miles down Highway 76 toward Española from Eppie and Ray's, near the neighborhood known as Plaza de Dolores or Plaza Abajo, Bobby Chacón and his partners run quite a different kind of car operation. The yard beside Bobby's double-wide trailer—like Eppie's, a dusty lot surrounded by venerable cottonwoods—is filled with a crazy assortment of old vehicles, the raw material for the polished products that will someday take shape as lowriders. White lettering on the door of one old vehicle, a 1950s-era dump truck, spells out "Los Guys," the name of a local car club to which Bobby belongs.

Bobby and his cousin Chris Martínez greet me as a shiny black 1950 Chevy, driven by Elmo Sánchez, from Velarde, rumbles into the yard. The three introduce themselves, but before we can talk, a small foreign car pulls up and a woman gets out, announcing, "I'm the mom," as she hurries into the home. Bobby explains that the woman, Candie, is his mother and that when he and his brothers and cousins were out playing in the fields around their home in Chimayó as kids, she

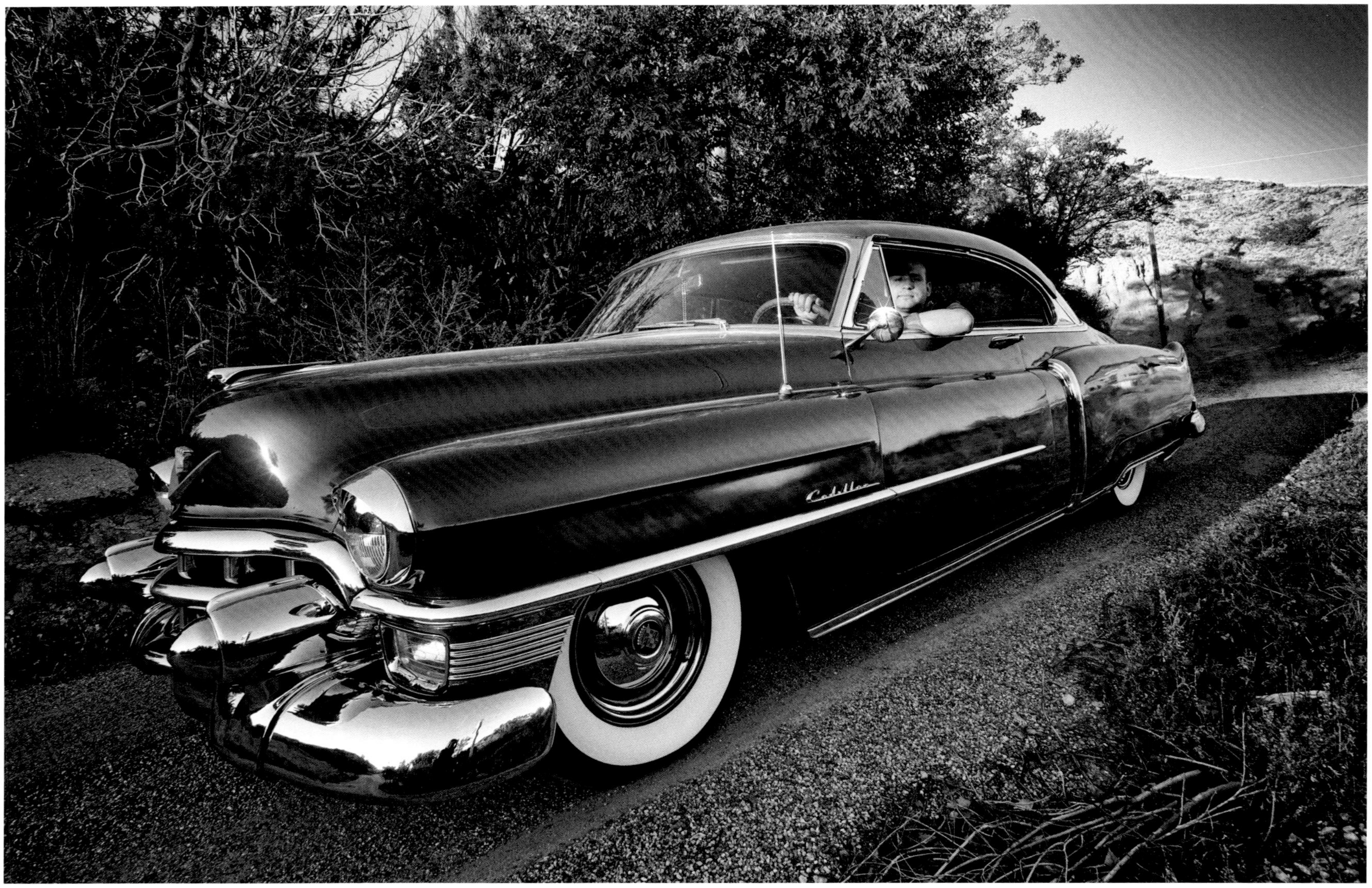

Chris Martínez in His '53 Cadillac, 2015

was like a mom to all of them and would call them in with a loud, "Come on in, you guys!" And hence when the guys later became involved with cars and decided to form a club, the name Los Guys seemed appropriate.

Candie is a grandmother now, and she's coming to see Bobby's new child, only two days old. Bobby and the others follow her inside to have a look at the infant. "I'll be right back," Bobby apologizes. Family is a high priority, even among the most fanatic lowrider creators.

When Bobby and his companions come back from the trailer, it's all about cars again. These three Los Guys are best known for their classic "bombs"—American cars made from about 1930 to 1955—and they pull them out to show me. First Chris glides by in his dazzling 1953 Cadillac, painted a rich maroon and restored meticulously. It gleams in the sun like a time capsule from a bygone era, as if it had just rolled off the lot to the cool clinking of change in an L.A. high roller's pocket. Such a painstakingly restored gem would never be subjected to the rigors of hopping, but Chris has installed on its suspension inflatable bags that raise and lower the car the way hydraulic pumps do on other lowriders. As the Caddy comes to a stop, Chris flicks a switch and the car sinks nearly to the ground with a smooth hissing sound as the airbags deflate.

Bobby motors up and parks his blue '51 Chevy bomb, also "slammed"—lowered, that is—and then retrieves from the yard a rich orange '61 Chevy Impala, which isn't a bomb at all but is considered a "traditional" lowrider— a term that refers to favored lowrider models from the late 1950s through the 1980s. Impalas rank among the favorite cars of all time for lowriders, because of their long, sleek lines, but also because their chassis design makes them ideal for lowering. Impalas are so popular that they go by the shorthand slang "deuce" for a 1962 model, "trey" for a 1963, and "foe" for a 1964. Any Impala, and especially a convertible, is a prize, but Bobby is particularly proud of this one because it was recently used in a Hollywood movie. He'll be taking it in the Good Friday entourage to the Santuario with Elmo, Eppie, and his friends from La Cuchilla.

Next, Elmo fires up his Chevy, a dark black beauty of a bomb, and drives slowly around the dirt lot. When he stops, he climbs out of the behemoth and extracts a life-size Elmo Muppet doll from the back seat, placing it in the front passenger seat so that its head hangs out the window as if it were cruising in the car. As Elmo the person backs out of the vehicle, I notice among his numerous tattoos an image of Elmo the Muppet on his shaved head, and another on his shirtless torso. Elmo's broad smile, and the whimsical images of the Muppet, completely deflate the stereotype of danger associated with the shaved, tattooed man in baggy pants driving a lowrider, a caricature that long—and unfairly, many would argue—haunted lowriders.

As Eppie's and Bobby's stories suggest, in northern New Mexico lowriders make a statement not only about individual car owners, but about cultural identity. In this holy land of sacred earth and tongue-biting chile, the craft of the lowrider is deeply embedded in family and place. An obsession for building lowriders has been passed through networks of extended families reaching across generations. There are many other types of customized cars in New Mexico, from hot rods to custom cars to classic cars and "Euros" (small cars that aren't necessarily European), but over the past half century the lowrider has become a symbol as evocative of the region's Hispano identity as homegrown chile and the local dialect of Spanish. It's an apt juxtaposition, that mural at Ray's garage of the lowriders and the legendary church, for both are symbols with potent resonance throughout northern New Mexico.

Almost any kind of vehicle can be made to ride low, but a lowrider requires several features besides the signature low-slung profile. Just exactly which characteristics are essential to "lowrider" status may be debatable, but renowned lowrider Fred Rael, from Española—whom *Lowrider* magazine calls "a time-tested and true veteran of Lowrider culture"—sums up the basics by stating his idea of what a traditional lowrider is not: "If it isn't low, doesn't have small-spoke rims, whitewall tires, and a nice paint job, it isn't a lowrider."

A drive through Chimayó or any other small town in northern New Mexico reveals numerous rusting relics waiting to be resurrected as lowriders. They're propped up on blocks beside double-wide trailers, half-covered with tarps in apple orchards, or lined up in rows along flowing acequias. Just about every make and model of car and truck is represented in the weathering

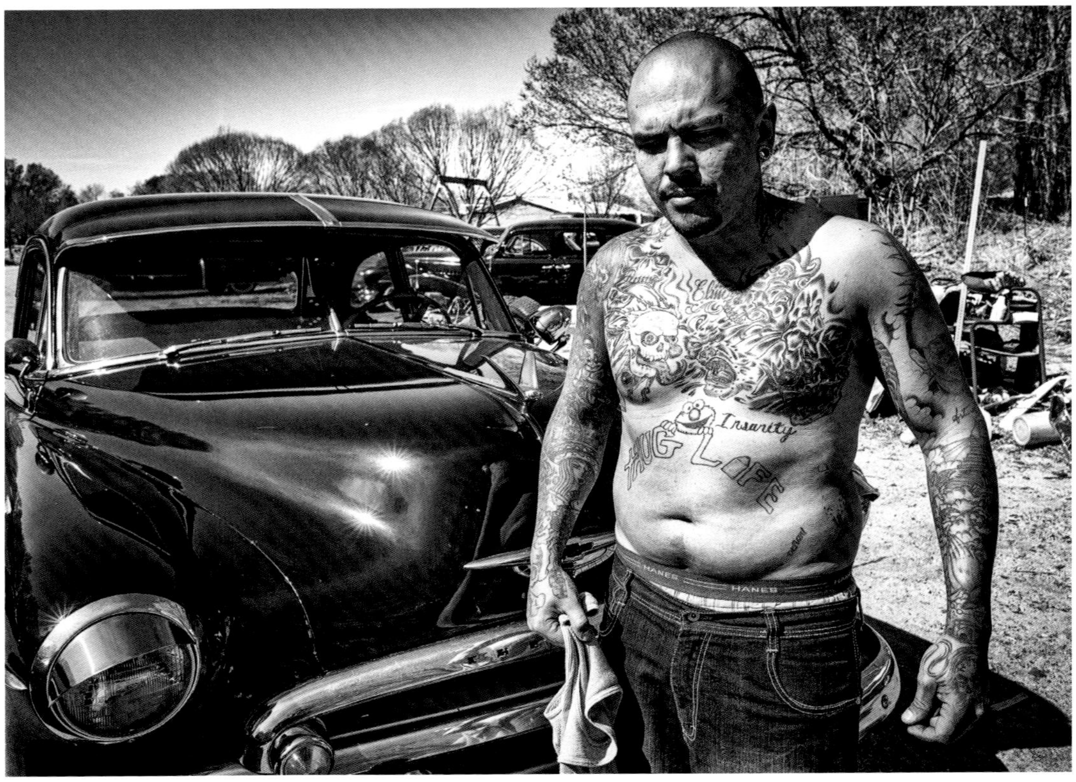

Elmo Sánchez with his '50 Chevy, 2012

assemblages. Each vehicle comes with its own history and an imagined future as a lowrider painted and chromed to perfection.

Finished lowriders abound, too, but they remain tucked away in garages, sheltered in carports, or carefully protected with covers. ("You wouldn't believe what's behind those garage doors in Chimayó," Eppie says. "There are a lot of prizewinning lowriders hidden around this valley.") The lowriders may emerge for organized cruises like the one to the Santuario, or on weekends on popular cruising streets in Española, Santa Fe, or Albuquerque. Some scarcely see the light of day, as their time to shine comes only at big regional shows, to which they're transported in closed trailers. But no matter their stature, cruiser or show car, lowriders are treasures to their owners, personal prizes that they cherish and often regard as family heirlooms. Their owners may fire them up only once a year, but when they do, it is with great pride.

Lowrider aficionados, like their cars, themselves are called lowriders, and there's a brotherhood of them in northern New Mexico. Throughout the region they cultivate and celebrate a fixation with transforming cars and trucks into lowriders. Individual lowrider owners are recognized by the cars they drive, also known as their "rides," so many conversations include references such as, "You know Fred—he drives the silver '64 Impala." Or, "Do you know Johnny?" "Maybe—what's his ride?" The cars are not so much status symbols as identifiers, totems that say much about the taste as well as the talent and style of the owners.

Lowriders also carry with them a weighty personal significance. Although lowrider craftsmen aim to impress with glitter and gleam, to show off artistry and technical prowess, they also express through their creations passion and pain, faith and sorrow—and humor. Each vehicle embodies a story, sometimes in a painted mural memorializing a lost loved one or depicting a narrative of struggle and redemption. They are all redolent with memories of extended family, community, and place.

"We show what we have inside," says Eppie. "When you see a lowrider's car, it's his style, his charisma. Our cars are our life. You work so hard for it, and show what you've got, show your people. We survive inside ourselves in different ways, and we show ourselves in our art. Our cars are art. It's always been that way and always will."

Most lowrider devotees make the cars as a hobby, although that word doesn't do justice to the devotion involved. Some do much or all of the work themselves in home garages, or they may turn to specialists—body workers, mechanics, painters, upholsterers—to take care of various phases of the car modification. Others hire out shops like Eppie and Ray's, or David Vigil's across the valley, Carmelito Martínez's in La Puebla, or one of several in Española, Santa Fe, and Albuquerque, to make their rides to their own specifications. Whatever route they choose, it can take many years to save up money, buy parts (or scavenge them from those aging vehicles stashed around the property), and put in the countless hours of work, usually on nights and weekends, to make one of these elegant mechanical marvels. There is a lifelong learning curve involved in becoming adept at the complicated technical aspects of taking apart and reassembling vehicles, often from the ground up. To say this is a labor of love would be an understatement. It's a preoccupation that demands much of the car owner and his or her family members, who are attached to their lowriders and give them names.

Each lowrider is a one-of-a-kind creation, and the care that lowrider owners show for building and caring for these cars can be summed up best by a simple expression in Spanish: *con mucho cariño*, "with much affection." The phrase certainly applies to the way Johnny Martínez feels about working on his cars. Martínez, who is from Chimayó, has built and owned lowriders, and although he has a penchant for hot rods, his comments ring true for all who spend their time working on old cars.

"I love to work on cars," he says. "I love to touch them. I like to put my hands on these cars, just to be around them, build them, and then see them again and what comes out at the end. Because I can stay in the garage there—I can lock myself in there and it's just like another world. Just being in there with the old cars. Sometimes I go in there, they don't know where I'm at. I just open the door and close it and I sit down in there and just look at the cars and I say, 'Dude, wow.' It takes me back into the fifties. That's what I like about it."

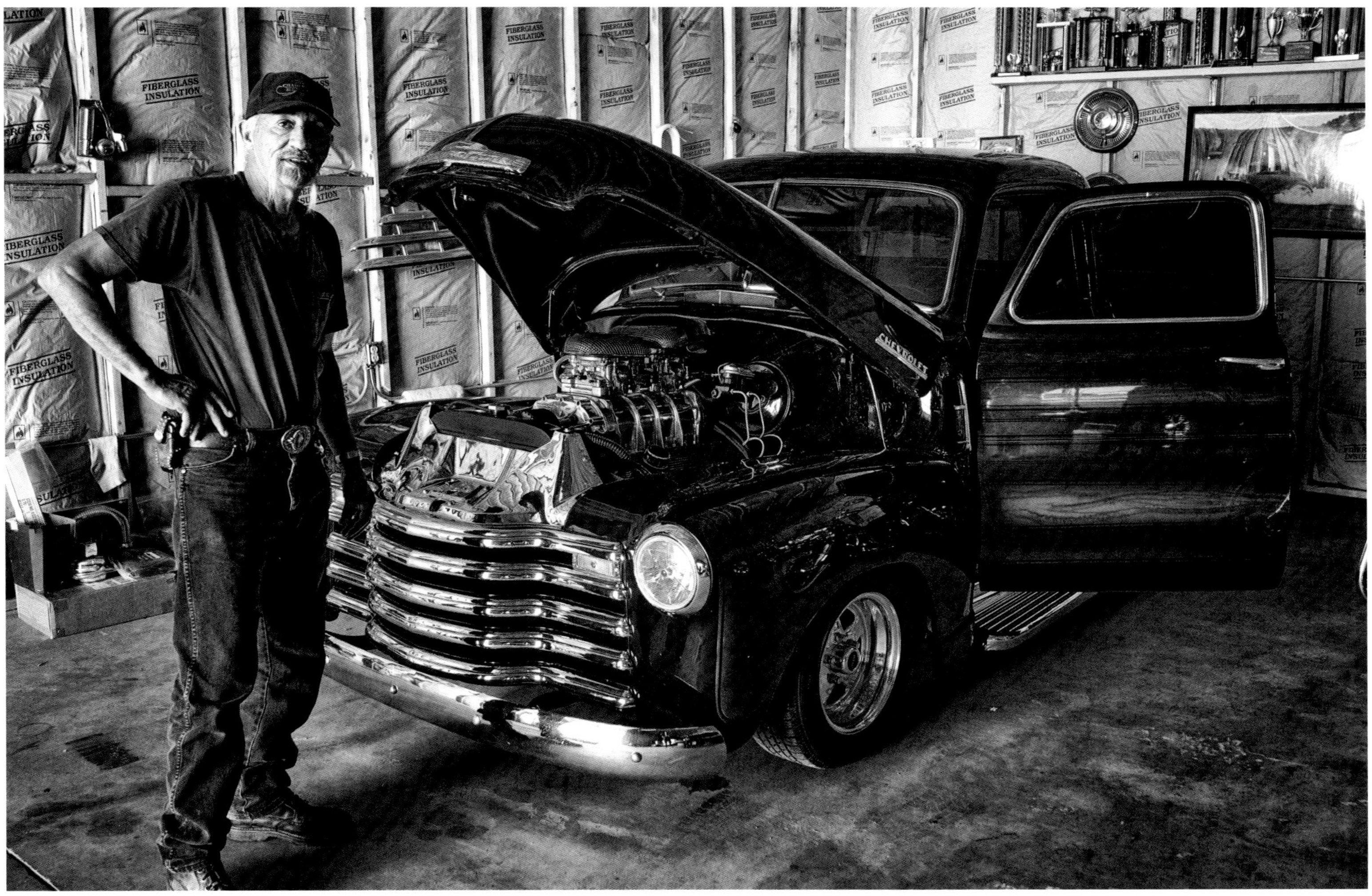

Johnny Martínez with His '50 Chevy Pickup Street Rod, 2015

Lowriders are by no means unique to one ethnic group, but since their beginnings they have found a particular richness of expression among Mexican Americans in the Southwest and on the West Coast. As Desiree Duda, the organizer of an Española car show held in conjunction with annual fiestas, told a reporter for the *New York Times* in 2004, "Lowriding is part of who we are as Latinos and Latinas. It's our history." The microcosm of northern New Mexico belongs to this expansive Latino cultural sphere, even as New Mexicans have developed their own expressions of their ethnicity and culture, including a particular lowrider style.

When I was growing up in the 1960s, lowriders only occasionally plied the dirt roads in Chimayó, where I spent summers at my grandmother's house. These curiously altered cars were to become a frequent sight there and on the highways, main streets, and plazas throughout northern New Mexico, but in those days they were not common—and they were not always welcome. The Chimayó *viejitos* who schooled me in the ways of the world associated lowriders with pachucos, and therefore regarded the cars as the inventions of miscreants, hardly worth a passing glance. They frequently reminded me to steer clear of them and everything else connected with pachucos, by which they meant any nonconforming or troublemaking youth in Chimayó. In fact, the word "pachuco" had become little more than a pejorative for such a character.

I remember my sister racing home wild-eyed to Grandma's once to report that some "pachucos in a lowrider" had stopped on the highway to offer her a ride. Her fear resonated with me, and I shuddered to think how close she had come to misfortune, but I realize now that the apprehension we felt was merely a manifestation of a widespread stereotyping of young Hispano men in lowriders. I wish now that those supposed pachucos had offered me a lift. They were probably just out for a cruise and meant no harm at all, and I'm sure I would have loved their car. Perhaps I would have caught the lowrider bug myself.

Little did I know then that the so-called pachucos of northern New Mexico represented a faint echo of a dynamic cultural movement that had begun in the 1930s in the barrios of Juárez, Mexico, and El Paso, Texas (aka Chuco Town), and had taken root in East L.A. Nor did I know that many people attribute to pachucos the invention of the lowrider car, as well as the habit of cruising low and slow.

The urban pachucos were best known for their attire, their Mexican streetwise panache, and their peculiar dialect of Mexican Spanish, *caló*, which blended Spanish (including archaic vocabulary from the fifteenth century), English, Nahuatl, and a dialect spoken by Spanish gypsies. Their zoot-suit "drapes" were composed of baggy pants that narrowed at the ankles, loose jackets, long pocket chains, and fedoras. The women, too—*pachucas*—embraced a distinctive style, sporting teased hair, plenty of makeup, short skirts, and long coats. Occasionally they, too, put on zoot suits, in defiance of feminine standards of the day. As an additional style statement, pachucos drove lowriders.

In northern New Mexico, early lowriders took up the car style but rarely adopted the full pachuco getup. More typically, they would wear baggy pants with plain white T-shirts, sometimes suspenders. Fedoras and zoot suits rarely appeared here except perhaps on special occasions. The local pachuco attire reflected the isolation of the region from urban centers where the style originated. Still, New Mexicans shared the urban pachucos' desire to carve out an authentic identity in an Anglo-dominated world.

John González, from Las Vegas, New Mexico, isn't a lowrider, strictly speaking, but he has put on a zoot suit on more than one occasion. He has a passion for building custom cars, vehicles that have been altered in significant ways that may or may not include lowering them. One of John's prizes is a 1951 Buick that exemplifies the approach of a custom car builder: the frame, engine, dash, and seats all come from a 1978 Oldsmobile, while the top is chopped and the rear lowered, giving the car a kind of stance that has "attitude" written all over it. "When I finished chopping it," John says, "and slammed it and did all kinds of old-school stuff on it, I saw it just leaning back like that, and I looked at it, and I said, 'That guy looks like a pachuco! Too cool!' So that's how I got the name El Pachuco for the car, and that car has won all kinds of awards." To emphasize his point, John painted a zoot-suit figure on the side. Similar imagery adorns lowriders and has become iconic in lowrider culture.

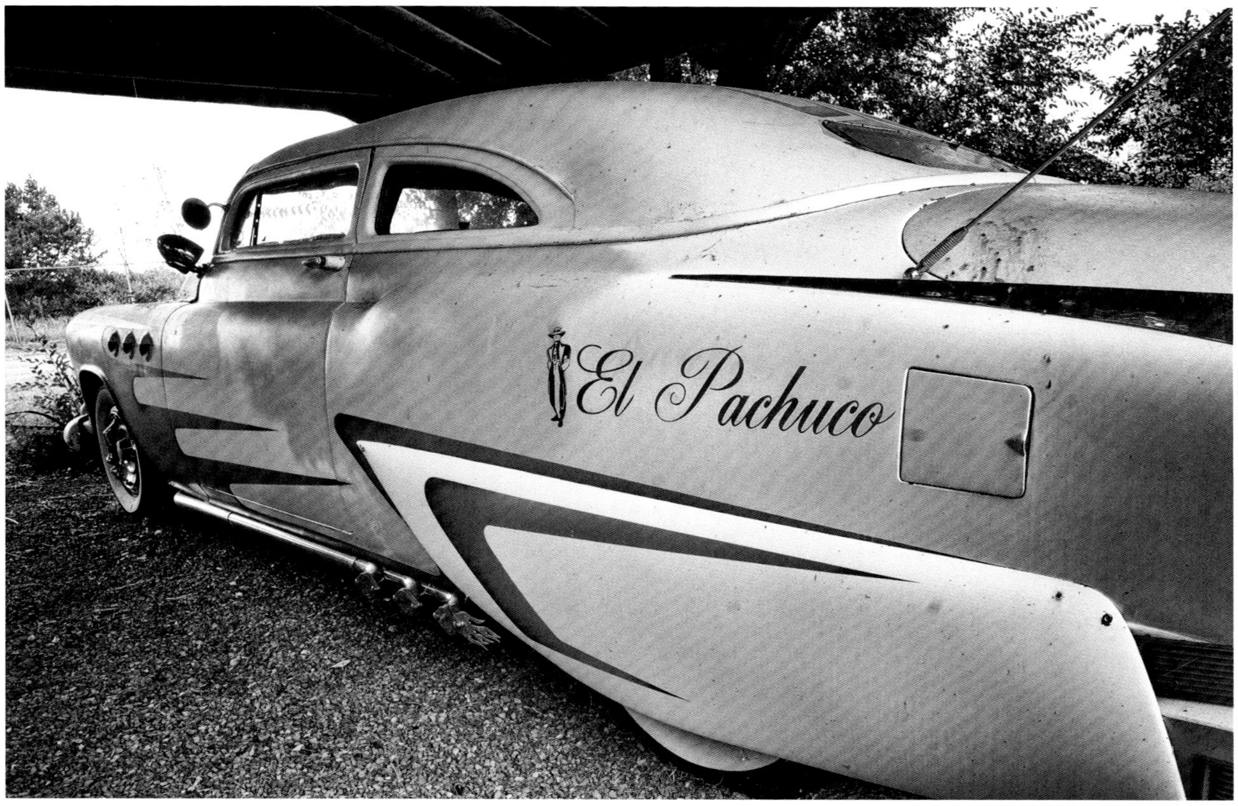

John González's '51 Buick, El Pachuco, 2015

In the beginning, lowriders, zoot-suited or not, simply loaded cars' trunks with sandbags so that the cars dropped low to the road, or they used torches to heat up the springs and compress them to let the car sink low into that striking, belly-scraping stance. In the street slang, this was called *tumbándolo*, "dropping it," and a lowered car was *tumbado*, "dropped." Small wheels added to the effect. These putative first lowriders emerged in Juárez and El Paso around 1939 and carried with them the original lowrider aesthetic when they moved to southern California in the late 1940s.

Some lowriders dispute this history, placing the style's origin among Mexican Americans in southern California. Some claim that lowriders had their beginnings in northern New Mexico. It's hard to say for sure, but perhaps Española lowrider Fred Rael has it right when he says, "Nobody's really sure how lowriding really started or who really started it, because you've got to figure, a lot of the people in Los Angeles weren't from Los Angeles. Half of my family was out there already. So there were people from New Mexico out there, and people were going back and forth—to El Paso, or San Antonio, too. And they'd see something in one place or the other and say, 'Hey, I want to try that,' and it kind of evolved from there."

Wherever lowriding started, lowriders from the beginning incorporated a pachuco flair into their dress and manner. That style and lowrider cars were inseparable and *pachuquismo* was to remain characteristic of lowriding for a long time after Mexican Americans had moved on to other expressions of social identity.

After World War II, L.A. car manufacturers, auto parts manufacturers, aircraft industries, and other businesses welcomed an influx of war veterans, many of them possessing mechanical skills they had learned in the service. A number of these were New Mexicans, who had moved to L.A. for the abundant jobs. There, the customized car trend focused on hot rods, but in contrast to the hot- rodders, who beefed up cars—mostly Fords—with large engines and jacked them up for better traction, working-class Mexicans across the river in East L.A. advanced an aesthetic in direct contravention of these norms. Instead of raising cars and driving them fast, they chose to build lowered cars—using mostly Chevrolets—and drive them very slowly. As Fred Rael puts it, "The lowriders never wanted to go fast; they just wanted to look good when they got there."

The main defining feature of early lowriders was the position of the vehicle—as close to the ground as possible. Little else was required. Lowriders then lacked fancy paint jobs, but they made up for it in other ways. Whereas hot-rodders eliminated fenders and other heavy pieces and extraneous parts, lowriders embraced decoration. They freely added or retained trappings like fender skirts, curb feelers, visors, spotlights, and headlight eyebrows—and plenty of glinting chrome. If you could get one, an ice-can window air cooler was a plus, and it was best to have plush upholstery (preferably from Tijuana), the dangling fringes known as dingle balls, and "flipper bar" hubcaps (chrome hubcaps with raised bars cutting across them). Some of the vehicles of choice for early lowriders were the 1939 Chevy Deluxe, the 1948 Chevy Fleetline, and the 1950 Chevy Bel Air hardtop. These cars, readily available as inexpensive used vehicles, were easy to modify, and parts for them were plentiful.

Just as important as the lowriding car for making a public pronouncement of style was the cruise. And the L.A. lowrider phenomenon, car and costume and cruising included, was not lost on car enthusiasts in northern New Mexico. After all, L.A. was just a long ride on Route 66 from Albuquerque, and many New Mexicans, as Fred Rael points out, had family in southern California. In northern New Mexico the lowrider habit took off a bit later than in California, but, pollinated by the fervor in L.A., it found fertile ground among car enthusiasts here, especially in the Española Valley.

Eppie's father, Ray, drove to visit relatives in California on Route 66 in the very car—the '53 Bel Air—that he would later give to Eppie. And it was precisely along this legendary road that Calletano Martínez drove his lowrider when he took a break from his job in L.A. to visit his family in Chimayó. His nephew Carmelito Martínez—now one of northern New Mexico's best-known lowriders and the proprietor of a La Puebla garage—was immediately smitten. "I saw my first lowrider when my uncle Calletano came home from working in California," says Carmelito. "He had a lowrider and he took me for a ride, and I decided right there that I wanted one of those. My first car was a '41 Chevy. I paid eighty bucks for it."

Vince Trujillo also remembers lowriders coming to Chimayó from California, the first driven by another Eppie Martínez (no relation to Eppie of hopper fame). "It was my cousin Eppie Martínez. He came from California, driving a 1956 Chevy. It was the first lowrider here in Chimayó, from California—that's when everything started here in Chimayó. He used to live

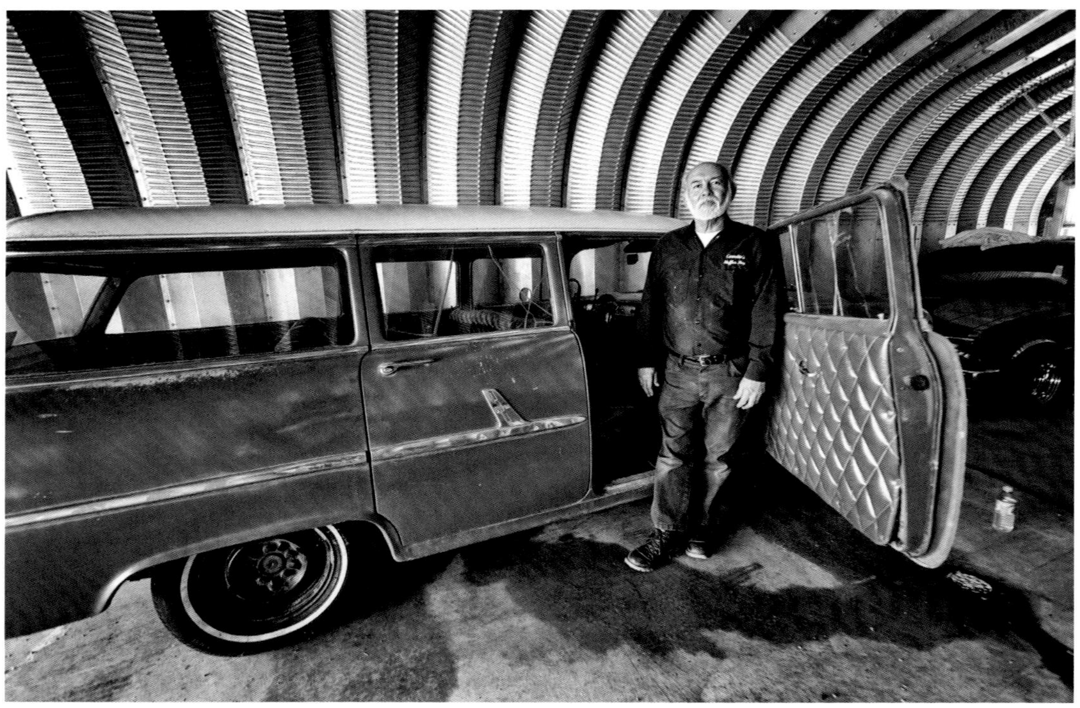

Carmelito Martínez and His '55 Chevy Wagon, 2012

in California; then he moved back to New Mexico many, many years ago. He brought that 1956 Chevy, a black one, I remember. It was lowered. Yeah, it was a beautiful car. That was about 1960. And me, growing up seeing him and other guys coming back from California and playing with the hydraulics, I said, 'I'm gonna have one one of these days. I'm gonna have one."

David Vigil, who for decades has been building lowriders, hot rods, and other kinds of cars out of his Chimayó garage, remembers clearly the first lowriders he saw, which also came from California in the early 1960s. "Some guys came from California driving lowriders. It was Medardo Martínez and Margarito De Agüero—who they called Maggie. Medardo, he had a dark blue '54 Chevy with dark blue, diamond-tuck upholstery. Oh, it was *bien bonito*! And Maggie, he had a '58 Chevy that was lowered, too. They showed us how to do it, and we started making lowriders right after that."

The California pipeline was a two-way street, with New Mexicans going back and forth and carrying with them ideas and techniques for car customizing. As Eppie recalls, "These guys lived in California, worked out there, and they would come back to Chimayó and show everybody their cars, and everybody was like, 'Wow, no way!'"

"I went to California in a '49 Ford," recalls Ray Martínez, "with my brother and my grandma. That was the first lowrider I remember seeing. It was in '53. I was only about seven years old, but I can remember it was blue. And it was low, dropped. I didn't think much of them then."

"My family would often go see Orlie Coca when he had his shop in Long Beach, California," Mike Roybal, from Las Vegas, New Mexico, recalls. "I got family in California there from my mom's side. So we'd go visit Orlie in Long Beach—he was from here in Vegas, you know, and our families were real close. And then we'd see all his hoppers and everything there."

Johnny Martínez tells a similar tale, although in California he discovered hot rods as well as lowriders, and ended up building and owning both. "When we were kids we were barely making it," he tells me, "so my mom used to take us to California to the fields to pick strawberries to make money to buy our school clothes, to prepare for school. We were nine kids, so my mom and all the aunties went out there. We were in elementary school up to about high school. Every day, Sunday, Saturday—all summer long until the strawberry season was over—we picked strawberries.

"We were at Santa Ana, and right there was a booming town of lowriders and all that," Johnny continues. "But it was mostly like hot-rodder style, with real skinny tires in the front and big fat ones in the back. And that was the car of my dreams. And then some of them had lowriders, and we used to see them there, too, and say, 'Wow, look at those cars!'

"So when we came home, my mom told me, 'You can get a car if you want it, but you have to work for it. I'm not giving you nothing.' And so I did—I started working. As a matter of fact, I quit school in the eleventh grade just to buy a car. I paid $100 for it. It was a '63 Chevy Impala."

By the 1960s, when the term "lowrider" was coined, L.A. lowriders had learned to make a car's height adjustable by adding hydraulic lifts to the suspension. This was a response to harassment by law enforcement authorities, who tended to regard lowriders as troublesome gangsters. A California law enacted in 1958 outlawed cars whose frames or bodies were lower than the wheel rims. Vehicles that were "juiced"—equipped with hydraulic systems—could be lowered to cruise the streets and quickly lifted back up to legal height when the heat came into view.

The practice of "scraping" also came to New Mexico from California, or at least it was demonstrated first by a visitor from California that Eppie (the hopper) remembers seeing. "One of those guys who came back from California, he was Joe Romero. They used to call him Scrap Iron, because he had this '66 Capri—black, beautiful—and he used to put this iron thing on the bottom of his car. They called it a scrape plate, and you'd see him at night and he'd put that car right down on the road, and you'd see all these sparks coming flying out and you were like, 'Wow!' And that's how he got his nickname, Joe Scrap Iron."

Hydraulics caught on quickly in the lowrider community. Orlie Coca, the Godfather of Hydraulics, came from Las Vegas, New Mexico, although he lived and worked in California, where he developed hydraulics for lowriders and brought them to wide recognition and use. He organized the first car-hopping contests and eventually developed his own brand of hydraulic systems for lowriders.

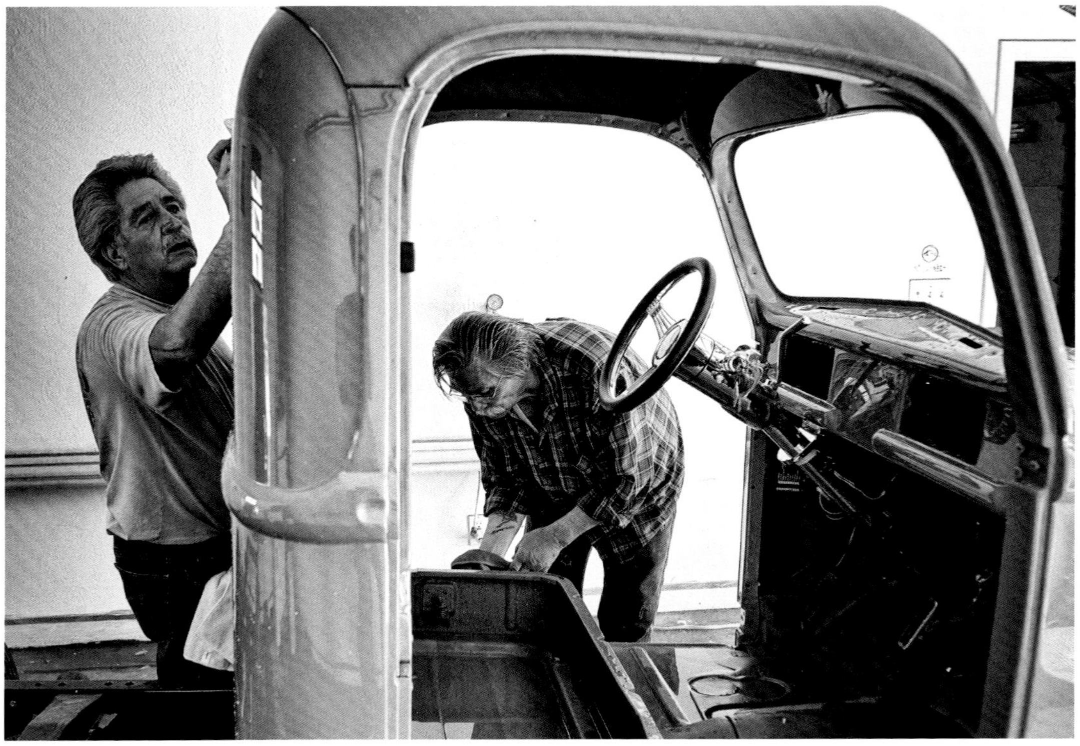

David Vigil and Ramón Esquibel, Chimayó, 2015

"I remember the day when I first saw lowriders with hydraulics," says David Vigil. "It was about 1969, when this guy, Timba—I think his full name was Alfredo San Cristóbal—brought a car with hydraulics from L.A. Me and my sister were cruising in Española. We stopped at a light and this '56 next to us just jumped up and then back down in front, and we said, 'Wow. What was that?' So we stopped the guy, pulled over at the Chevron station, and he and this other guy they called Tábano—Eppie Martínez, but not the one here from Chimayó—they showed us how they did it. They had worked with aircraft companies," David adds, "and they took these hydraulic lifters that planes use for raising and lowering the flaps, and they put them in the shocks. We had to have those."

Eppie Martínez says that in northern New Mexico, the hydraulics were quickly adopted, not so much to avoid the authorities but to increase the cars' clearance when navigating dirt roads. "It started out because we have rough roads in Chimayó, you know," Eppie says. "So we wanted to bring our lowriders to shows, but they'd get banged up on the bumps and ruts and rocks here, so we figured out ways to jack them up, take them to cruise in the shows, you can drive any road that you have here, and then you can go back to the highway and just lay it down."

About the time lowriders were making their first appearance in the Española Valley, the Chicano movement was introducing a distinctly political, activist tone into Mexican American youth culture. By then the pachuco style had morphed into a cholo identity. The appellation "cholo" had been around since seventeenth-century Spanish America, when it referred to a person of mixed, mostly indigenous blood, and in most contexts it has long carried a negative connotation. "Pachuco" and "cholo" had been used in the Southwest since at least the early 1900s, but as the pachucos faded in the late 1940s, Mexican American youth began to embrace the cholo as a kind of analog of the pachuco, complete with undertones of nonconformity and an unmistakable statement of style.

Many New Mexican lowriders took on this cholo affectation, which required a less elaborate wardrobe than the pachucos' drapes. Cholos left behind the zoot suit and instead wore loose-fitting khaki pants (always pressed, with a crease), military belts, loose T-shirts (sometimes ironed), button-up flannel shirts fastened only at the top, and "winos" canvas shoes (Zig-Zag brand). Fedoras sometimes remained as elements of the outfit, but folded bandannas over shaved heads or "fade" haircuts generally took their place. Tattoos, a minor element of pachuco style, became popular among cholos. Not all cholos were lowriders, but if a driver rode low and wore a bandanna, it was sufficient evidence to call him a cholo, his female companion a chola.

Cholos retained elements of the pachuco vernacular, typically using the standard greeting *¡órale!* and appending it with a modern *bro!* On the street it was common to hear *simón* for "yes," *guátchate* for "be careful," and *que hubo* or *quihubo* for "what's up?" A cholo's lowrider was his *ranfla*, while he'd refer to his girlfriend as his *ruca* or *güisa*. He himself might be called a *vato*, a caló term for "dude." A *vato loco* would signify a wild young man, literally a crazy dude.

Having caught the lowrider bug, enthused northern New Mexico mechanics began turning out the cars one at a time, typically in their backyards or home garages. The word spread, creating a cadre of zealous and adept devotees. By the 1970s, they were numerous enough that lowriders cruised regularly on weekends down Main Street and Riverside Drive in Española and around the Plaza in Santa Fe. They were wildly popular throughout the region, showing up for small-town fiestas, weddings, even funerals.

"In Chimayó, we were always known for our chile, our apples, but most of all, the cars," says Eppie, who grew up in Chimayó in the seventies. "We'd see these older guys driving their lowriders and we'd say, 'Wow, look at that!' No matter where we went there was always one or two lowriders—always badass guys to us—guys we looked to with respect."

As Fred Rael remembers, "The scene—the lowrider scene in the seventies in Española—was just intense. I mean it was every Sunday at the car wash, you'd just see everybody out there shining the chrome and all that, and I think that's what got me hooked. We'd be out there on our bikes, you know, thirteen or fourteen years old. We'd be out there at the car wash on Sundays, watching everybody clean their cars, and it was like, 'I want to be a part of this.' So as soon as I started driving, when I was fifteen years old, first thing I did was to put some 5.20s [small, narrow tires] on my car, and I went out there and hung out with the lowriders. And it was like some kind of magic just to be a part of it, you know."

"Everyone drove a lowrider in those days," David Vigil affirms. "People took them to work, to the bank, wherever, but we would especially gather on weekends. We would all park at the Chevron station, cruise down the street, come back. Or park in front of the old J. W. Owens department store, in the big empty lot there, and we'd watch the other cruisers go by. We'd pull into the Big Burger to park and wait and see which girls would come talk to us and check out our cars. Then, when I got a job in Albuquerque," David continues, "all the Chimayó guys living in Albuquerque would get together to cruise around Roosevelt Park. We were the only lowriders in Albuquerque. There weren't any there before."

Lowriders began to make an appearance in mainstream media in the seventies, too. By then, the major features defining a modern lowrider were in place: lowered chassis, hydraulic systems to adjust height, colorful paint jobs, and small rims. Diminutive steering wheels, often formed from chains, were in fashion, as were plush interiors. Scraping along the road to set off showers of sparks—as introduced by Joe Scrap Iron—had also become popular, as had dropping the cars' seats to make the drivers sit even lower. The hydraulics were now more powerful—not only strong enough to raise and lower vehicles but also capable of making the front end jump as much as six feet off the ground. The lowrider hopper was born.

Most New Mexicans making lowriders still did it on a budget, working with old cars or recovering discarded vehicles. With a suspension drop, a little spit and polish, and perhaps the addition of new rims, an ordinary car could become a lowrider. "Back then, if you found an Impala, even a '58 Impala, it might have the original paint, or have been repainted the same color, and you'd buy the car, put rims on it, tires, put a stereo in it, drop it down from the back end—and that's all you needed," Fred Rael remembers. "You drove it and started saving up for more expensive rims, maybe some hydraulics."

In the seventies, many New Mexicans outside of the insular lowrider culture began to recognize the cars as more than the creations of dangerous gang members. Once regarded as old, ground-scraping jalopies driven by gang-affiliated cholos, lowriders were recast as stylish anachronisms of the road. Marking this shift, Española hosted its first lowrider show in 1975,

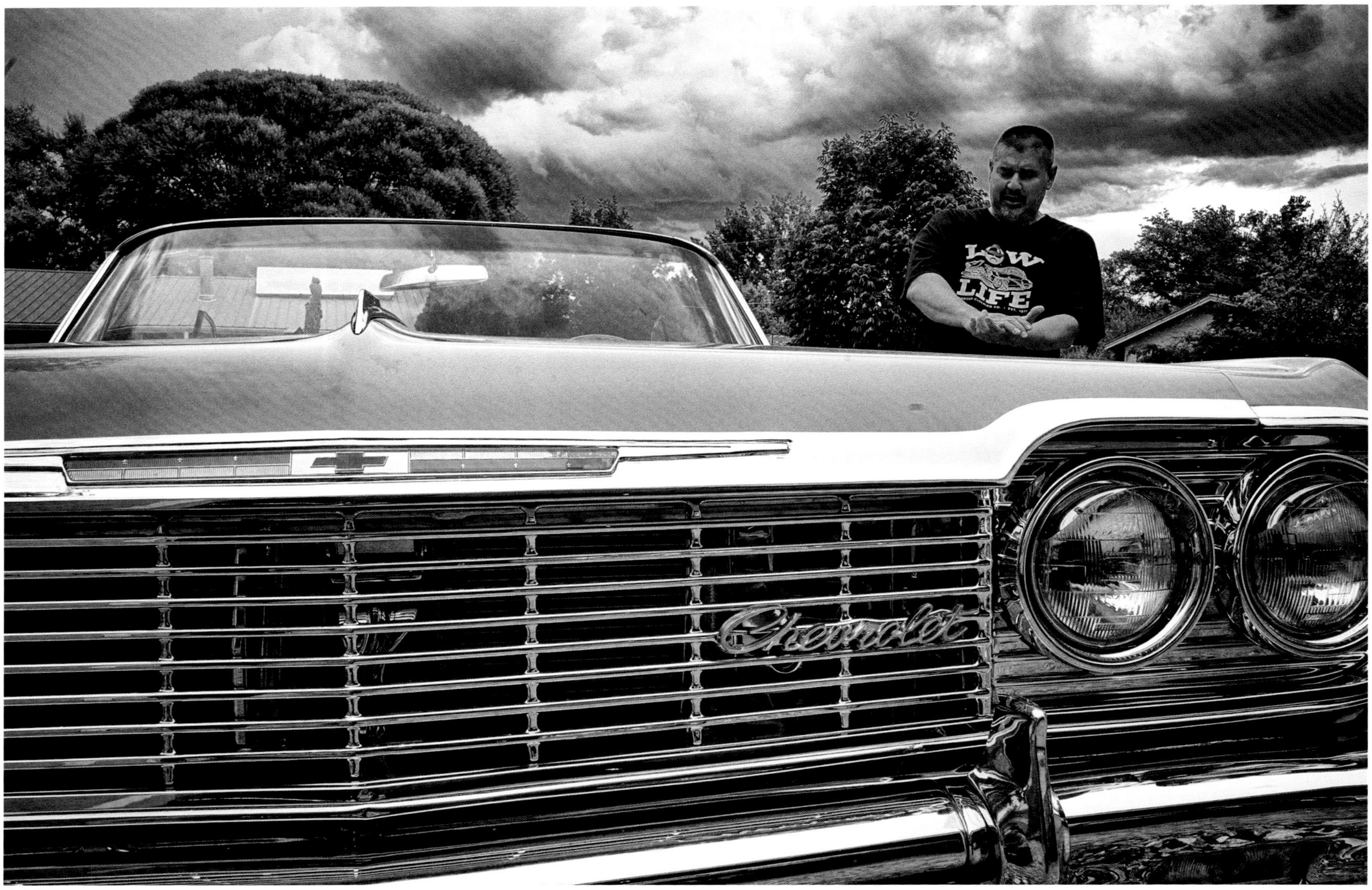

Fred Rael and His '64 Impala, Española, 2015

bringing attention and appreciation to the cars and the lowrider culture and establishing Española as a major center of lowrider activity.

In 1975 the band called War released its song "Low Rider," which reached number one on the Billboard R&B charts (and remains a kind of anthem among lowriders). Articles in national magazines reported on the spread of lowriding, and television got in on the act, too, when a Chevrolet Impala lowrider christened "Gypsy Rose" appeared, cruising down Whittier Boulevard, in the opening credits of NBC's *Chico and the Man.*

The fame energized the New Mexico lowrider scene. "I remember when I watched *Chico and the Man,*" Fred Rael recalls of his youth in L.A. "That was the first time I saw the car called Gypsy Rose, and I had actually seen that car on the street, and it was just like, wow! To see something I'd seen on the street on television? I kind of got hooked on the lowriders right there."

The image of the cholo or the vato loco was still associated with lowriders, regardless of the lowrider's actual character, but many lowriders preferred not to be associated with the stereotype and sought to distance themselves from it. As Fred Rael points out, not all cholos were lowriders, and vice versa. Being a cholo had become a lifestyle choice. "People would look at me and say, 'Hey, are you a cholo?'" Fred recalls. "And I'd say, 'No, I'm a lowrider. I've got a car.'"

The first lowrider car clubs formed in L.A. in the early sixties, and New Mexico followed suit. By the 1970s numerous car clubs had formed in New Mexico, in part to counter the tendency to conflate lowriders with cholos, gang-related activities, and crime. Violence and gang activities had plagued lowrider communities, especially in large, urban areas, and incidents of public disturbance riled law enforcement and alarmed residents at times. But gang culture was scarcely known in northern New Mexico then.

"We all would stick together," Eppie recalls. "It was just Chimayó, you know, maybe the 'Chimayó locos' or the 'Chimayó boys'—or the 'Chimayó dummies' sometimes because we did some crazy stuff—but we took care of each other. It wasn't like you hear stories now, or see in movies where there's different sides, like West Side, Eighteenth Street, gangs like that. It was never like that in our place. It was always strictly Chimayó. Seven miles of it."

By the seventies the New Mexico lowrider community was making an effort to shun gang-related elements and wanted recognition as a respectable group of hardworking car enthusiasts—making a distinctive style assertion, to be sure. Around Española and Chimayó, clubs like Amigos, Paisanos, Chimayó Valley Cruisers, and Del Norte sought to promulgate a more wholesome image for lowriders. Some required that members refrain from using drugs and alcohol.

The seventies saw a great increase in the kinds of vehicles that were popular for lowriders. In addition to the perennially favorite traditionals—including the most-favored sixties-era Impalas and the older bombs—lowriders applied their skills to General Motors Bonneville, Cutlass, Regal, Cadillac, Grand Prix, Monte Carlo, Malibu, El Camino, Caprice, and Impala cars, and to Ford's Lincoln, Thunderbird, Cougar, and LTD. From this expanded selection, lowriders fashioned a whole new generation of vehicles, widely varied in body type but still expressing the characteristic low-riding profile.

"When I first started out in the seventies, any car you got your hands on, you would make into a lowrider," recalls Fred Rael. "It didn't matter what it was, because you worked with what you had. If your parents had a Mercury Cougar and they passed it down to you, you would make that into your first lowrider. Of course, you'd preferably want the Chevrolet or the Cadillac or something. But back in the seventies, anything that you had, if you could put some thirteens [narrow rims] on it, some fourteens on it, and some 5.20s, you put some side pipes on it, and a stereo in it, and you were cruising."

Lowriders began to paint murals on their rides in the sixties and seventies, soon after mural art appeared in barrios in East L.A. and other urban centers. Descending from the Mexican muralist tradition popularized by Diego Rivera many years before, urban lowrider painters used religious figures, images of personal narratives, women (usually in provocative poses), and symbols common to the Chicano movement and the Mexican Revolution. The murals on New Mexico lowriders featured similar imagery as well as depictions of local landscapes, landmarks, and icons.

"Murals here in New Mexico tended to be either religious or traditional," states Fred Rael. "Like mine. Any mural that I'm going to get done, it's going to be of scenes from New Mexico, because I'm proud to be from New Mexico, and I'd like to show that anywhere I go."

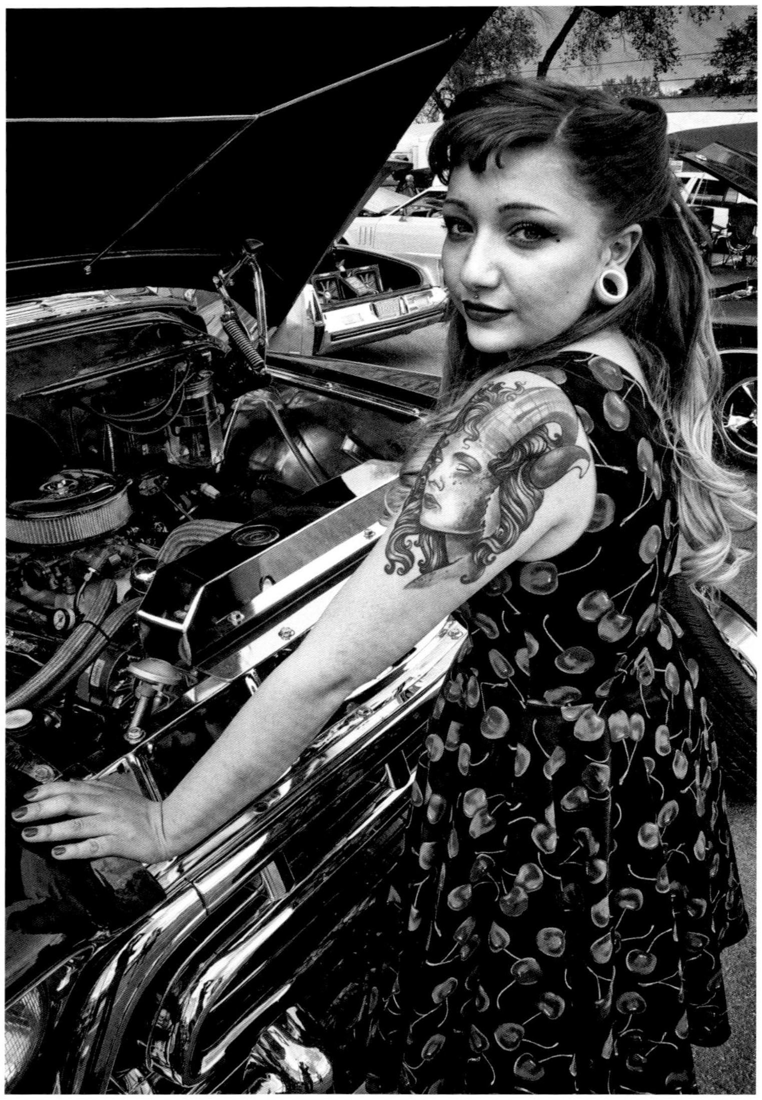

Woman with Her Chevy Street Rod, Mainstreet Showdown, Española, 2015

Lowriding had for decades been a man's game, but women's involvement began to increase in the 1970s. Until then women had been seen primarily as adornments to lowriders and companions to the cars' owners. Scantily clad women were foundational in the lowrider imagery projected in popular media (especially on the cover of *Lowrider*), and it was a struggle for females with an interest in cars to break out of established stereotypes. Now lowrider clubs began to accept women for the first time, and women also formed their own, women-only clubs. Female lowriders began to build their own cars and show them—and win prizes—alongside their male counterparts.

A seminal event in bringing New Mexico lowriders to a bigger cultural stage in a positive light took place in 1980 when New Mexico's premier public art venue, the Museum of Fine Arts, sponsored an exhibit of photographs of lowriders by Meridel Rubenstein. Presented in conjunction with a car show on the Santa Fe Plaza, the exhibit effectively gave lowriders the imprimatur of the Santa Fe art establishment. At the time Rubenstein opined, "Lowriders are an art form, and their makers are artists of the highest order."

This kind of talk was a long way from the scornful comments I had grown up hearing about pachucos and cholos and their cars. Lowriders assumed a kind of legitimacy as a contemporary folk art form. Suddenly lowriders were bestowed with cachet, and a much diminished bad-boy image.

As the lowrider trend caught on, an industry grew to service devotees and provide them with parts and materials for building their rides. Buying a car might well be the least of the investment required. The all-important small wheels alone could cost three times as much as the car. Most coveted were Dayton rims—"D's" or "killer Daytons," as they were known—in thirteen- or fourteen-inch sizes. A used car might go for $700 to $1,000, the rims $1,600 to $3,000. "People were getting hijacked for their wheels back then—or their cars were getting stolen just for the wheels," Fred Rael says.

In 1990 the Smithsonian Institution in Washington, DC, purchased the classic lowrider Dave's Dream, a 1969 Ford LTD created by Chimayó resident David Jaramillo. Jaramillo's family finished the car upon his untimely death and sold it to the museum, which put it on display in the National Museum of American History—after it was blessed by Father Casimiro Roca, the parish priest at the Santuario in Chimayó.

Española's distinguished poet Jim Sagel expressed well the thoughts of many passersby, heads turning as they watched the lowriders rumble past—or as they waited, trapped behind the tortoise-paced processions:

> smooth and sleek as a great blue whale
> the low rider crawls down the narrow state highway
> six barely visible curly heads
> jolt up and down in perfect unison
> to the rhythm of the shockless Chevy
> tracking every wave and asphalt imperfection of the road
> and I'm caught in the most frustrating position
> next to introducing an old friend
> whose name you've forgotten
> I'm late for work and stuck
> behind lowriders

Some New Mexicans began to respond to lowriders in much the way suggested by the last lines of the poem, wherein Sagel, forced to "forget his watch and look at the mountains," finds enlightenment in the slipstream of the lowriders:

> and although I'm hopelessly late
> I continue putting down the road
> barely in high
> delicately bouncing off potholes
> mirando las nubes
> and building my own proud line
> of blistering mad commuters

These words and events placed iconic images of New Mexico lowriders firmly in the popular imagination. The lowrider phenomenon thrived. Numerous publications sprang up to celebrate and promote the cars and the industry that grew up around their production. *Lowrider* magazine, which had launched in San Jose, California, in 1977, was joined by many other serial publications that highlighted lowriders as emblematic of Chicano culture, such as *Q-Vo* (short for the cholo slang "que hubo") and *Firme. Orlie's Lowriding Magazine*, published by Orlie Coca when he moved to Corrales, New Mexico, in 1991, kept the pulse of the vibrant lowrider community in New Mexico. These magazines did much to counter the negative reputation of lowriders and to spread enthusiasm and support for lowrider culture.

The publicity about lowrider culture sparked enthusiasm among cultures far removed from those in the western United States. The cars caught on in Japan, the United Kingdom, Sweden, and Brazil, among other places. Back in the USA, rap artists such as Dr. Dre, Ice Cube, and Snoop Dogg purchased lowriders and featured them in music videos, popularizing the car style in the African American hip-hop scene. This affiliation brought African American street-gang styles—sports jerseys, team jackets, baseball hats, and Nike Cortez running shoes—into Latino lowrider communities.

Cruising continued at a fever pitch in Española, with bumper-to-bumper lowriders jamming Riverside Drive, their sound systems throbbing as traffic slowed to a standstill. In Santa Fe, the Friday night cruise remained extremely popular, with East Alameda Street clogged with lowriders. Las Vegas, New Mexico, had its favored lowrider cruising circuit, too, as Mike Roybal recalls, "The main cruise was Douglas Avenue from Grand to Eighth Street right there at the Safeway parking lot. Everybody used to gather there. And then you would cruise up Eighth Street, down National around the plaza park and then back down National, and then on Twelfth Street and back on Douglas. Then sometimes they would go up Grand all the way up to the old train. Friday, Saturday nights that thing was bumper to bumper. That was the best."

Car clubs proliferated throughout northern New Mexico: Tru Rydaz, Prestigious, Los Guys, Vicious Dreams, and Laying Low, among others, in Española; Latin Dezire in Las Vegas; and Enchanted Expressions and Good Times in Santa Fe. All of these added to the national groups that had a local, New Mexico presence, such as RollerzOnly and Goodtimes.

Mike Roybal captures the spirit of the many small lowrider car clubs in New Mexico when he describes his own experience cofounding Latin Dezire. "Here in Las Vegas when I was a kid I remember a car club—Sombra Car Club—and Infatuation Car Club, and I remember seeing the clubs over in California when we'd visit—the Hijos, the Imperials. These guys were of course older than us and we just looked up to them and I just liked their style, their cars. And then as the lowriding started getting big and we had our own cars, we were at the Santa Rosa car show in 1989, probably twenty of us [from Vegas] and my friend Cider Esquibel asked us, 'Do you guys have a name of a car—are you guys a club or what?' And we were like looking at each other and, 'You know, maybe we should be a club.' That's when we started the club.

"But in our car club," Roybal states, "we don't have requirements and stuff and you don't have to pay dues. It's more like, 'Let's hang out and not be real technical about things.' We allow any kind of vehicle. As long as you have a good attitude and you represent the club name in a good way, and you're not out there with a plaque on your car making trouble. That's what I like about this club. We're still like family, you know? We're just so close."

In the opinion of many in the lowrider community in New Mexico, the "big family" feel of car clubs helped curb gang membership and averted serious problems. Speaking of an emerging gang problem in Las Vegas in the 1990s, Roybal recalls his club getting involved in activities like graffiti cleanups, participating in the Toys for Tots toy drive with the Hermanos Bikers club, and providing money for Highlands University students to buy textbooks. The object, he says, was to keep kids out of gangs and to get them to stay in Las Vegas for their college education and for work afterward. "So we did help out a lot," he says. "People would stereotype lowriding, thinking it was part of gangs and drug dealing or stuff, but we in our club never allowed stuff like that. We've just been straightforward people, and there are guys that were gang members that would tell you that lowriding got them out of the gang."

The late Nolan Martínez, one of Española's most respected lowrider artists, worked hard to encourage young people to embrace lowriding as an antidote to the prevalent crime and violence in the valley. In a paean to lowriders and a plea to youth, he wrote a poem in which he says, "Keep your heart and mind clean, like a lowrider."

In spite of lowriders' increasing popularity in the nineties, and the wholesome image that lowrider clubs were promoting, in 1995 New Mexico governor Gary Johnson saw fit to criticize them publicly, commenting that he was afraid of them. Lowriders felt that he had implied that they were all dangerous criminals. A lowrider protest ensued, with a large group of them doing what they do best: cruising, this time around the capitol in Santa Fe.

Recognizing his error, Governor Johnson quickly did an about-face and sponsored a show of lowrider photography at the capitol. He invited lowrider clubs to attend, declared a Lowrider Day in Santa Fe, donned wraparound sunglasses, and took a spin in a low-slung vintage car. He also made public comments about the importance of lowriders in New Mexico culture. Lowriders showed up for the exhibit in large numbers, hoping that the publicity would once and for all extinguish stereotypes that had long haunted them.

In contrast to the negative comments made in many places, really high culture gave a nod to lowriders when the composer Robert Ashley wrote and staged an opera called *Now Eleanor's Idea.* Part of the story in the 1993 opera focuses on a young woman making a documentary about low-

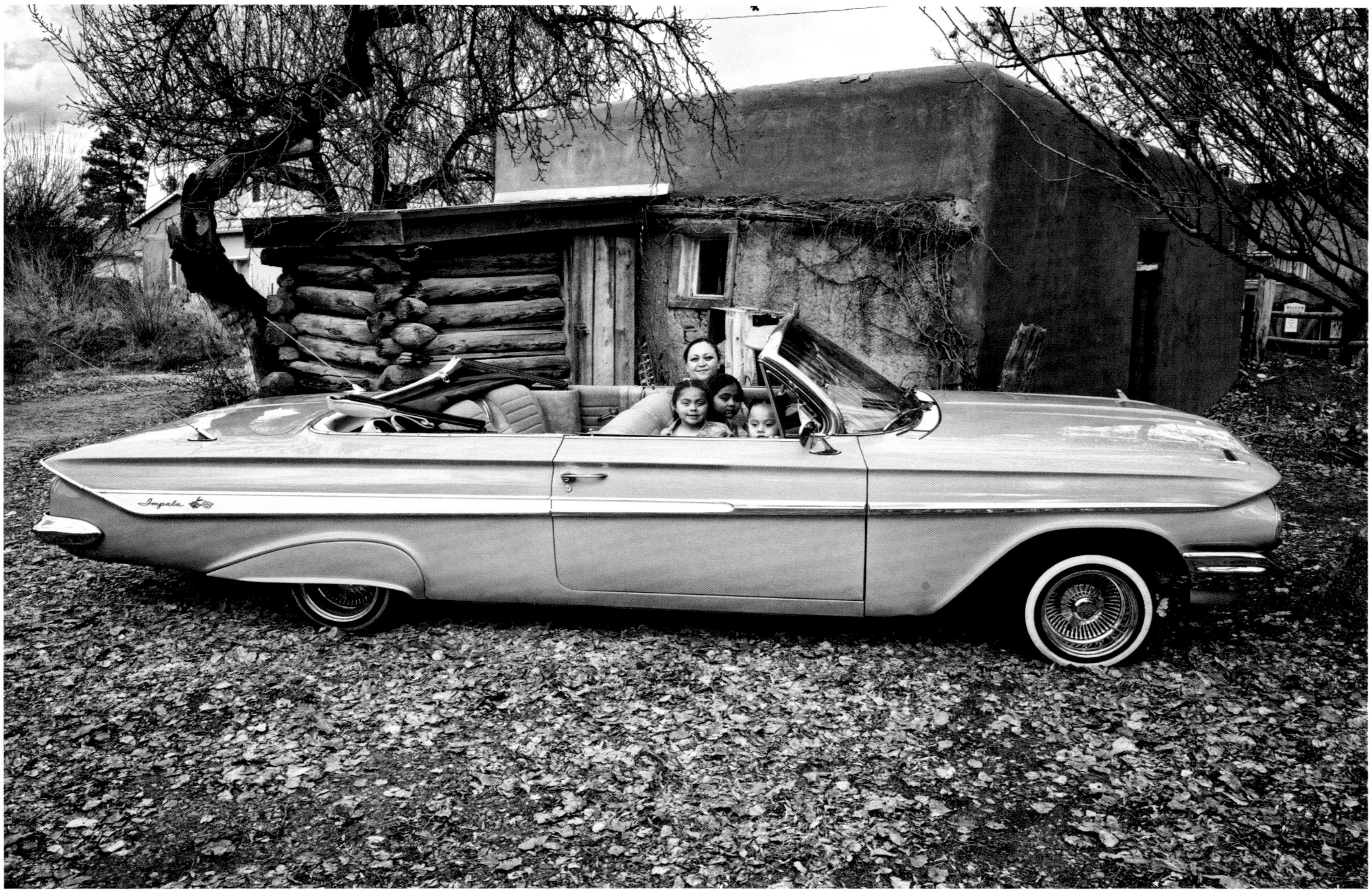

Bobbie, Heaven, and Angel Chacón with Their Mother Pam Jaramillo, Chimayó, 2016

riders who falls in love with Chicano lowrider culture. The opera makes references to lowriders made by Chimayó's own Arturo "Lowlow" Medina. Ashley said that he drew his inspiration for this avant-garde opera partly from articles in *Lowrider* magazine, and he called Chimayó "the spiritual center of the lowrider world."

Lowriders, it seemed, were everywhere in the 1990s. They received positive press and international exposure, and many places could rightfully claim ownership of a strong lowrider presence, but northern New Mexico remained indisputably one of the most homegrown and community-based lowrider scenes of them all. The epicenter of lowrider culture remained the Española Valley, which was touted as having the most lowriders per capita of any American town or city. In 1993 an MTV news broadcast declared outright that Española was the "Lowrider Capital of the World," giving it a higher ranking than L.A. The legend caught on, though it galled the rank and file of longtime car clubs in L.A. and other cities. Lowriding, it seemed, had taken its place as a permanent feature of northern New Mexico's cultural landscape.

Aided by the Internet as it penetrated rural New Mexico, lowriders developed and shared new styles and technologies more quickly and across a broader landscape than ever before. Rather than traveling with workers commuting to and from the automotive centers in L.A., ideas and innovations could be communicated instantly online. Videos and streaming TV shows also disseminated information to and from remote corners of the international lowrider realms.

The increased publicity and improved communications stimulated a boom in lowrider technology that reached New Mexico quickly. The hydraulic systems became stronger and more outrageous, no longer assembled from scavenged airplane parts but available off-the-shelf as products made specifically for lowrider enthusiasts. Hopping contests became the rage, with records for the highest front-end lift exceeding ten feet. The systems grew more complex, too. Originally, they featured two switches, one for lifting the front and the other for the back of the vehicle. Then the fad was four switches, one for each wheel, which allowed the cars to jump front, back, and one side or the other side. By the nineties, hydraulic systems utilized as many as sixteen switches, which let lowriders "dance." Car dancing contests, alongside hopping competitions, became standard features of car shows.

Paint and exterior finish remained, as it had been in the eighties, an important aspect of the lowrider look. Flashy exteriors continued to dominate with bright paints, multiple colors, extensive pinstriping, and metal flake paint (with bits of shiny metal that make the car sparkle). "Candy" finishes, fade paint jobs, layered patterns, and metal flake gave rise to a generation of dazzling lowriders, still showing off as much chrome as possible.

The nineties brought an increase in mural painting on lowriders, inspired in New Mexico by the outstanding works of artists like Chimayó's Randy Martínez, who saw lowriders as rolling canvases for his soulful paintings. Most of Martínez's murals were strongly religious in theme. He brought the art to a new level, working feverishly to crank out mural after mural for lowriders from around the state. His vivid, realistic, and yet hauntingly evocative murals inspired a style of lowrider art that distinguished northern New Mexico's lowriders. Strongly religious lowrider murals by Arturo "Lowlow" Medina also attracted wide media attention and were featured in *National Geographic* and *New Mexico* magazine.

Mike Roybal painted his well-known ride, "the New Mexico 505 car," in an entirely different style, without any religious imagery at all. His car shows off numerous symbols related to New Mexico history and culture, including representations of the Zia sun symbol (on the New Mexico state flag), roadrunners (the New Mexico state bird), an Aztec goddess, thunderbirds, and faces painted for Día de los Muertos. It also features inside the trunk painted imagery of the Aztec god Montezuma, a shout out to Montoya's family in the New Mexico town of the same name near Las Vegas. "My mom grew up in Montezuma, New Mexico," he says. "My grandpa had a church there, and he was the justice of the peace up there, and my mom went to school at that monastery. So I wanted to include that for my mom, and my cousins in California like that, too, because they're from there, too. It goes back to the family thing."

At the same time mural art was blossoming, Rob Vanderslice was revolutionizing abstract painting on lowriders, developing an instantly recognizable style of multilayered ribbons in patterns that wind in hypnotic tangles. Vanderslice, working out of Albuquerque but painting cars from all over the state and beyond, worked his way to prominence and became nationally known, although his affection for northern New Mexico remained strong. "I give Española the utmost respect," he told *New West* digital magazine in 2015, "because they keep lowriding traditional. In Española, you'll see grandma, grandpa, mom, dad, the whole family rolling a lowrider. They give me respect when I go to the shows and I love them for that."

A number of other stylistic trends started in New Mexico and some became emblematic of the area. As Fred Rael explains, "Back when Española was at its peak, we had our own style, you know, the big whitewalls, and white diamond-tuck interiors—everybody had white diamond-tuck interiors, no matter what color the outside was. In Los Angeles, if you had a blue car, you had a blue interior; you had a red car, you had a red interior. But over here, if you had a red car, you had a white interior, if you had a blue car, you had a white interior, if you had a gold car, you had a white interior, if you had a black car, you had a white interior—and a white top. And that was the style that was really, like, New Mexico."

Lowrider bicycles, which had been around for a long time, went more mainstream in the nineties, starting to become regular features of lowrider shows. These bicycles incorporated the

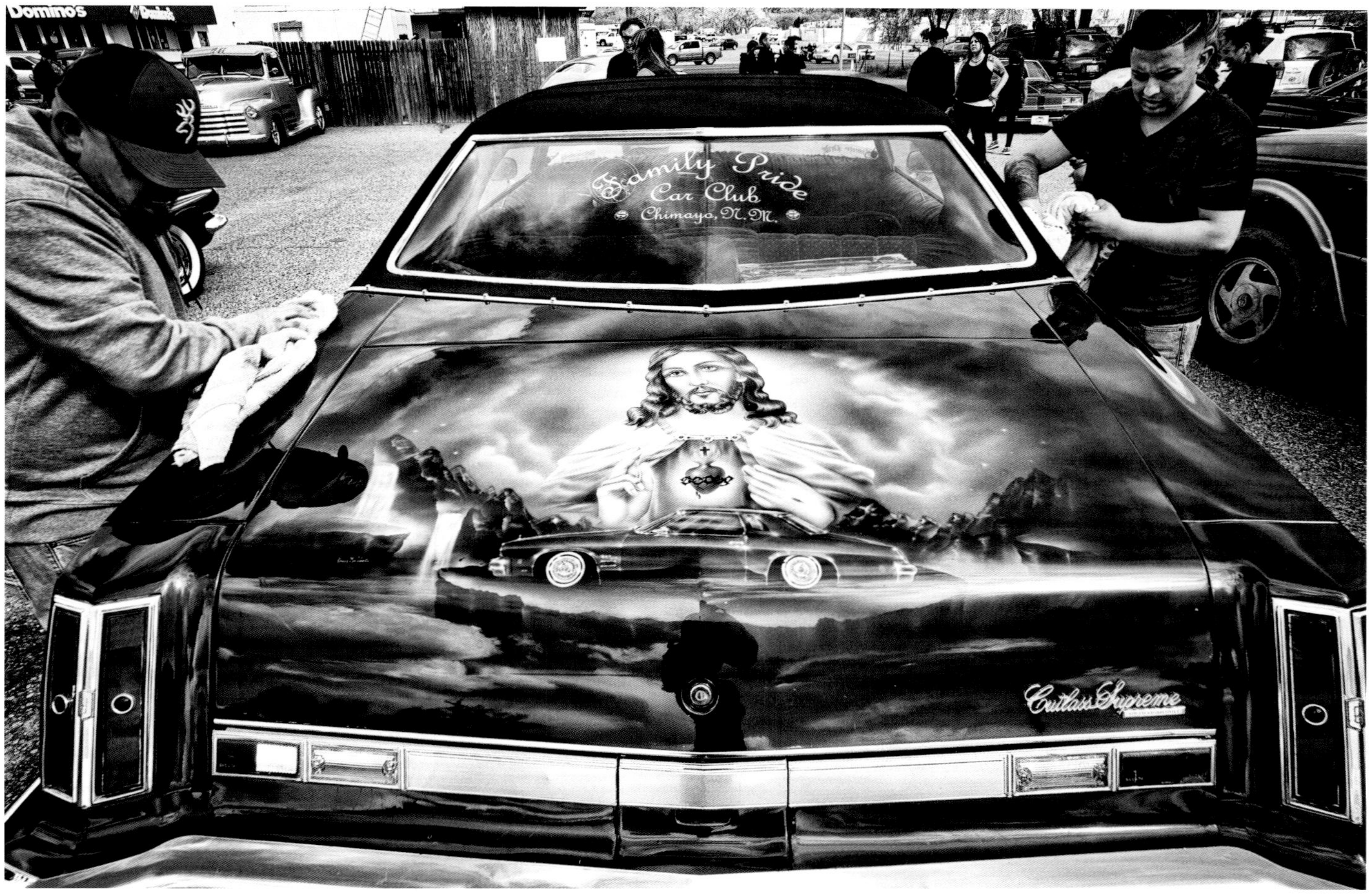

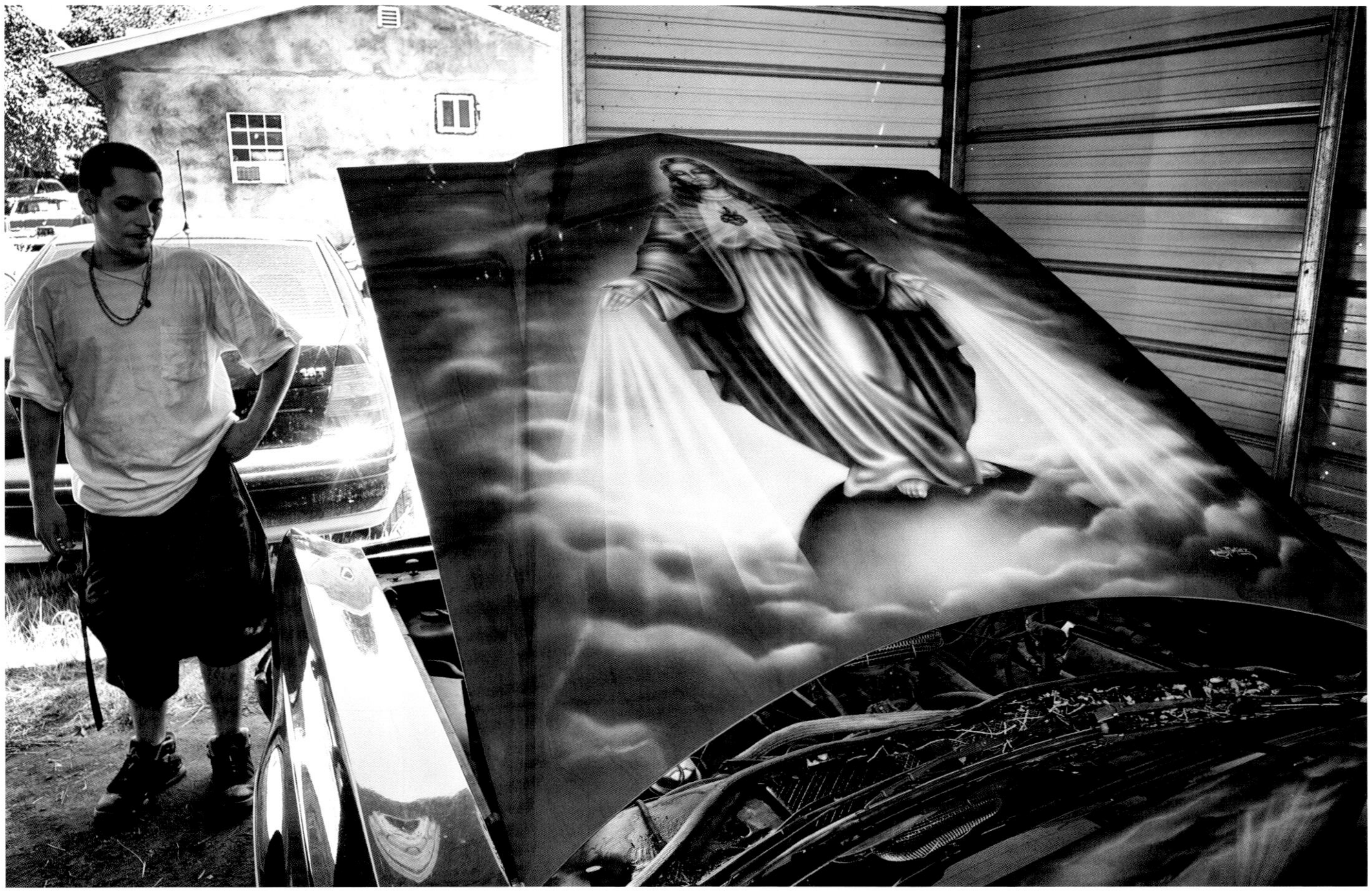

(top) *Randy Martínez Mural*, 2012. (bottom) *Randy Martínez Mural*, 2015

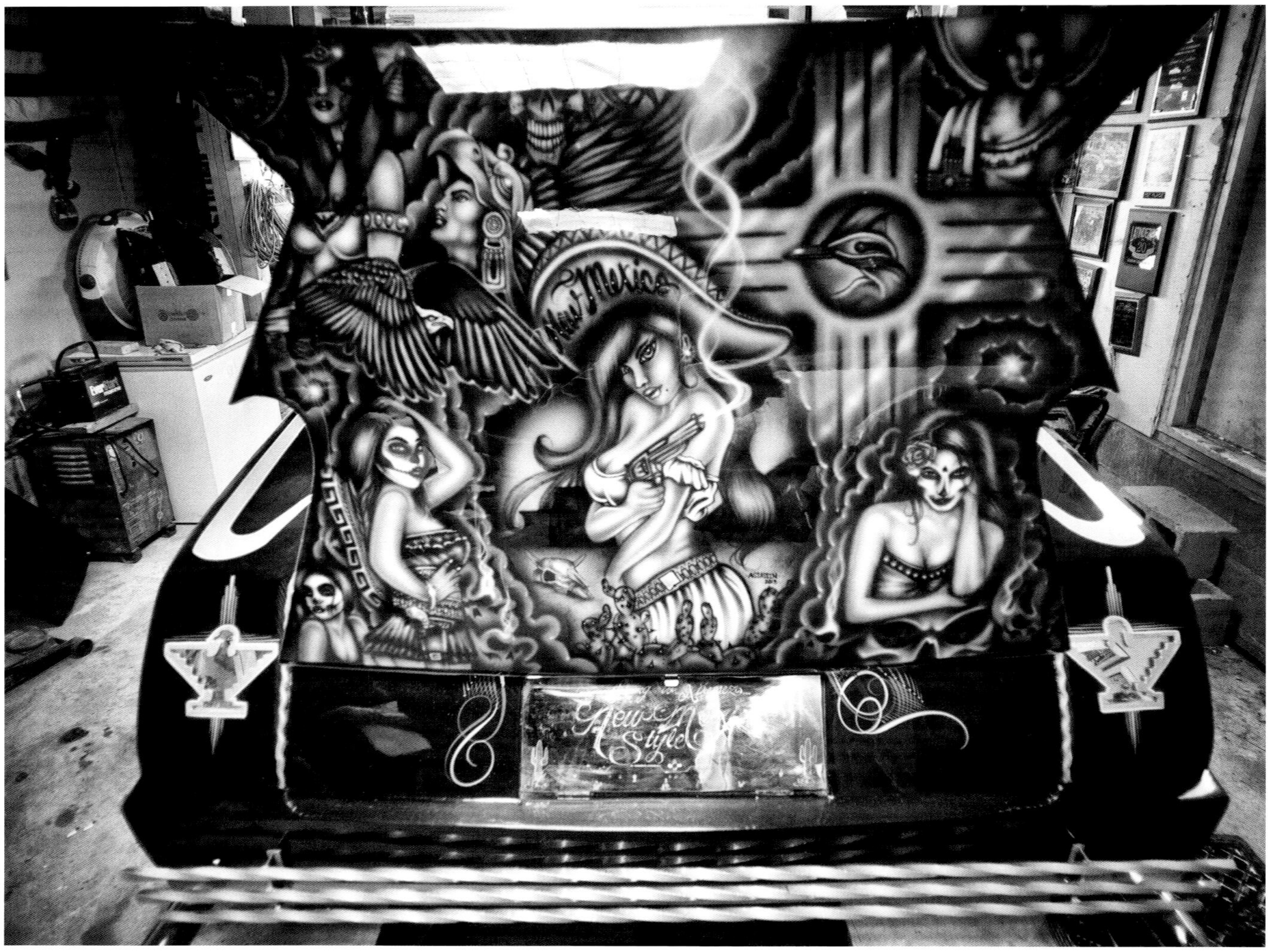

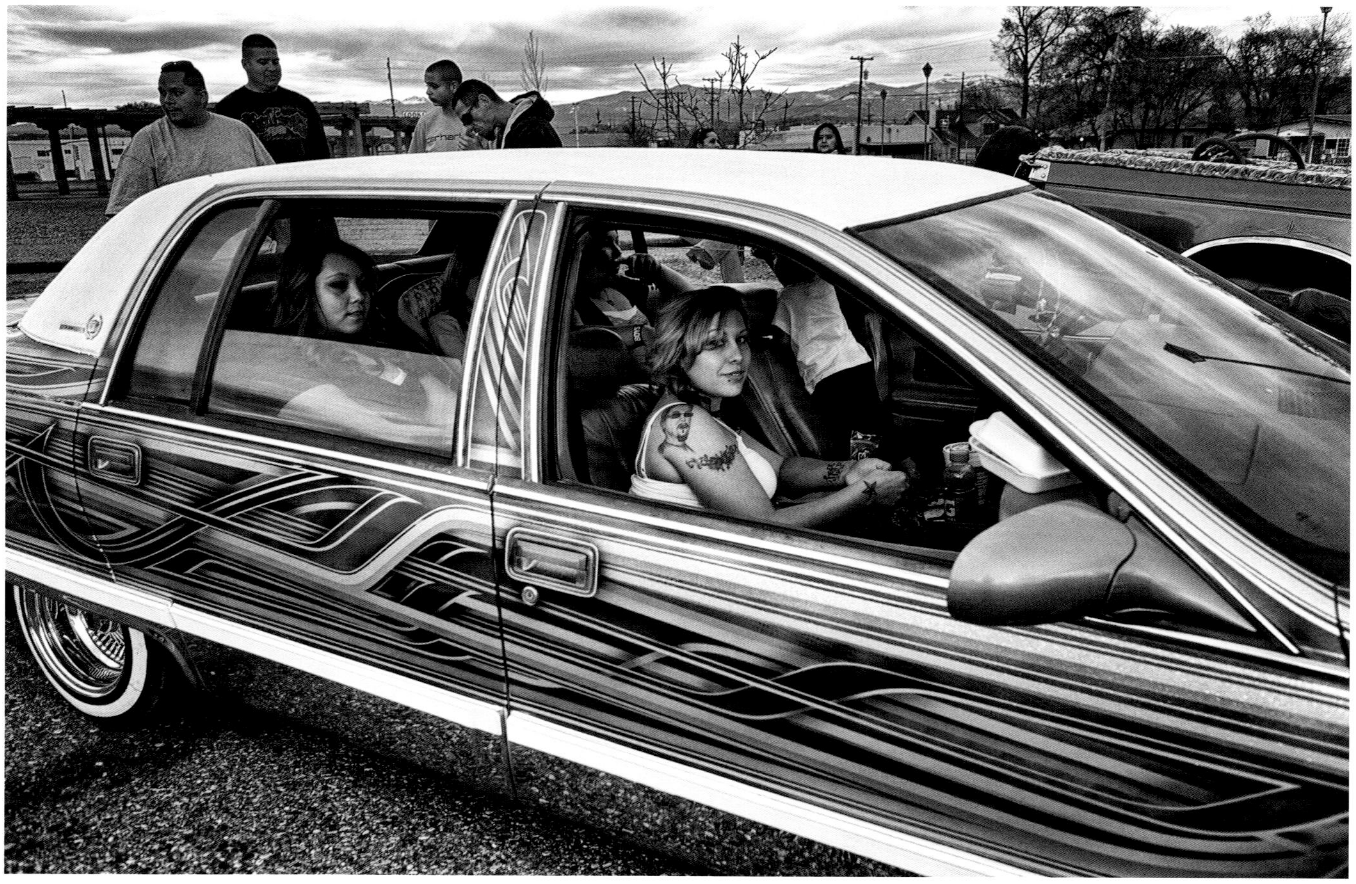

(top) *Mike Roybal's New Mexico 505 Car*, Las Vegas, 2015. (bottom) *Amanda Sherwood and Friends in a '95 Fleetwood Brougham with Rob Vanderslice Paint Job*, Plaza de Española, 2012

basic lowrider feature of riding low, and they usually featured long "banana" seats, spoke wheels, whitewall tires, fenders, and sometimes a chain steering wheel. Very "tricked out" bikes might include hydraulic or airbag suspension.

Much has changed since those heady days in the nineties when lowriders made their way to national prominence. The cars continue to get more sophisticated. Advanced hydraulics make it possible for hoppers to jump higher than ever (current record: more than 130 inches) and to "three wheel," lifting one front tire off the ground. "Bagging" cars—that is, adding airbags that rely on compressed air instead of pressurized hydraulic fluid—makes raising and lowering cars easier and smoother and eliminates the need to carry heavy batteries for hydraulic systems. Both airbag systems and advanced hydraulics now make it possible for cars to "bunny hop," audaciously jumping up with all four wheels at a time. (Some lowriders have even coaxed their rides to jump rope, bunny hopping repeatedly over a suspended line!)

Technological advances aside, some lowriders see the 1990s as the peak of the lowrider sensation in New Mexico, and most everyone agrees that since then there has been a steep drop in the number of lowriders cruising northern New Mexico. Certainly the days are gone when most lowriders drove their cars to work.

"All of us lowriders, we've just gotten older," says Fred Rael. "Back in the day, we could just work on our cars and cruise all we wanted. We didn't have much responsibility. Now, we've got jobs, our kids are in school . . . we just can't hang out like we used to.

"And think about it. Back then, there were no lowriders dying of old age, but now, like look at that book *Low 'n Slow*, most of those guys are gone. It's sad."

"We have a lot of club members that are retired," says Mike Roybal of Latin Dezire. "But they still have their cars from back in the day. You know a lot of us guys from here, we're putting our kids through college now. We're getting ready to have grandkids, and we're retiring. For some it's like, 'I used to be a lowrider and sold it and it's over.' But others still have their lowriders and still have the passion. The old members still hang out with each other but it's just life, and you have to take care of what's first, your kids."

Other lowriders attribute the decline in street cruising to other factors besides an aging demographic. They point out that traffic and congestion are worse on streets that used to be ideal for cruising. Downtown Santa Fe, around the old Plaza, is now closed to vehicles on two sides, and nearby streets are jammed with tourists in the summer. Also, there has been a deliberate attempt to prevent lowriders from cruising in some places. Not all drivers have come to Jim Sagel's conclusion that it's a blessing to slow down behind lowriders. Their complaints have moved law enforcement to discourage cruising on favorite routes, like East Alameda Street in Santa Fe, where the Santa Fe City Council attempted for years to restrict lowriding.

As cruising diminished, many lowriders have turned to car shows to show off their vehicles. "Lowriders have left the road for the show," the *Los Angeles Times* opined in 2006, pointing out that cruisers were choosing to pull their cars off the street and invest in them as purely show cars. This has been true in New Mexico as well. By far the biggest competition happens at the Lowrider Supershow, sponsored by *Lowrider* magazine in Albuquerque each summer. There, hundreds of lowriders from all over the state and beyond gather to present their finest, admire the work of others, and compete for prizes. Serious competitors also haul their cars in trailers to shows in Colorado, Texas, Arizona, California, and Nevada.

At the same time, the small shows in northern New Mexico continue, attracting lowriders from throughout the region. Monthly car shows in Española draw a local group of lowriders, hot-rodders, and other car enthusiasts to the Española Plaza. The annual Main Street Showdown in Española brings life to Española's nearly abandoned main drag, and gatherings on the Santa Fe Plaza draw locals back to a place that has become largely a venue for tourism. Large car shows at Buffalo Thunder Casino have attracted crowds in recent years, accepting more than five hundred entries in 2013. Additionally, car shows at small-town fiestas bring out the cruisers, who, notified through Facebook postings and texting alerts, also turn out spontaneously, sometimes for memorials or fundraisers for local charities. The cars always bring out crowds.

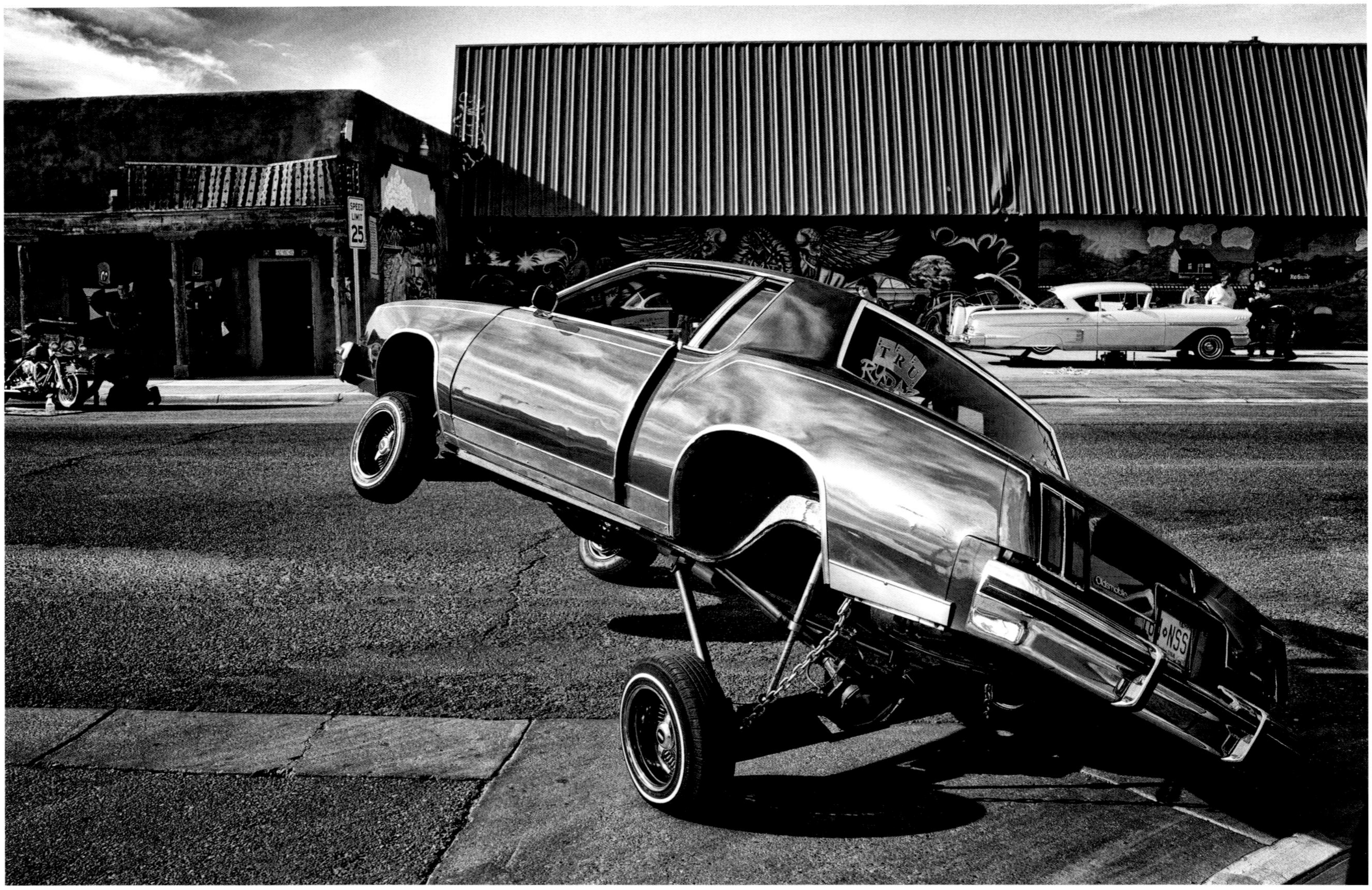

Oldsmobile Cutlass Three-Wheeling at Mainstreet Showdown, Española, 2015

Local shows may lack the ostentation and excitement of the Vegas show and other super shows, but they serve another purpose: bringing together lowriders from Chimayó, Alcalde, El Rito, Rio Chiquito, Española, and dozens of other small places to exchange stories, look at each other's latest experiments, watch some hopping, and, most of all, share in the camaraderie of the local lowrider community. Here the gatherings serve to reinforce a common bond between people who come from similar cultural backgrounds, giving them the time and space to reaffirm their identities as Hispanos.

The sense of brotherhood among lowriders—and other kinds of car enthusiasts—persists at car shows, which for New Mexicans are anything but cutthroat competitions. Many lowriders speak of the camaraderie they feel at these gatherings. "Through my years of lowriding I've met so many guys out of Española, Albuquerque," says Mike Montoya. "You can go to a car show and you don't have to worry about anything. It's all just together. I tell my members, 'Don't go with an attitude that if you don't win you're going to be throwing things around.' It's all fun. We hang out together and we have a blast. That's what makes people tight, hanging out together—not Facebook or calling each other, but actually hanging out."

Although a sense of solidarity prevails at the small shows, lowriders are more competitive at the bigger, regional shows. Strict guidelines determine what cars can enter, with limits on the total number of cars. On the high-end cars that are built to compete in these big shows, ever more elaboration has become the rule. Paint jobs spread into trunks, around engines, and even to the belly of the car. Chroming extends far beyond bumpers and rims to include engines and undercarriages, and the chrome sometimes bears fine engraving. The chassis may also be covered in chrome or glazed with gold—even the nuts and bolts. Show cars may be made to break apart to expose the undercarriage, suspension, and wheels. The wheels are often removed to make the suspension more visible, with the car up on lifts and mirrors placed underneath to allow views of the undercarriage. Doors can be made to flip up to show off custom interiors, and Plexiglas hoods show off engines.

As Chuck Montoya says of these show cars, "Back in the day, people didn't get so technical with the cars. We would just paint them and make them look kind of good. You'd just put some rims—and cruise. But as time has gone on, everybody's gotten way more technical. They're chroming, detailing, putting in high-performance motors, rear ends, engraved, masterpiece rims. You gotta have a radical paint job, a bunch of Kool-Aid colors, and the car surfaces gotta be super straight, no waves, no dents in the moldings. The glass has gotta be perfect, all the chrome. Now it's a lot more technical at the lowrider shows than cruising."

Even as he acknowledges the elaboration in car painting and detailing techniques, Fred Rael also sees a countertrend in recent years toward simplicity—although that doesn't necessarily mean less expense. As Fred puts it, "Now the new cars come stock with such really nice colors that a lot of people are just using the base coats, clear coats of the new cars, and instead of doing a lot of patterns and doing a lot of flakes, they're doing a lot of straight-line pinstripes and gold leaf—but it still costs a bundle."

The increasing complexity and elegance in the art and craft of lowriding has raised the bar and compelled many to pull back from investing in a car. Lowriding used to be a poor man's pastime, but keeping up with the sophistication of show cars demands more money than ever before. Says Montoya, "It's just a lot of money now. You can put a couple hundred thousand dollars in a lowrider now, believe it or not. I've seen people do that." Once car owners have spent this kind of money to make their lowriders suitable for competition, they are unlikely to drive them and risk damaging the paint or other features of the cars. Instead, they transport them in closed trailers so they are never exposed to the elements.

The lowrider community in New Mexico has no doubt matured into a more middle-class, show-oriented identity, but poets continue to celebrate lowriders and their meaning to Latino culture. No one expresses nostalgia for lowriding in New Mexico more passionately than Levi Romero, a native of Dixon:

> how can I tell you
> baby, oh honey
> you'll never know the ride
> the ride of a lowered Chevy
> slithering through
> the blue dotted night
> along Riverside Drive Española

"Old-school" lowriders find themselves faced with a dilemma as they see changes in the community and look to the future. They want to preserve the traditions of lowriding but keep young people interested in joining their ranks. Others in the lowrider scene of northern New Mexico see no cause for concern about lowriding disappearing. "No way will it go away," says Vince Trujillo. "There's a lot of young people who want to keep it going." "You look around the car shows," avers David Vigil, "and you see the old guys, like me, going into street rods, but the younger kids are getting back into lowriders now."

"It's never going to die," Johnny Martínez agrees, nodding toward his son, Johnny Jr., who is three-wheeling with his Monte Carlo in the driveway. "I'll just put it that way. Sure, there's all of those noise burners and all that, like in *The Fast and the Furious.* A lot of young kids are into that. They just buy a new car, they slap on a muffler that makes noise, and that's about it. And they put a stereo system there and they go boom-ba-boom-boom. And that's all they do.

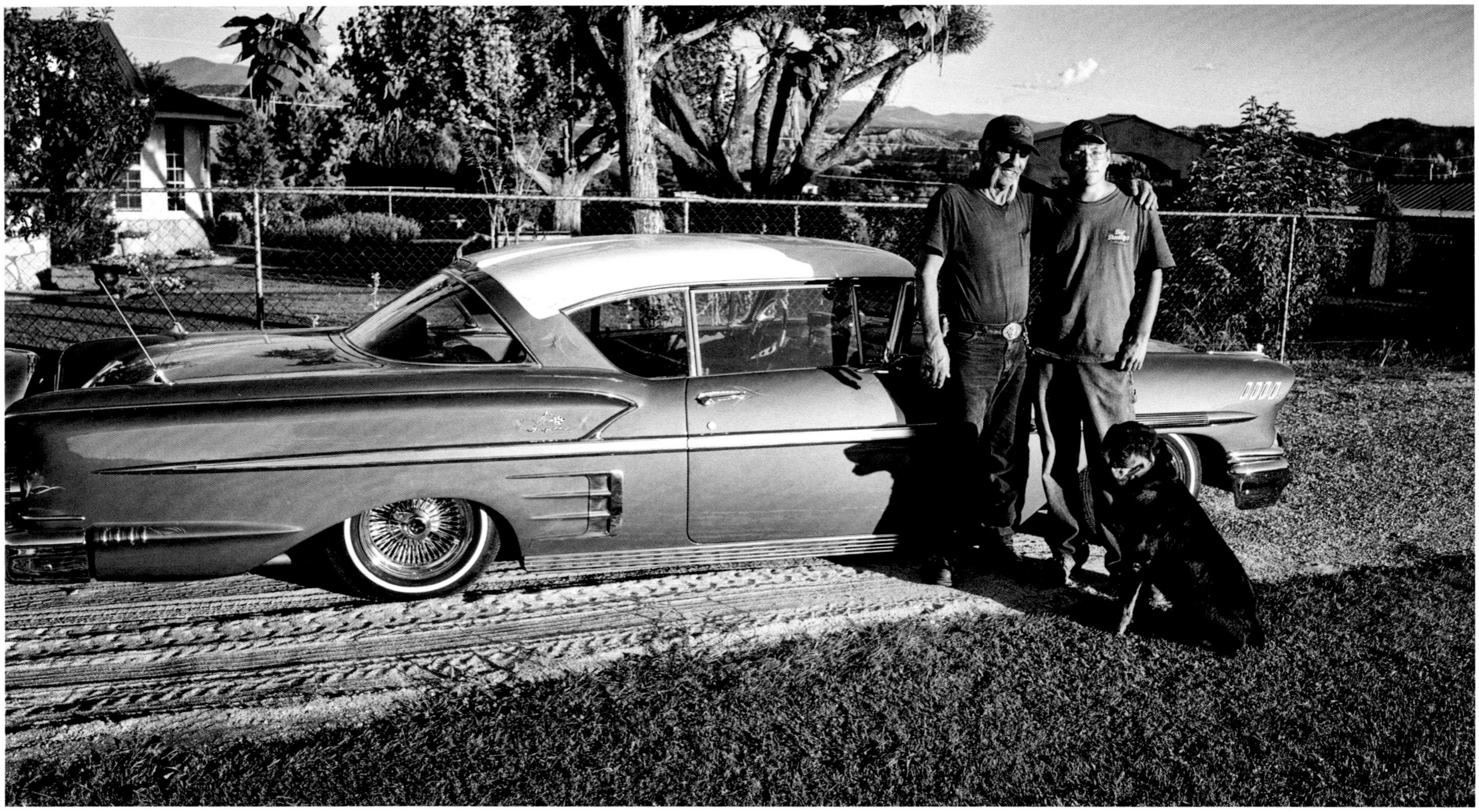

Johnny Martínez and Johnny Jr. with Their '58 Impala, Chimayó, 2015

"But there's also a lot of kids interested in lowriders, hot rods, old cars—like our kid is interested in it, and then when he has kids they're going to see him and they're going to want to be doing the same thing. So I think it's here to stay." Mike Roybal seems to agree with Johnny's assessment. "To me lowriding is going to be forever. It's not a phase to me. It's forever, you know."

Forever is a long time, but after nearly seventy years, the lowrider phenomenon is still around, and it has reached far beyond car enthusiasts. Lowrider culture includes many people who don't own a lowrider at all but embrace the lifestyle and its accoutrements. Lowrider model cars sell by the hundreds, as well as small "homie" dolls, including the lowriding, zoot-suit-wearing "Chuco," dressed to represent a cholo. An industry built around this and other lowrider paraphernalia—car-club T-shirts and hats, car-show swag, music, movies—celebrates and perpetuates the style. This kind of gear is on display in most extravagant form at the largest lowrider show in the nation, the Las Vegas Supershow, sponsored by *Lowrider* magazine and held every year in Las Vegas, Nevada. There, thousands of lowriders and spectators come together in an atmosphere of glitz and glamor that inspires lowriders to reach ever higher in their quest to perfect their rides.

From the streets of Juárez to the glittering lights of Las Vegas, Nevada, lowriders have come a long way—very slowly and very much in style. Elements of those foundational times persist even as the cars have become so extravagant and high-tech that a sixties cholo from Española would hardly recognize them. But although the cars may now bloom with lush, extravagant color, and they can dance and hop like no car has ever before, they're still low and they're not in a hurry to get anywhere.

And though the focus may have shifted from the streets to the shows, even tried and true competitive lowriders like Fred Rael, who love the car shows and do well at them, still succumb to the charms of the ride. "Lowriding is just a way of life," he says. "Like the other night, we were here in Santa Fe, my girlfriend and me, and she says, 'Let's go get some ice cream, like from McDonald's.' And I say, 'Well, tell you what, let's go in the Cadillac.'

"So we go down, and the weather is just perfect. Perfect evening—no wind, no rain, no dust. And so I say, 'No—we're going in the convertible.' So we took the '64 [Impala] out for the first time since I'd redone it, and we drove it to Sonic, had an ice cream, went to the gas station and talked to some friends at the car wash, then drove back home. We didn't even make it across town. We just went around the block—it took us about an hour to get around, real slow. And that was really fun."

It's been three years since I visited Eppie at his father's garage in Chimayó, when he and other lowriders from around the valley were getting ready for a cruise to the Santuario. But now I notice that the '53 Bel Air that was parked in front of the garage is inside the bay. It's been repainted and has a rebuilt motor and new hydraulics. It turns out that there's more to that car than I had realized, as Ray and Eppie explain to me now.

"Thirty, forty years ago when I gave him this car," Ray says, "he dropped the damn thing! And he did it without my permission. I had told him, 'It's yours, *m'hijo*, as long as you don't abuse it.' And sure enough, I went to Albuquerque one time and came back—and there's the car and it's lowered!"

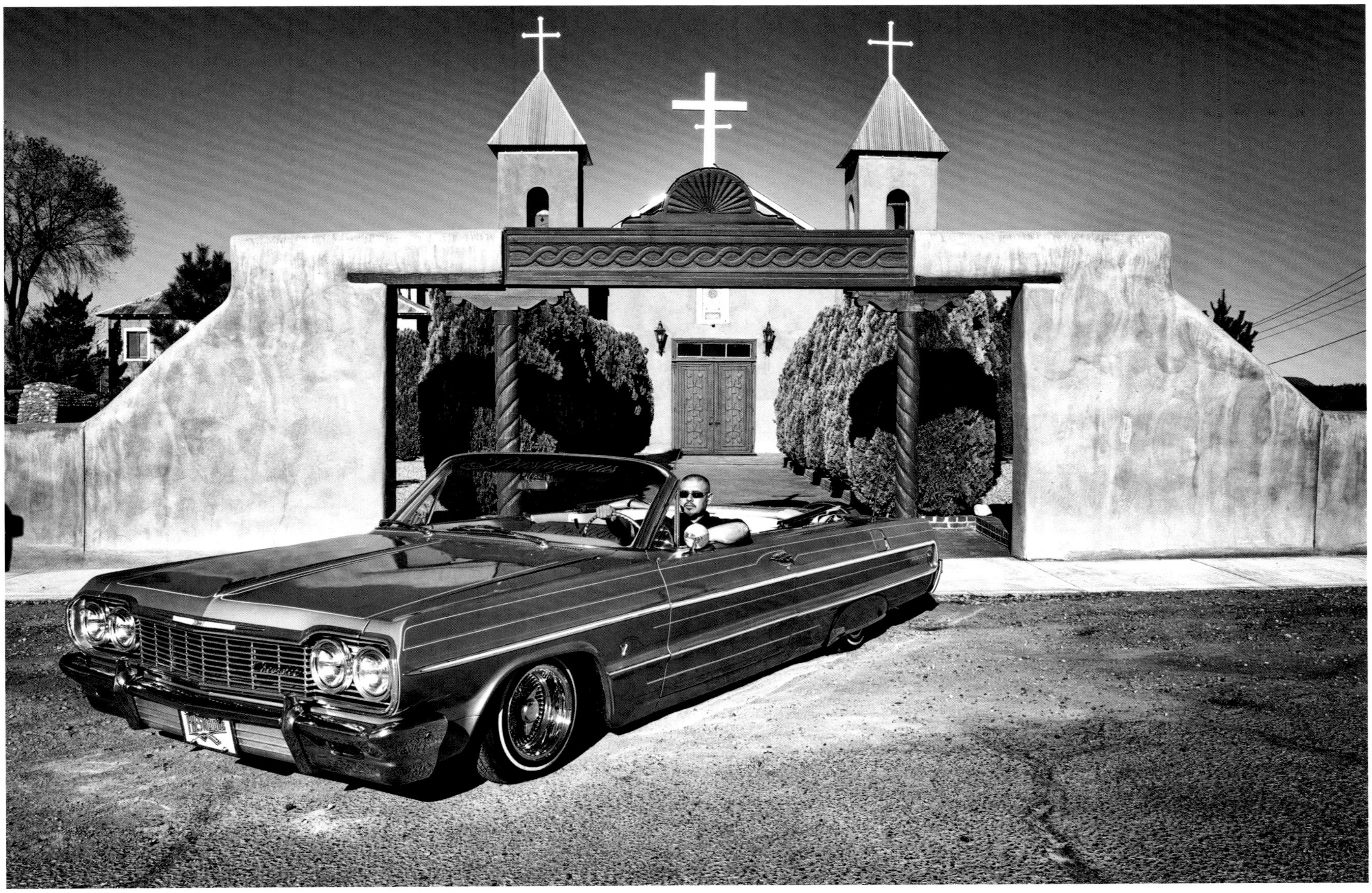

Fred Rael with His '64 Impala at the Santa Cruz Church, 2012

So perturbed was Ray with Eppie's remaking of his old car that he decreed, "You broke my first commandment!" and took it back from Eppie. It's only now, decades later, that Eppie and Ray have rebuilt the Bel Air and prepared it to show and drive.

Eppie and Ray's conflict over the lowrider reflects a long-term trend in attitudes. The car culture of northern New Mexico has always included a diversity of passions, but to an old-school hot-rodder like Ray, lowering a car represented an act of rebellion. Among the general public, too, lowriders were stereotyped as the creations of a rebellious fringe element of Latino culture. It took decades for Ray to accept his son's decision, just as it took a long time for lowriders to come into their own and gain acceptance as a bona fide—and now dominant—part of New Mexico car culture.

Eppie has his own shop now, on Albuquerque's Central Avenue, where people come to have him slam, juice, paint, and overhaul their cars to the owners' specifications. Ray has gotten over any resentment he had about Eppie embarking on a life devoted to lowriders. In fact, he is proud of his son, and he drives down a few times a week to help out in the shop. Eppie appreciates every visit. "I don't know what I'll do when he's gone," says Eppie, choking up, "because he got me started, and he has supported me all along here in my own shop. That's what it's all about, and I think I'll be done with all this when I don't have him anymore."

Watching Eppie at work, Ray beams, saying, "Some people just don't know how to do this right. It takes a lot of learning. It takes doing this so long that you know how to do it. That's the way with Eppie. He can throw a set of hydraulics on your car in the matter of quick. If somebody says, 'Juice up this car for me,' boom, boom, he takes batteries off the racks in the shop, says, 'How many batteries you need?' And boom, boom, boom he's got your ten, eight batteries, whatever, in there. And there you have your lowrider, and it's done right."

"Doing it right," building cars with great care and attention to detail, showing them to the world with great pride—this is the kind of *cariño* that lowriders bring to their craft, and among the dozens of lowriders I've met and come to know, it's the same attitude that they bring to their families, community, and culture. That's something to be admired as much as the paint job on a beautifully restored and tricked-out Impala at a car show, or the lines of a bomb cruising the back roads of northern New Mexico.

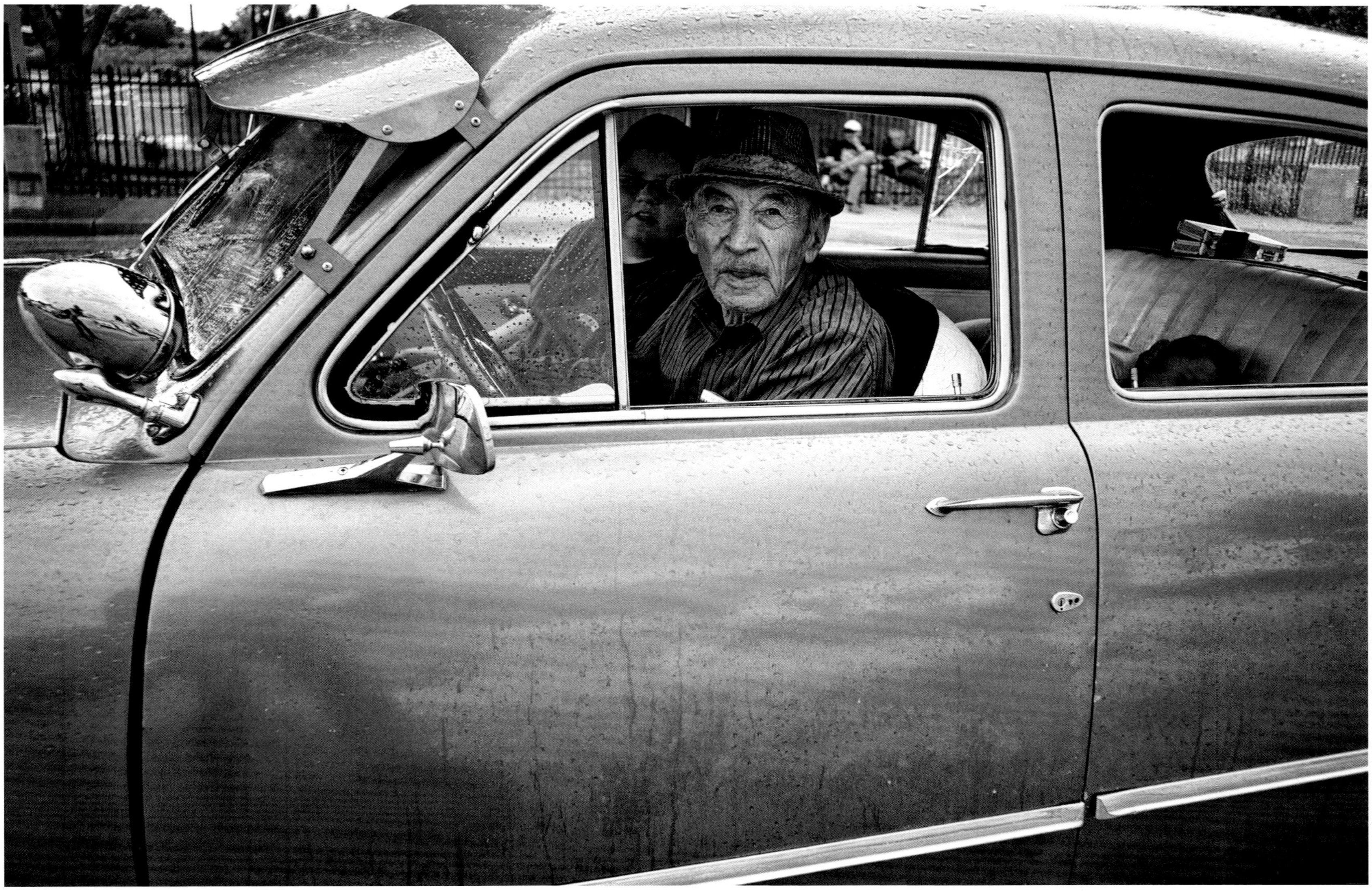

Plaza de Española, 2015

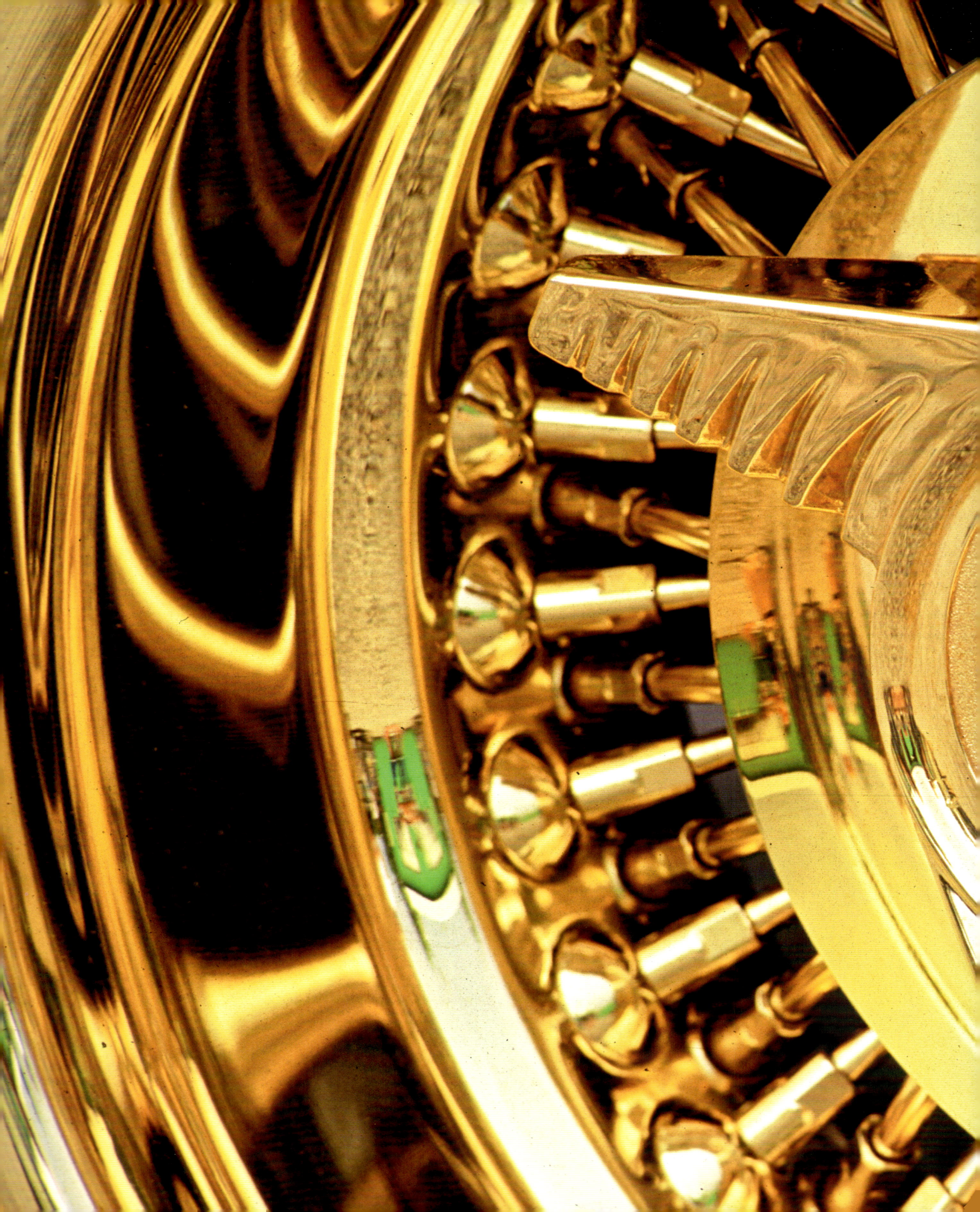

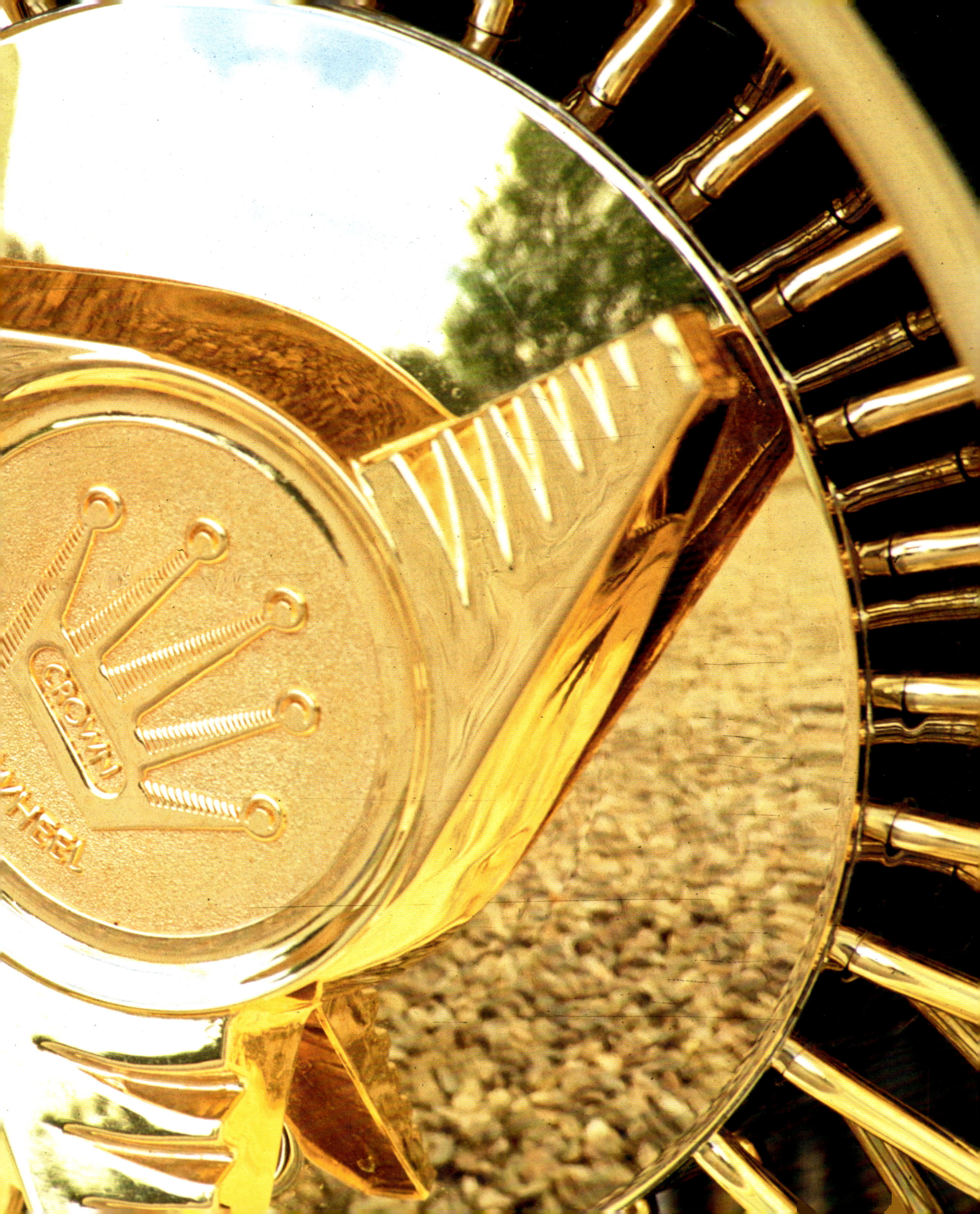
CROWN

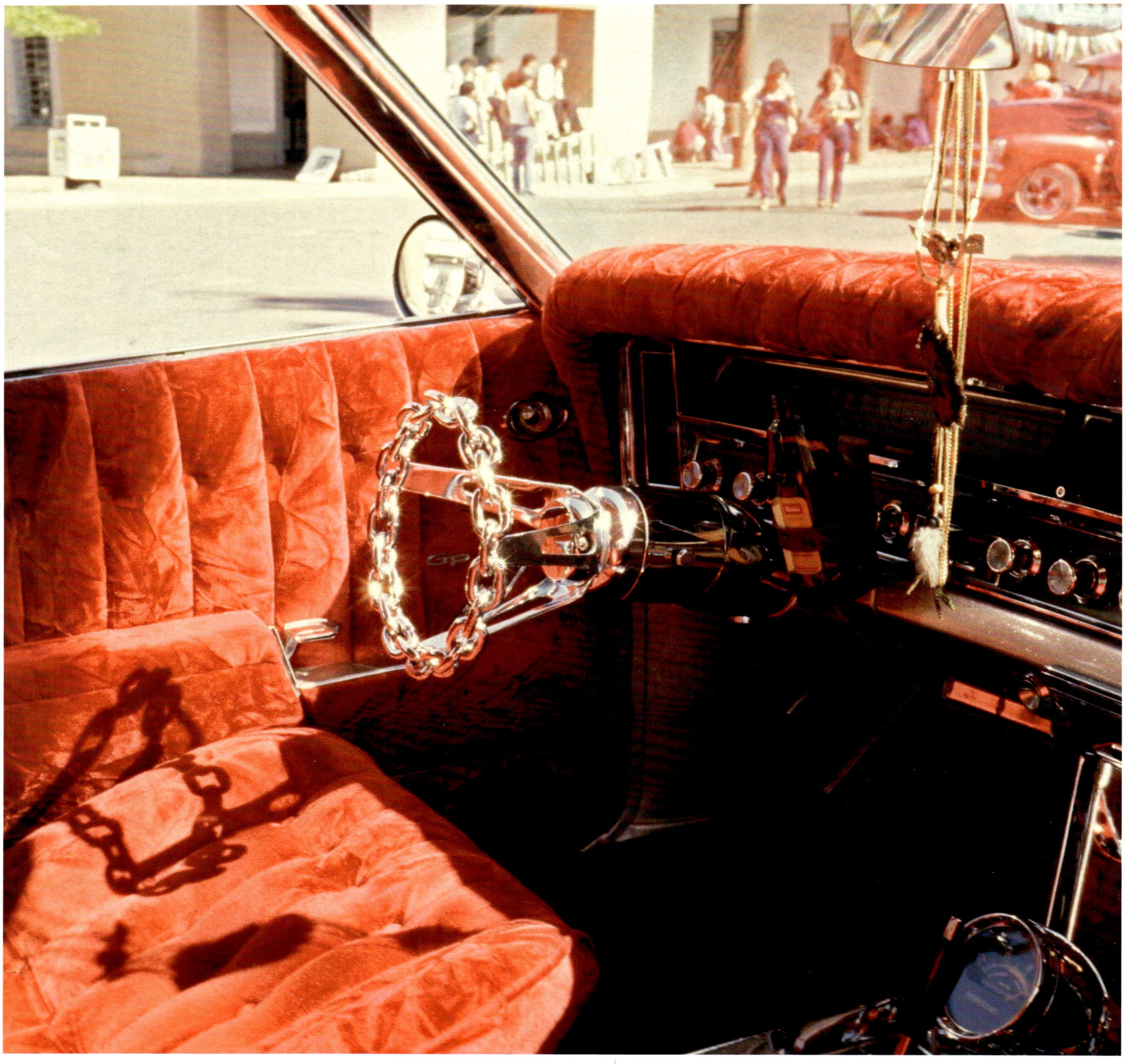

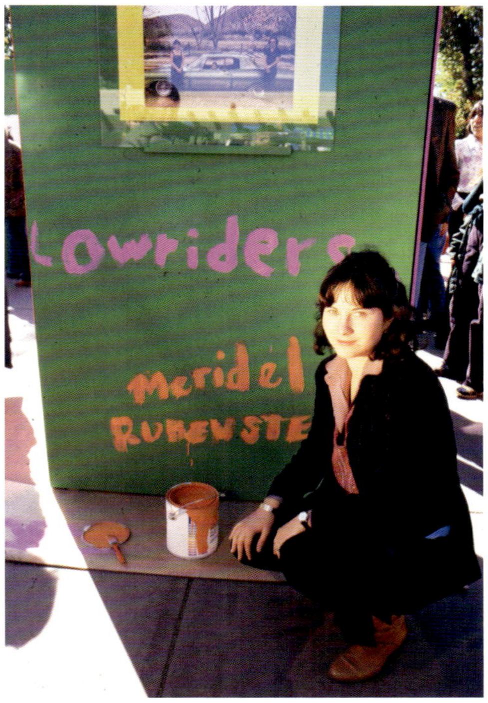

the art of the lowrider: interview with meridel rubenstein

KATHERINE WARE

Meridel Rubenstein moved to New Mexico as a young artist in 1973 to attend the MFA program in photography and art history at the University of New Mexico. In 1980–1981 she made a series of photographs of some of the state's lowriders, both the cars and their owners. Rubenstein approached the lowriders as fellow artists, and her time with them had a deep and lasting impact on her work over the years. Katherine Ware, curator of photography at the New Mexico Museum of Art, talked with Rubenstein at her studio in July 2015 about the adventure of making the photographs as an outsider to the culture, the museum's remarkable outdoor show of those portraits in 1980, what she learned about art from lowriders, and her interpretation of these extraordinary "cathedrals on wheels."

KATHERINE WARE (KW): Meridel, you're now well established as an artist, but about thirty-five years ago, when you were fairly new to New Mexico and just getting started in your career, you decided to photograph lowriders, and that became a really important event in your career, both in its influence on your later work and also in terms of people continuing to be very interested in the pictures. How did you get involved in this project?

MERIDEL RUBENSTEIN (MR): In about 1978, I was commissioned to make portraits for an exhibition and book about New Mexico craftspeople for the inaugural exhibition in the Albuquerque Museum's new building, *One Space, Three Visions*. For me, the work was a sequel to the 1976 series *La Gente de la Luz* that I did for the Museum of Fine Arts [now the New Mexico Museum of Art] in Santa Fe, that were portraits of people from the dominant three cultures [Anglo, Hispano, Native American] in the state.

above
Meridel Rubenstein painting the title panel at the opening of *The Lowriders* exhibition, Santa Fe Plaza, October 19, 1980

opposite
Meridel Rubenstein, *Lowrider Interior*, Santa Fe, October 19, 1980

For the Albuquerque project, I traveled with artist Ramona Sakiestewa, and we had the greatest time on the road all over the state, meeting the craftspeople. For the grand opening of the new building in 1979, all the crafts by these artists were on display with the portraits I made. Ray Graham, who is a patron of the arts in Albuquerque, looked at the work and said, "Meridel, those are not the true craftspeople of New Mexico—the lowriders are!" And he said he would pay me to make three portraits of the lowriders. I didn't think this was a great idea, but I needed the money. I had no interest in going up to these tough guys to make portraits for a collector, but I thought I might be willing to do it for a museum. So I talked to Director Ellen Bradbury and Curator of Photography Steve Yates at Fine Arts about it.

KW: What made you think you'd be interested enough in lowriders to make more than three portraits, enough for a museum show?

MR: I'm not crazy about cars. My friend Sal, an upholsterer here in Santa Fe, got the first three guys together for me to photograph. These cars were not connected to lowrider culture—just custom cars. Next I went to a car show in Albuquerque, which I wasn't so excited about. You have to imagine the big, steamy convention center. There were girls having a wet T-shirt contest, and the boys were down on their hands and knees with rulers measuring how high their car could hop with its hydraulic system.

KW: The portraits weren't clicking and the car show wasn't your scene, so what was your next move?

MR: I understood the sexy aspects of it right away, but I didn't yet understand the religious signifiers of the lowriders. So I had made those first three portraits, and I felt like something was not working. And then Jerry [West, her partner] said, "Just go to Española."

KW: Sure, Española is the lowrider capital of New Mexico, if not the world! An easy drive from Santa Fe. But for some folks, it had the reputation as a tough town.

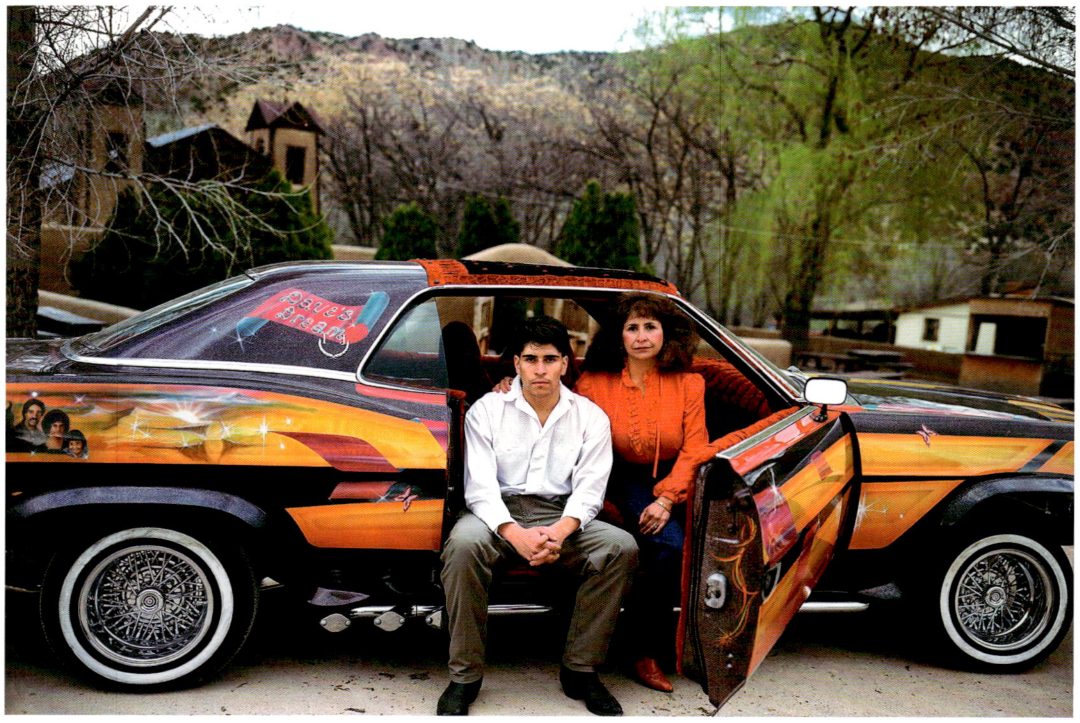

Meridel Rubenstein, *Irene Jaramillo and Dave Jaramillo Jr., Dave's Dream 2, '60 Ford LTD,* Santuario de Chimayó, New Mexico, 1992

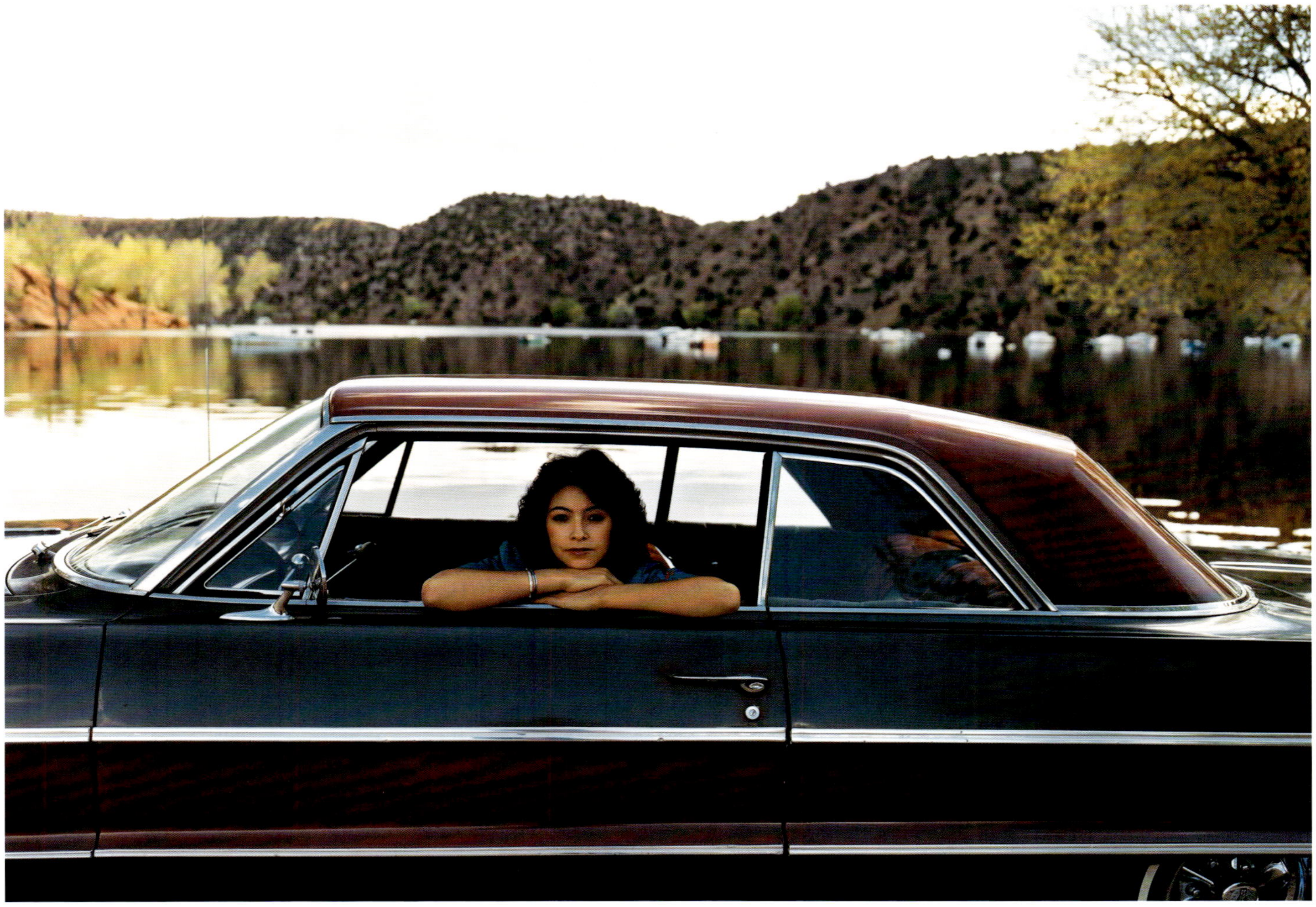

Meridel Rubenstein, *Peggy Martínez, '64 Chevy Two-Tone,* Santa Cruz Lake, 1980

MR: I was a little scared. I drove up to Española, and right away I saw a really colorful car in the Safeway parking lot with the owner standing there. I think Jerry was with me and he said, "Just go talk to him." I jumped out of the car, introduced myself, and met Charlie [Villareal], who turned out to be the sweetest guy in the world. I made his portrait that day. (At the Lowrider show on the Plaza a year later a woman from New York bought this car.) After I met Charlie, he introduced me to Benino Martínez: "Call Benino, he's a car upholsterer, he'll know a lot of lowriders." I call Benino on the phone and describe what I'm trying to do and say, "Could you just meet me with a few cars? Next Saturday." He said, "Sure, meet me at Colonel Sanders."

And on Saturday I drove up to Española to the Kentucky Fried Chicken, this small restaurant parking lot, and two full car clubs—Los Bajitos and Los Unidos—had shown up each with about ten people, so twenty cars!

They were so amazing all together! I stood on my front bumper and told them what wonderful artists and craftspeople they were and that I'd like to have them be part of a museum show in Santa Fe.

Then the police showed up and said we couldn't have more than two cars here. There were rules to stop the lowriders from gathering in public places. I explained to them, "I'm from the museum, and these people are artists, and I need to photograph them." They said okay, we could drive over to the police station and set up in their parking lot in back. So I sat in my car, waiting for the cars to get moving, and it seemed to take forever. Finally, I rolled down my window to ask what was going on since I was supposed to follow them. Somebody said, "Don't worry. Los Bajitos invited us, and we're Los Unidos." Meaning that Los Bajitos had to go first. And their president and their vice president, their treasurer first and then the rest of the club, then we'll go next. They had a formation, rules of etiquette.

That's when I said "Yes!" These wonderful lowriders were sprawling out in formation from the parking lot, twenty cars all jammed together, and what they had to do was spiral out to get the right one in the right order out of that mass of cars. And they were going about one mile an hour.

KW: Why was that exciting? How did that experience change your perception of lowriders?

MR: It was a procession! Because I knew about the conquistadors and the Penitente Brotherhood and I make the pilgrimage to the Santuario de Chimayó every year. I walk every year when I'm here on Good Friday.

KW: It resonated with what you knew about the traditions connected with Spanish settlers in this country and Catholicism in northern New Mexico, things you learned after you moved here? You came to New Mexico to study photography at the University of New Mexico, but was that your only connection to the land?

MR: I'm not one of those people that fell in love with this place and gave up everything and moved here. I was here for school and I had to start learning who was here so I could make pictures. The first few years I was working on pictures I had already made in Newfoundland and Vermont, but meanwhile I was trying to find out where I was. You can't tell in Albuquerque what northern New Mexico is about, at least I couldn't.

KW: You're a Jewish woman from the East Coast. Did you have an awareness of yourself as an outsider, especially as you began photographing the art and culture of lowriders? That was a time when the culture wasn't in charge of how it was being seen by the outside world, but you went in to record your own perceptions of it.

MR: I want to paint a picture for you, about what was going on then in America about identity and culture. This was right on the cusp of people of color getting involved in representing themselves and their culture, but it hadn't happened yet. In 1980 there were very few Hispanic photographers starting to do some of this work, and I did the lowrider pictures, but that was about it. We didn't have the identity politics then. Later, when I was teaching at the Institute of American Indian Arts, artists were actively pursuing that. And self-representation was, and still is, a key part of that.

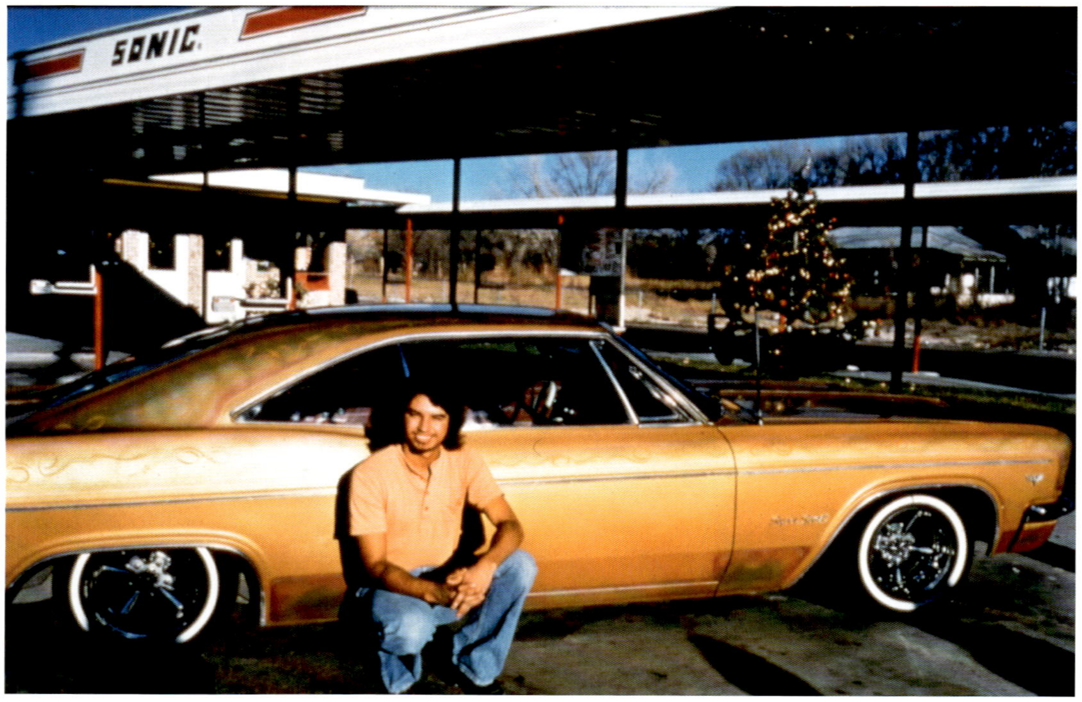

Meridel Rubenstein, *Carlos Archuleta Lowrider at Sonic*, Española, 1980

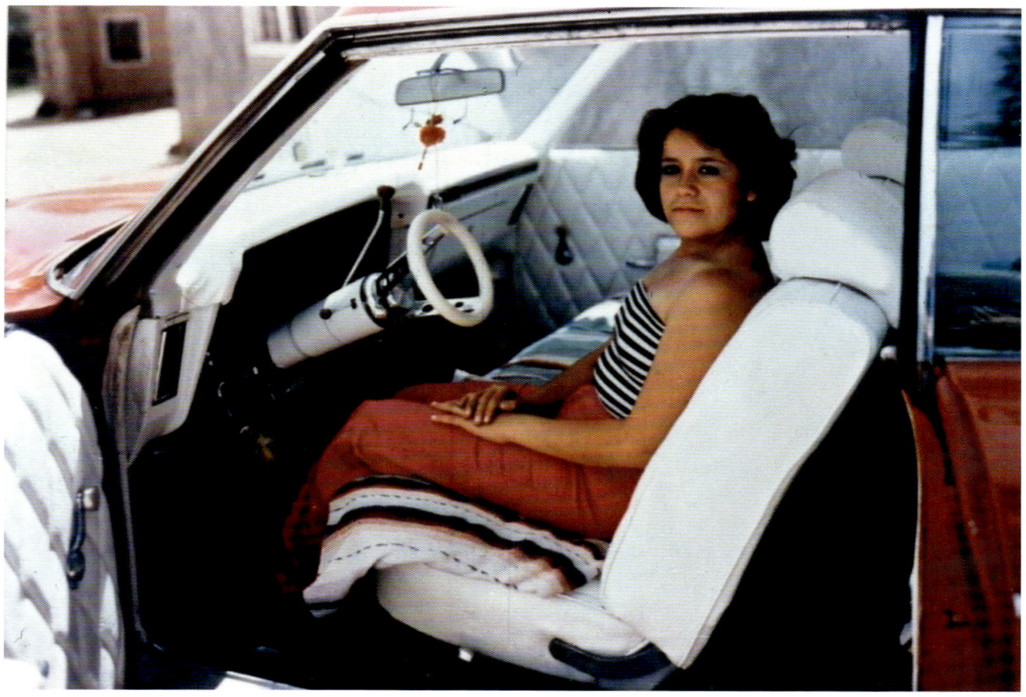

Meridel Rubenstein, *Anabelle Martínez in Her Cousin Petra Garduño's Lowrider*, Chimayó, 1980

KW: So in 1980, you found lowriders and their families receptive to your interest in photographing them?

MR: Think about artists. You want to come talk to me about what I do? I'll stop everything I'm doing. That's my art. I have to talk to you. My purpose is to communicate. Right? It's the same for the lowriders. That's their purpose. They're artists.

KW: They were excited to share their masterpieces.

MR: Once I got that they were artists, it was great. They were showing me their art and I was celebrating their art by photographing it. Totally reciprocal. I wanted to celebrate it; they wanted it to be seen. I photographed every weekend, because the lowriders have jobs, and they're only free on the weekend. By then I had met at least twenty people in the car clubs, so I made appointments to photograph them and they introduced me to other friends.

KW: The lowriders were willing to have you photograph their cars, because that was their art, but you're a portrait photographer. How did you manage to get them in the picture, too, to make it your art?

MR: I said, "You are the artist, you have to be in the picture, if you don't mind. I'm not a car photographer. I'm making a work about you."

KW: Yes, but many of these cars are worked on by a variety of talents, like the mural painters or the hydraulics guys, the upholsterers, and the whole production is really kind of a collaborative effort that involves not only the person who imagines the car but everyone who works on it and often their whole family.

MR: The owners are the conceptual artists who decide what the car will portray. Some of the photographs I took include the family, like the photo of the Bad Company car. And the Martínez family, each member of the family had a car, so I photographed them individually. But I guess that's a failing of the project, in a sense, that I was after each car maker and not the community of workers. (The photos on p. 45–47 are all of the Martínez family. The parents got a new car and their old cars went to their kids to turn into lowriders.)

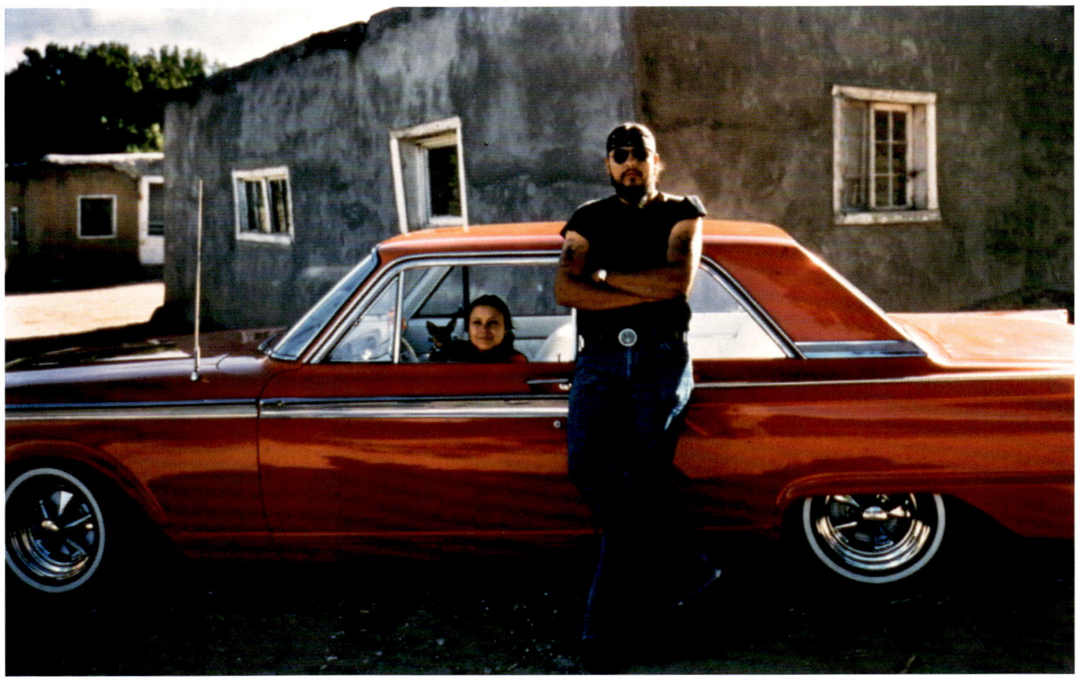

Meridel Rubenstein, *Vangie Martínez and Frankie Maestas*, Chimayó, 1980

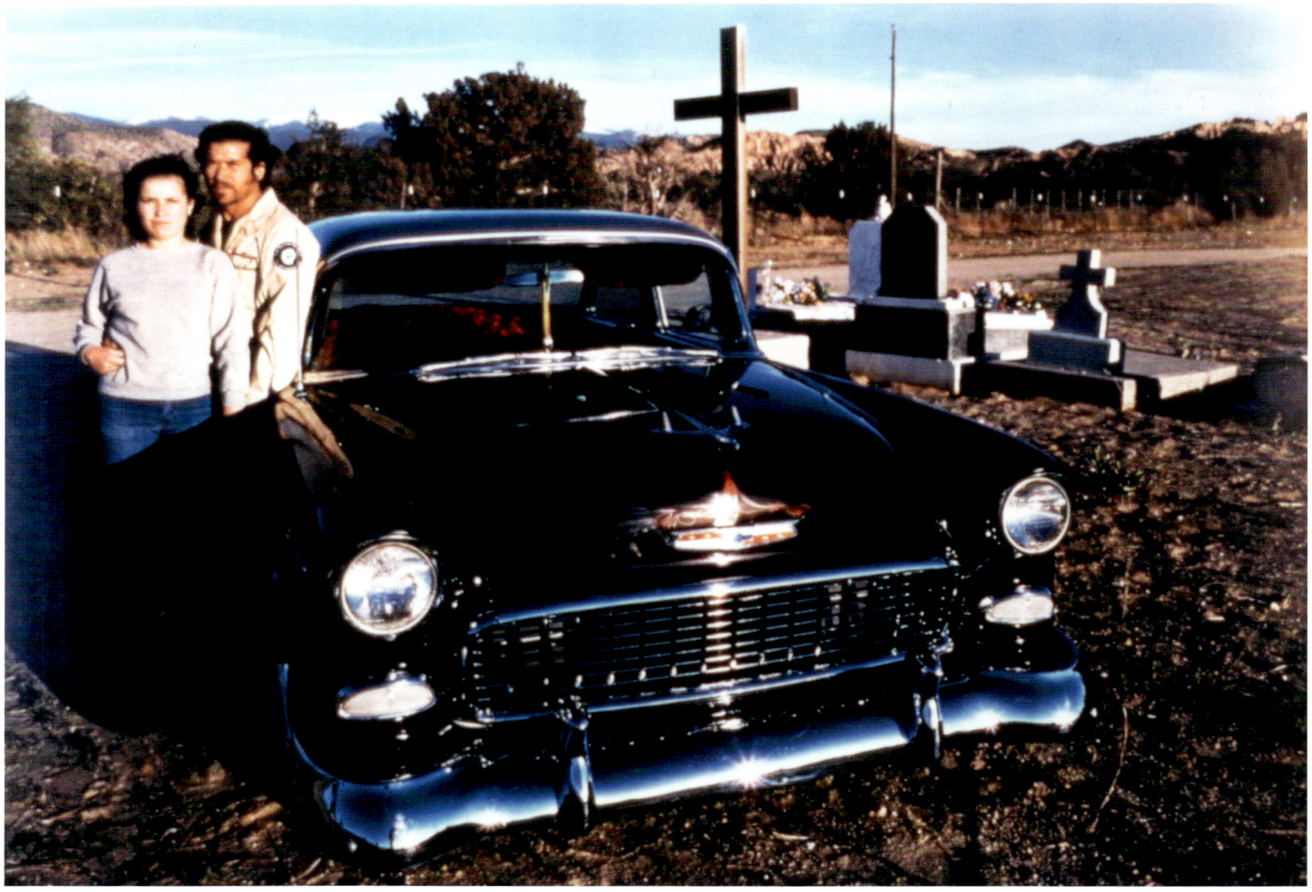

Meridel Rubenstein, *Jimmy and Clara Martínez at Jimmy's Grandmother's Grave*, Chimayó, 1980

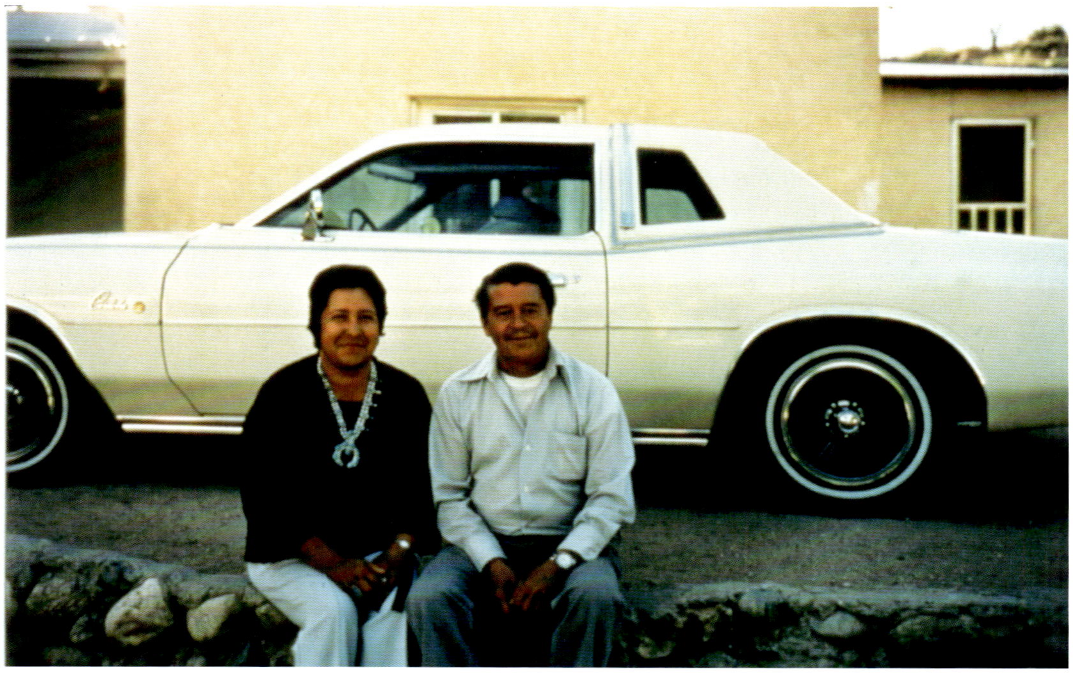

Meridel Rubenstein, *Martínez Parents with Their Car*, Chimayó, 1980

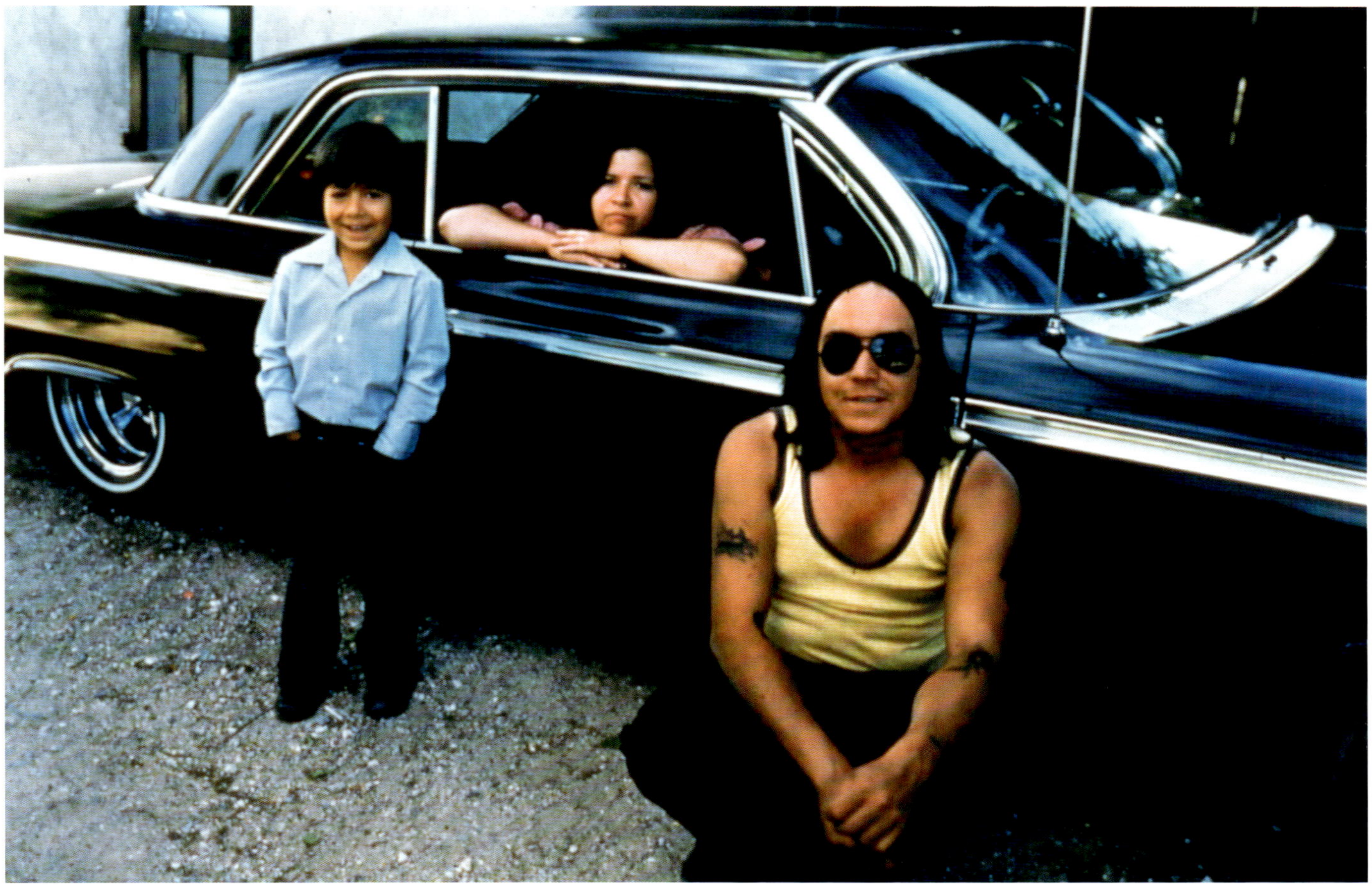

Meridel Rubenstein, *Chris Martínez and Family*, Chimayó, 1980

KW: Your approach was to portray the owners as individual artists—that's how you related to them personally. That's part of the issue with being an outside observer, an artist, because you always bring a vision or a perspective of your own, yet you want to be careful about imposing an idea on a situation you don't know much about.

MR: You want to give people what they need to be themselves, that's all. My job is to disappear when I am photographing.

KW: That's coming from your studies in social science and as a documentary photographer and filmmaker. In earlier work you used a 4x5 view camera, black-and-white film. Those were the tools, and the philosophy was for you to be an objective witness to whatever you photographed.

MR: Yes, monochrome prints for me, though elaborately toned. Color was only for commercial photographers! After my *La Gente* series, I thought I should have a bigger camera, a 5x7 field camera, which was a perfect format for photographing the lowriders.

KW: Do you remember what made you decide to start photographing in color? It was just starting to be used by artists in the late 1970s and early 1980s but it was still kind of edgy.

MR: The lowriders had to be in color. There was no choice.

KW: I love that you were using a big camera, the 5x7, for the lowriders, because that's a slow camera and you were taking pictures of slow cars. It's a really different experience from taking a snapshot.

MR: That was a thing people had to learn when we made the portraits. It's a strategy, too, because you don't really want to make a quick picture. I'm just looking through the ground glass on the back of the camera and I'm watching them. I'm tweaking it and fiddling with it and they're getting bored. They're looking at me. It's a very curious process. You need time till the people are ready to give you the picture themselves. Then we make the picture.

KW: How did you decide on the locations for the photographs? What were you looking for?

MR: Well, probably where they lived or somewhere we'd meet. We'd meet at Sonic or we'd meet at Colonel Sanders or at Safeway. A good one to talk about is Benino's car, the gold car. It's the color of the earth, *tierra madre*; I understood that connection was important. With Peggy, they suggested we go to Santa Cruz Lake. I'd never been to Santa Cruz before, but it was so perfect because there's the water and these lines on the chassis. They thought of that as the most scenic place to go but it also worked formally so perfectly for the picture.

KW: What about the evolution of the series, how the portraits may have changed over time as you got to know people and learned more about lowriders and the local culture?

MR: The *La Gente* series I did in the mid-1970s was totally about culture. And at the same time, I was also making pictures about Jerry's ranching family and their longtime relationship with this land, blending a portrait to a landscape and having writing with it. So in my own life, after I married, there I am with this very large family that I was astounded by. [laughs]

KW: A family with deep local roots.

MR: Yes, and I was a wandering Jew. [laughs]

KW: So working with the lowriders was an extension of your interest in the culture of New Mexico, then with its craftspeople, and then with the large extended family you married into, the West family. It sounds like there were a lot of levels of connection with the lowrider artists.

MR: The truth is, working with the lowriders was extremely influential for me.

KW: What do you mean by that? How did getting acquainted with lowriders and photographing them affect you as an artist?

MR: It completely changed me. Their use of velvet and chrome together was a powerful combination for me. Later I made work with palladium and steel, glass and wood, and copper and metal—that's all from understanding from the lowriders what two different materials do to your psyche. Even sandblasting on glass—I can't say I got that from sculptors. I did not learn any of this in art school because I was a photographer, so I learned about materials from the lowriders. It was from that point on that I began to work with disparate materials. To believe that a material has its own resonance as a signifier that can affect the viewer. There are probably more influences from them that I'm not even aware of.

KW: It's the juxtaposition of the differing materials that you feel is so powerful?

MR: It's the disparate nature, the contrariness they can suggest. They allow more than one idea to live in one work. With the lowriders, religion, family, sexuality, regeneration are experienced through velvet, chrome, glass, and a little imagery. The materials have to reflect what the work's about. In two later series, *Labyrinths* and *Critical Mass*, I used palladium and steel to mean very specific things. In *Critical Mass*—cold and hard, warm and soft, technological and earthbound issues. The *Labyrinths* were about a split self, male and female, old and young, animal and human, palladium and steel. I learned how to use materials conceptually from the lowriders. I'm so lucky that I had that experience.

KW: Not everyone would have learned that lesson though. You were receptive.

MR: Another important lesson they taught me has to do with procession. With my 1995 installation piece *Oppenheimer's Chair*, I was really interested in having people circumnavigate it, to keep their bodies moving as they were seeing it. That's what happens with the lowriders—everything's moving. I got really interested in building images, though I had already started doing it before meeting the lowriders, circling images with text and having one blend into another. I started piecing images together, because that lowrider event on the Plaza in 1980 was such a constructed tableau with the photographs and the cars and the music all together. It was a big event.

KW: That was the one-day exhibition you did with the museum on Sunday, October 19, with the Santa Fe Plaza closed down for the lowriders and all the visitors.

MR: Imagine the Santa Fe Plaza in the late 1970s. Each street on the square has two-way traffic going around it. You could hardly move on Friday or Saturday nights because the lowriders were there going one mile every hour! It was wonderful to see, and Jerry and I loved to go downtown and watch all these cars. But then the city council decided to make the streets one-way to stop

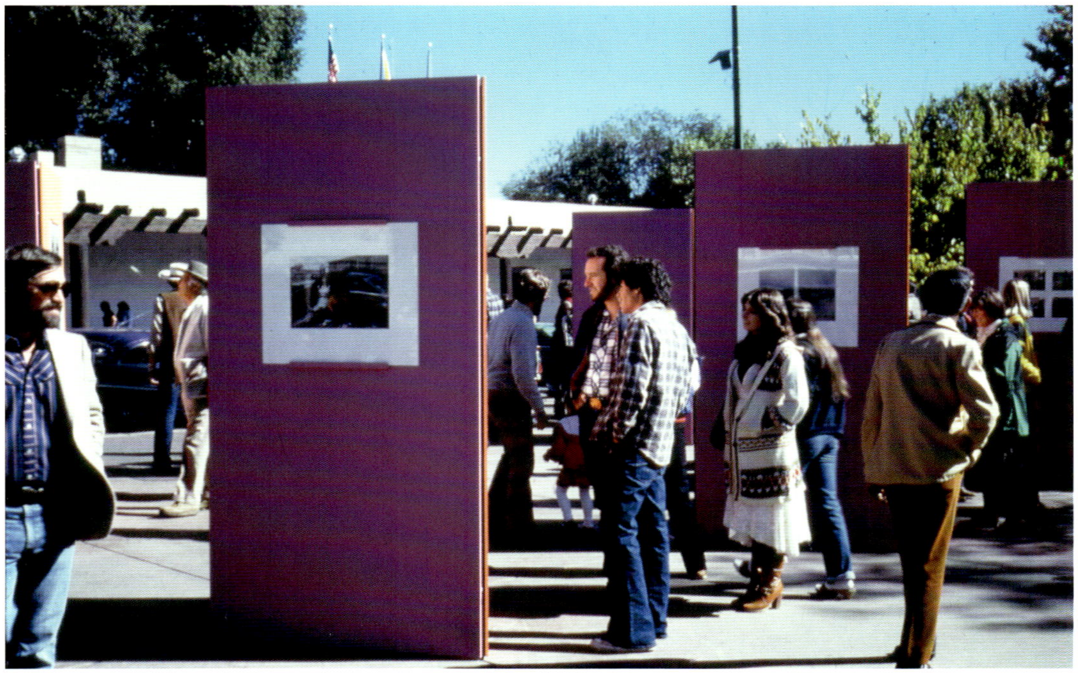

Meridel Rubenstein, The Lowriders *Exhibition*, 1980

this from happening, because some people had very negative feelings about the lowriders and the traffic. So for the museum show, we thought the idea of having the cars coming to the Plaza was a lost cause! But when we asked the city council, they said okay, and we got the Plaza for one day. Then Ellen [Bradbury, MFA director] went into action!

KW: A lot of people at that time thought of lowriders as outlaws and wrote letters to the newspaper complaining about them driving around downtown.

MR: That was the misconception, because it's not a gang culture at all. When you spend that much time and money on making something beautiful, you are not in a gang. You don't have time.

KW: Making these cars, it seems like a very positive impulse, of imagining and creating your own reality to inhabit. Making this absolutely one-of-a-kind jewel box out of some old junker car and listening to oldies music as you cruise the neighborhood at the speed of a snail, slowing the world down to that pace and traveling in that glorious style and luxury! It's like a bird of paradise in our brown, rocky landscape.

MR: The families are involved, everybody's putting the money in, and they're seeing what's going to be created. Think about some of the modest housing in rural New Mexico, and then in front of it, they've got this beautiful object. Everybody's invested in it.

KW: The family treasure and the family fortune, too, right?

MR: I'm amazed it's still going on. These are artists of the highest order; they're doing something profound.

KW: I'm really interested in that visionary aspect. That each of these owners is taking, often an old car, and they use this old American car partly because it's strong and well made and either cheap or free. They completely strip them. So they are really envisioning everything, every step of the way. And the incredible ingenuity that goes into these things.

MR: They had to create their own technology.

KW: It's interesting to me that you're originally from Detroit.

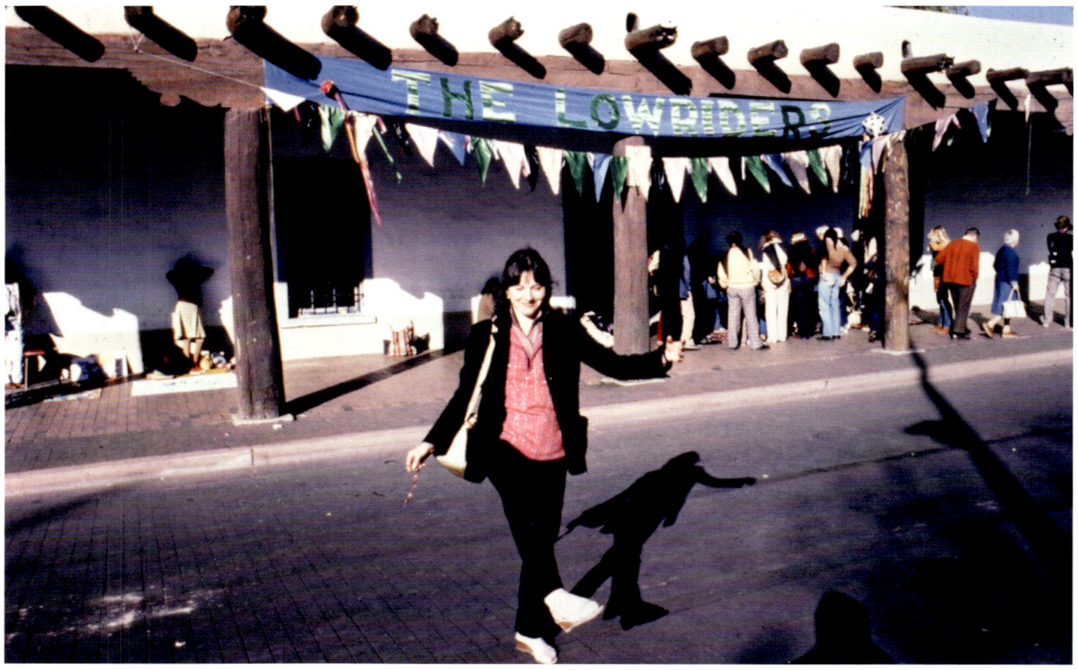

Meridel Rubenstein in Front of the Palace of the Governors, The Lowriders *Exhibition*, Santa Fe, 1980. (Banner made by Meridel's photography students at the University of Colorado, Boulder.)

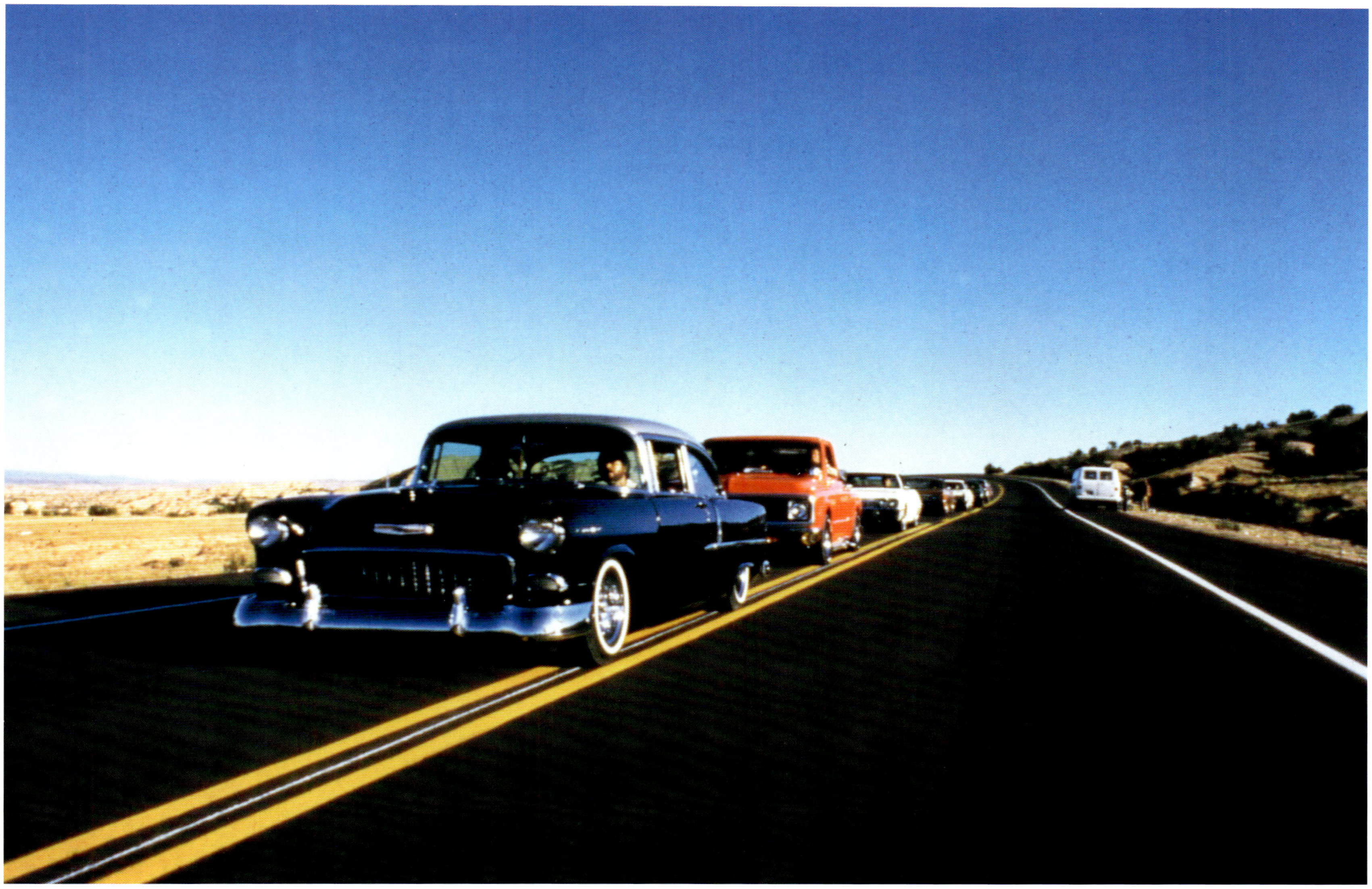

Meridel Rubenstein, *Lowriders Procession to Santa Fe Exhibition*, 1980

MR: What about that! I hadn't thought about that at all. My parents would have had those same models of cars.

KW: One of the things that really strikes me is how the cars are an assertion of identity in a sometimes hostile world, a strong message that "I am here," you have to look at me now. And because the cars are mobile it's a way of claiming space, of taking a piece of your community with you wherever you go. Everything stops when the lowriders go by. The traffic can't go. The people stop and stare, take pictures, and applaud. You can't ignore them.

MR: It's in public space, claiming public space as an art experience, as an aesthetic experience. If you think about it, that's what they do, they construct meaning. They're doing it in a mobile fashion. They're constructing meaning and they drive by. There they are and you have to stop.

KW: They pull you into their world, at least for a moment. That's powerful.

MR: Somebody said lowriders were invented in New Mexico, but I think it probably came from Los Angeles to here. So for the show on the Plaza, in addition to my photographs, I knew the cars should be there and we had seventy-five of them. I was teaching in Boulder, Colorado, at the time, and my students made this banner for the show, very long, that said "The Lowriders" with big satin dice hanging on the ends. I used that afterward, in all the other shows of the lowrider photos.

KW: That was the big sash that hung across the front of the Palace of the Governors on the day of the exhibition!

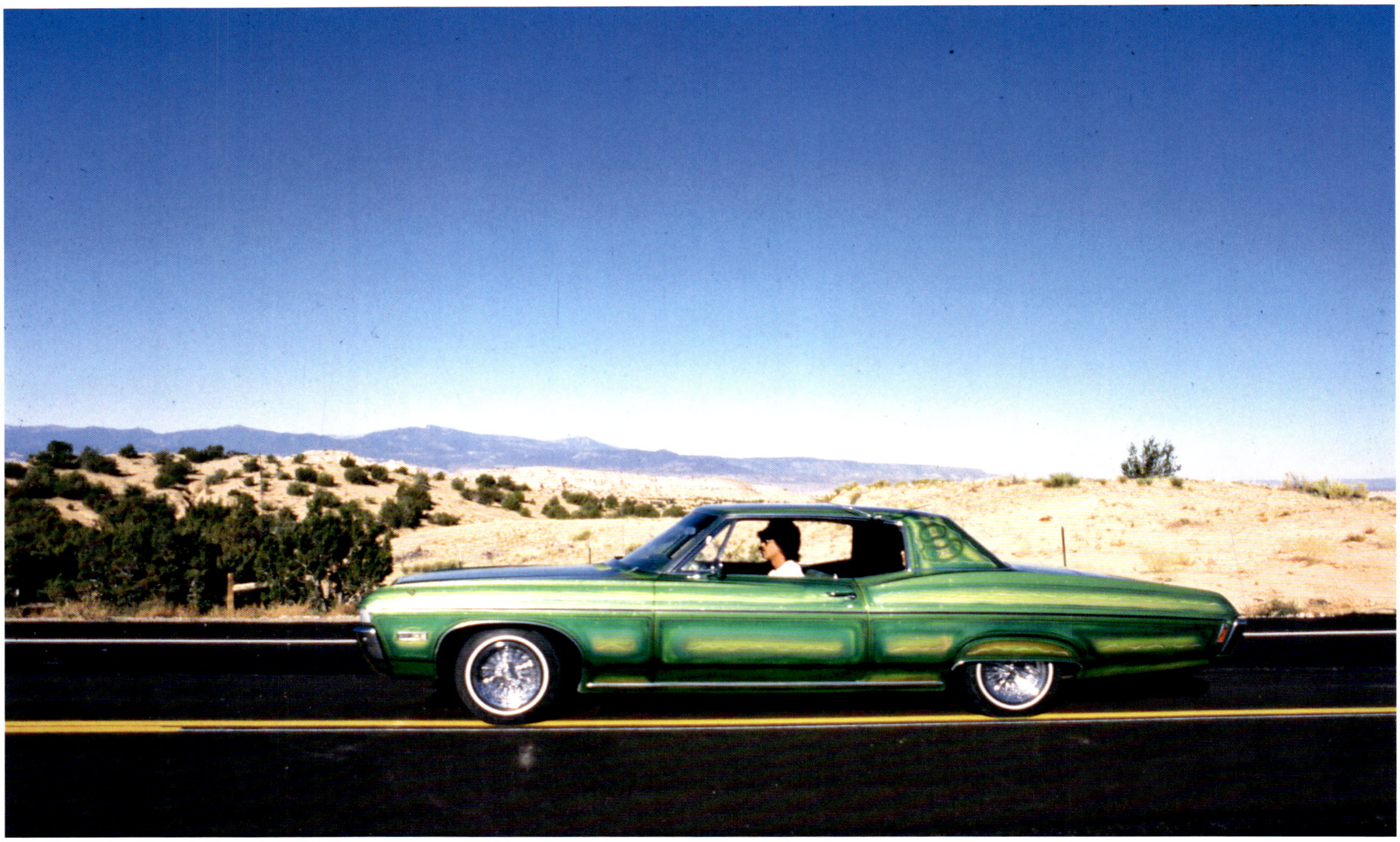

Meridel Rubenstein, *"Bad Company" Lowrider Driving to Santa Fe*, 1980

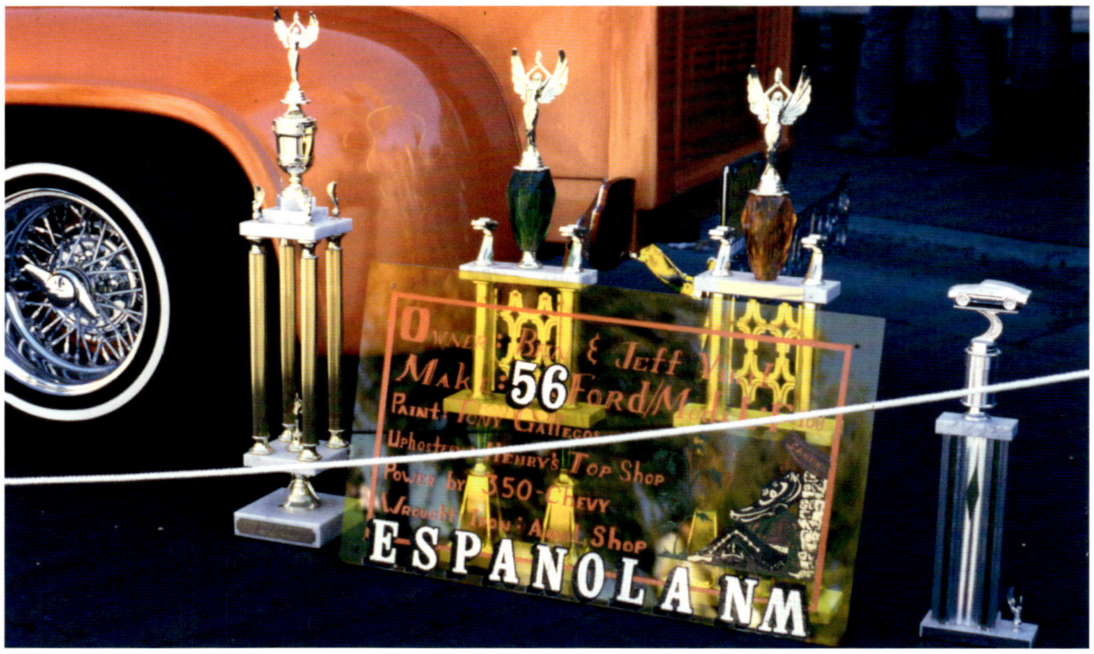

Meridel Rubenstein, *Trophies Displayed at* The Lowriders *Exhibition*, Santa Fe, 1980

MR: I had to organize all the car clubs and people to come down to Santa Fe for the show, but they invited other people, too. In the meantime, Gary DeWalt decided to make a film of the whole event. He had to get up early because the cars started leaving around six in the morning to get to the Plaza on time because they were going to go so slow. They had to stop in Española at the car wash, then again in Santa Fe at the car wash. They were cleaning and polishing up to the last minute so they could appear in their full glory!

When they arrived at the corner of Washington and Lincoln Streets in Santa Fe, there was a policeman to let them in to drive in front of the banner. Each car stopped to be admired, they hopped, and then they found their place in the circle around the Plaza. They were such great showmen. They opened their trunks and hoods. They put down carpets and brought out their trophies. They had fences, so you could put a little fence around your car.

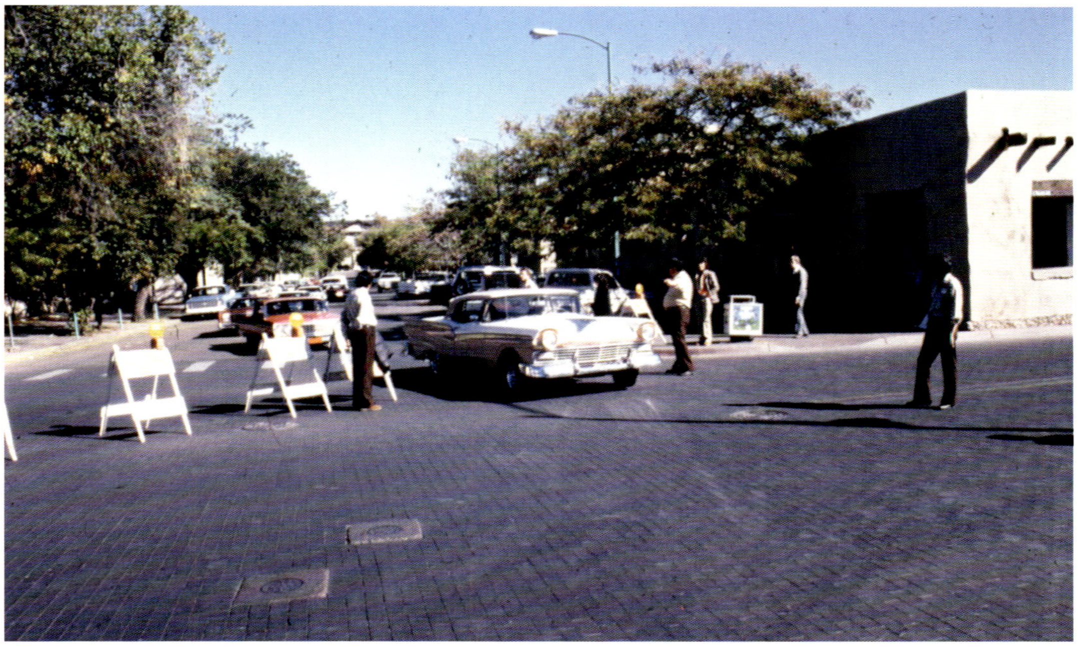

Meridel Rubenstein, *Lowrider Entering Plaza for* The Lowriders *Exhibition*, Santa Fe, 1980

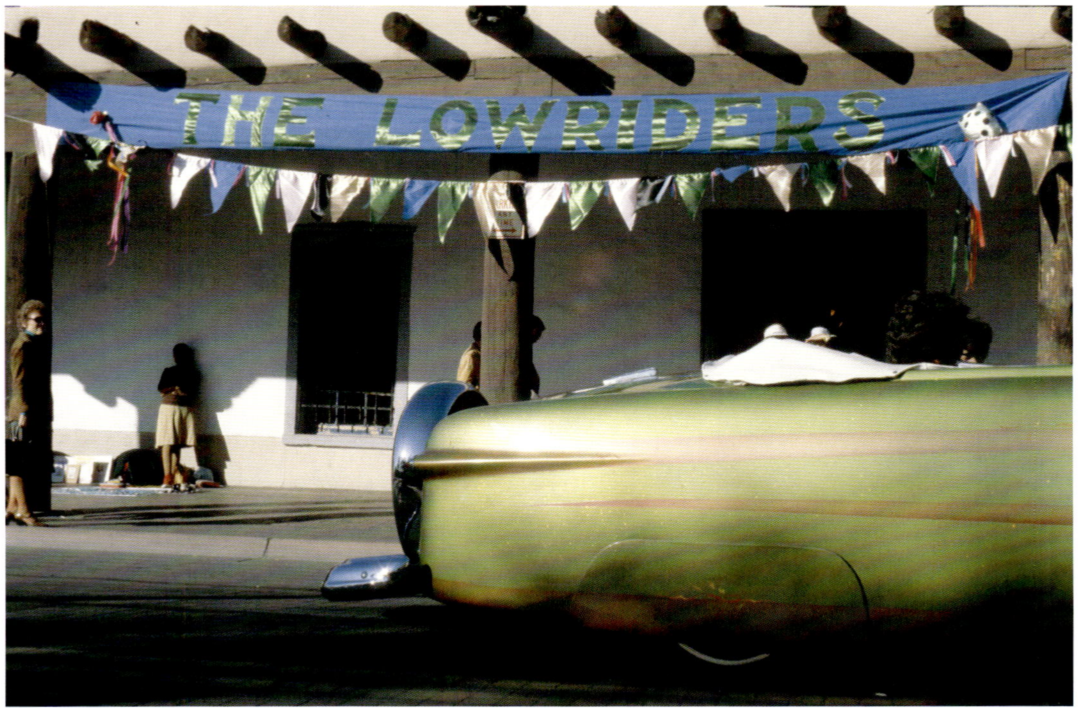

Meridel Rubenstein, The Lowriders *Exhibition*, Santa Fe, 1980

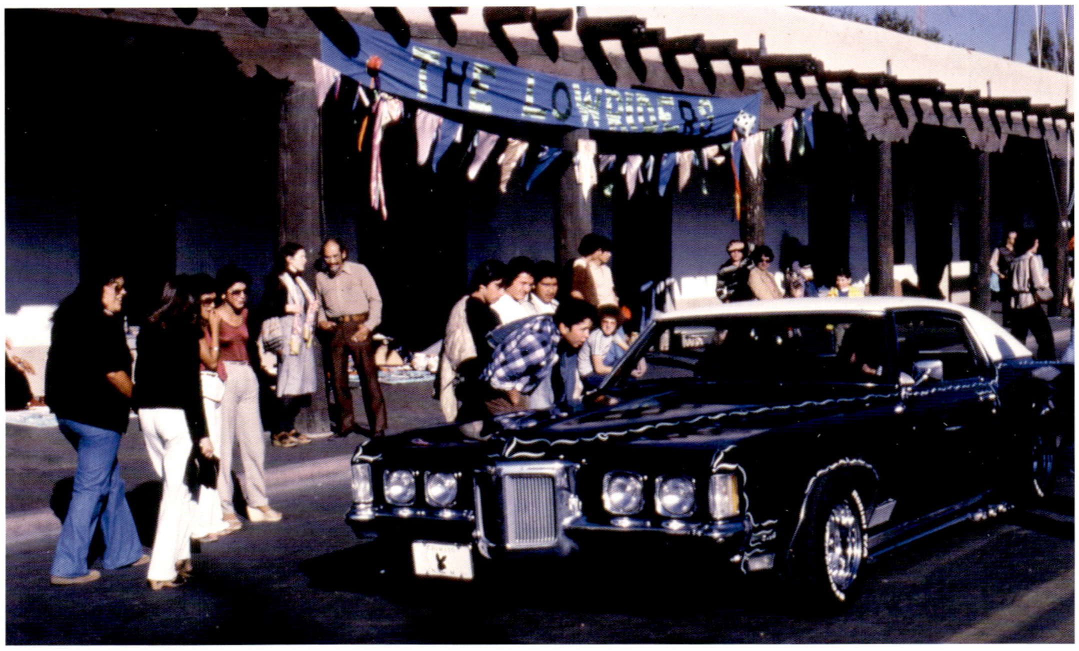

Meridel Rubenstein, *Lowrider in Front of the Palace of the Governors as It Leaves* The Lowriders *Exhibition at the Plaza*, Santa Fe, 1980

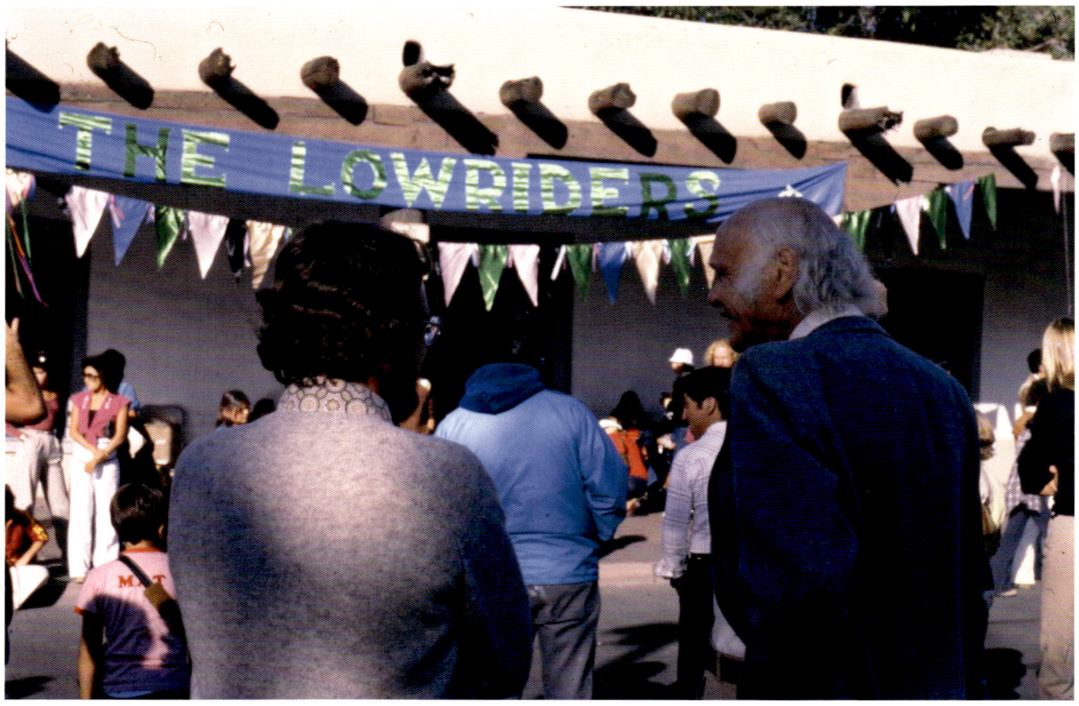

Meridel Rubenstein, *Photography Curator Steve Yates and Photo Historian Beaumont Newhall in Front of the Palace of the Governors*, Santa Fe, 1980

It was the largest single opening ever in Santa Fe up to that point, around three thousand people. There was an art festival going on for the first time at the Sweeney Convention Center, so a lot of people were in town for that. There were the car clubs and their families and friends from up north, and then there were the neighborhoods here. It was mobbed all day long.

KW: I love the twist that the police closed off the Plaza *for* the lowriders instead of closing it off to *keep out* the lowriders! It sounds like a party, a street fair, and an exhibition all in one. Quite a contrast with the stereotype of lowriders at that time! It seems that the exhibition offered an important opportunity for people in Santa Fe as well as tourists to have a firsthand experience with lowriders, to see the cars and meet the families personally and see what they were like. Ideally, that's what a public plaza is for, right? For everyone to come together as a town.

MR: The media really responded to this event. A German television station sent a crew, all these different reporters came, and everybody together. This was so amazing because they'd been getting such bad press for so long, and here they were having fun with the community and being ambassadors for New Mexico. The show went on all day. At an unappointed hour people started to just pack up. They brought in the rugs, the fences, and the trophies. They closed the trunks and the hoods. They got into their cars, and one by one, in formation, came around in front of the banner. They hopped, and then they peeled out.

KW: Just as they had come in.

MR: The cars left, and it was mid-October, a little bit windy. The last car left. I was standing there with Steve Yates and photo historian Beaumont Newhall, looking at the empty Plaza and feeling a little sad because it had been so alive. And then Beau says, "Look at those latent images." Where the cars had rested all day, they had blocked the dust. After they left there was a perfect rectangle for each car all around the Plaza, like a photographic trace.

One of the clubs that came was the Lowriders de Aztlán. They had their T-shirts, their cars, and their mural, and throughout the day they read their credo in Spanish and English: "We are united comrades forming a kinship that is fine and without envy, which we call the Lowriders de Aztlán, our lowriders, our way of speaking, our way of living and thinking represent a Pachuco-Chicano culture. We will form a Chicano nation called Aztlán, where we will live in harmony close to nature cruising in clean rides towards the sun together in a caravan, proud and driving very, very low."

KW: Aztlán, that's the legendary ancestral home of the Aztecs. So that gives this a utopian twist, at least for this club. So imagining and building the cars is an expression of personal and cultural vision, but also a vehicle for collectively imagining a better world. The club starts to make that world a reality by connecting the drivers, unifying them as a close-knit group engaged in the common pursuit of a unique and joyous experience that almost transcends space and time!

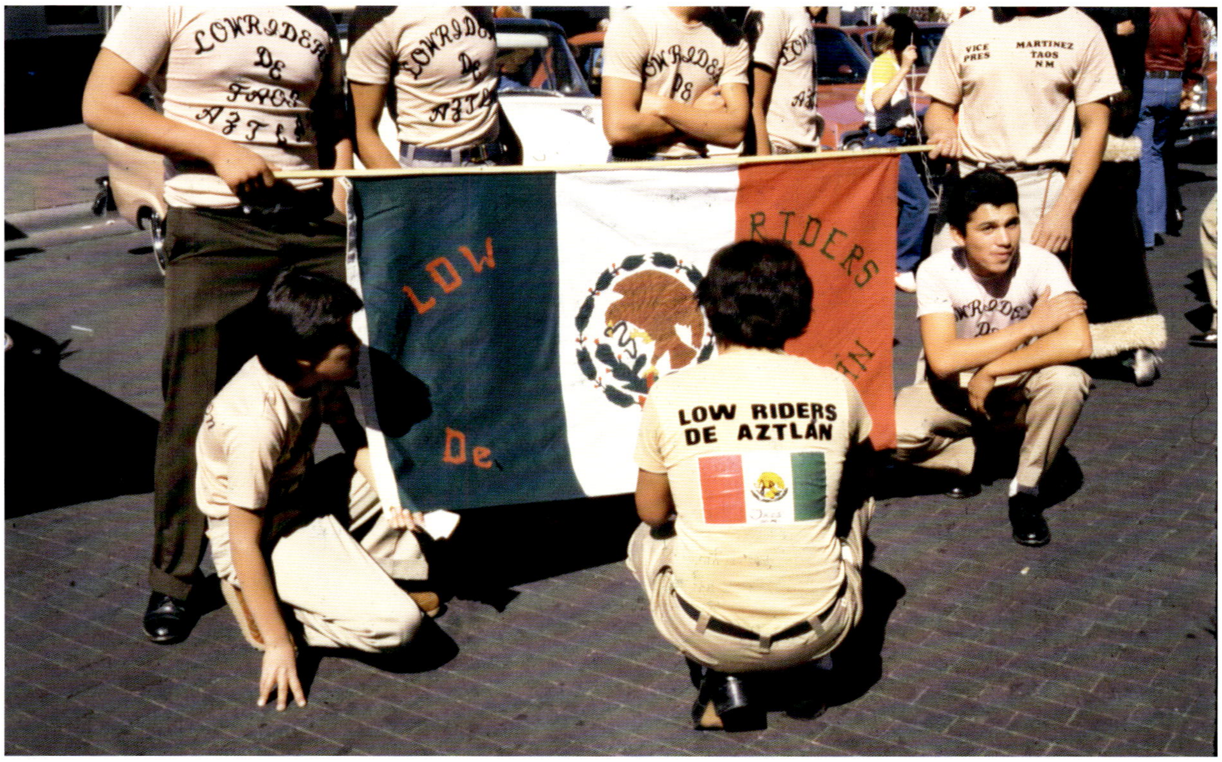

Meridel Rubenstein, *Low Riders de Aztlán from Taos*, Santa Fe Plaza, 1980

MR: So many realities are going on at once in these cars! They're not cars, they're reliquaries—the artist Rubén Ortiz Torres calls them "cathedrals on wheels." They are repositories for all sorts of information and messages about identity.

One thing we talked about is the sexy wet T-shirt and hopping thing going on. It gets imaged onto the cars with the glossy paint and the plush interior and the murals of the women. This sexual aspect is modern. But a casket also has velvet interiors, so that's another reference. And moving slow, *bajo*, is important. Moving slow is an act of defiance, going so slow we're not going to run from adversity. "I'm in no hurry. You can't push me. I'm not going to run." And there's the idea of not being afraid of death. It goes back in time to the Aztecs. In Mexican culture you have a tradition of celebrating death. I love that Mexican way of facing the fear of death and surviving it by celebrating life and spiritual union.

KW: Sure, in ancient Aztec culture, sacrificing your life to the gods was considered an honor. Now we have Día de los Muertos as a special time to visit and remember those who have passed away, but also for each of us to acknowledge our own mortality. And of course Jesus is believed to have sacrificed his life for the salvation of others—that's an important touchstone for the lowriders.

MR: Jesus and the Virgin of Guadalupe appear on so many of the lowriders, as murals, inside the car, Jesus's face sandblasted on the back window in between two chrome organ pipes for the music.

They're being created by people who have had to put these different traditions together to survive. I bet if we went to L.A. we could find the similar iconography. It's just the flashier ones get all the attention.

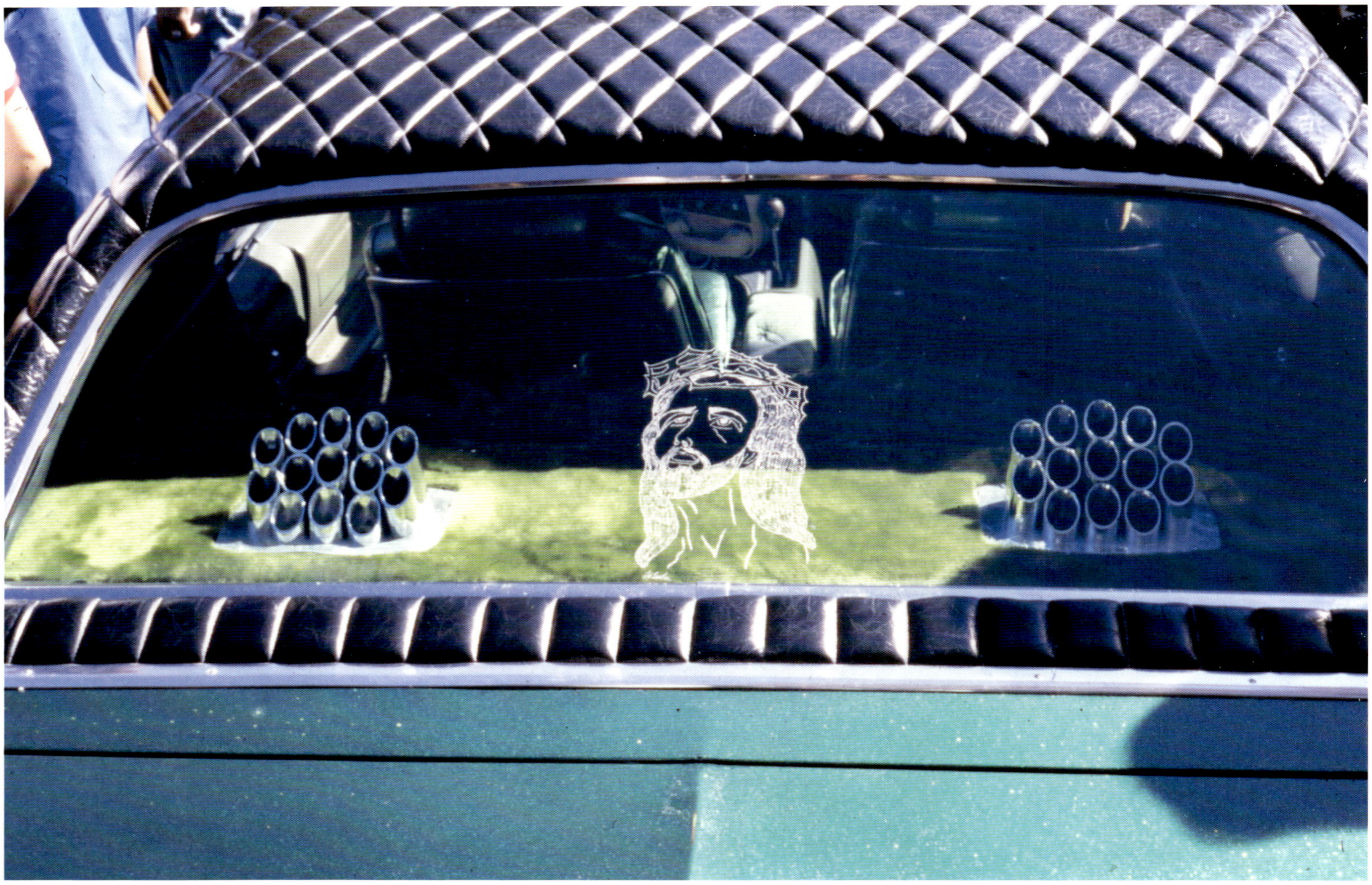

Meridel Rubenstein, *Image of Jesus Sandblasted on Rear Window of Lowrider*, Santa Fe, 1980

KW: What about the women lowriders? We talked about the murals with a sexy woman but also the religious imagery. Are the cars of the men and women different?

MR: The cars I photographed didn't have pictures of women on them. And it was great to meet women who had cars. The husbands and brothers were making the cars for them, but with the women's taste in mind. Petra's car was so feminine, that beautiful, delicate steering wheel and the white tuck-and-roll interior, and the roses hanging from the mirror.

KW: The decorative qualities or the elaborate qualities, the customization, in some ways, it feels kind of feminized.

MR: They do keep the interiors very feminine, even the men, in the sense that they are soft and luxurious, like a reference to the female body, the womb.

KW: I was thinking about ships, and historically a ship is usually a "she." These cars must be she's.

MR: The cars I encountered were called Bad Company and Dave's Dream, more masculine names. But I do think the car is she. It's a he-she because of the way it's all working. You know, it is made of both masculine hopping and feminine interiors—the regenerative act.

KW: That's right, the mechanics would represent the traditional male energy while the interior is the female element perhaps.

MR: You know, in the car Dave's Dream there's a bar in the back and a TV. That's after everything else going on in that car, there's a bar and a TV. That's where you would recline and rest. That's a feminine aspect. It's a kind of boudoir, a sexy bedroom that caters to your wishes and your comfort. And it's not just about sex, it's about regeneration. It's a body thing. The cars are these living bodies that are enacting regeneration, a sacred act. They're also symbols of death and of not being afraid of death. Mary is on the dashboard, Jesus is sandblasted on the rear window. It's all incorporated together in the cathedral on wheels. The mother and father are there but so are the bar and the television!

KW: All the important things in life!

NOTE:

Photographs of the exhibition *The Lowriders* and its related car show were made by many people and shared afterward. Authorship of individual works is now unknown but contributions were made by Meridel Rubenstein, Steve Fitch, Ray Graham, Chama Ruiz, Sam Samore, Jerry West, and some of Rubenstein's students from the University of Colorado, Boulder, including Lou Marcus. Rubenstein thanks the other photographers for the use of their images.

¡Órale! lowrider

PLATES

wheels

LEVI ROMERO

how can I tell you
baby, oh honey
you'll never know the ride
the ride of a lowered Chevy
slithering through
the blue dotted night
along Riverside Drive Española

poetry rides the wings
of a '59 Impala
yes, it does
and it points
chrome antennae towards

'Burque stations rocking
oldies Van Morrison
brown eyed girls
Creedence and a
bad moon rising
over Chimayó

and I guess
it also rides
on muddy Subarus
tuned into new-age radio
on the frigid road
to Taos on weekend
ski trips

yes, baby
you and I
are two kinds of wheels
on the same road

listen, listen
to the lonesome humming
of the tracks we leave
behind

1. Gabriella Marks, production still from *Spinners*, Chimayó, 2007

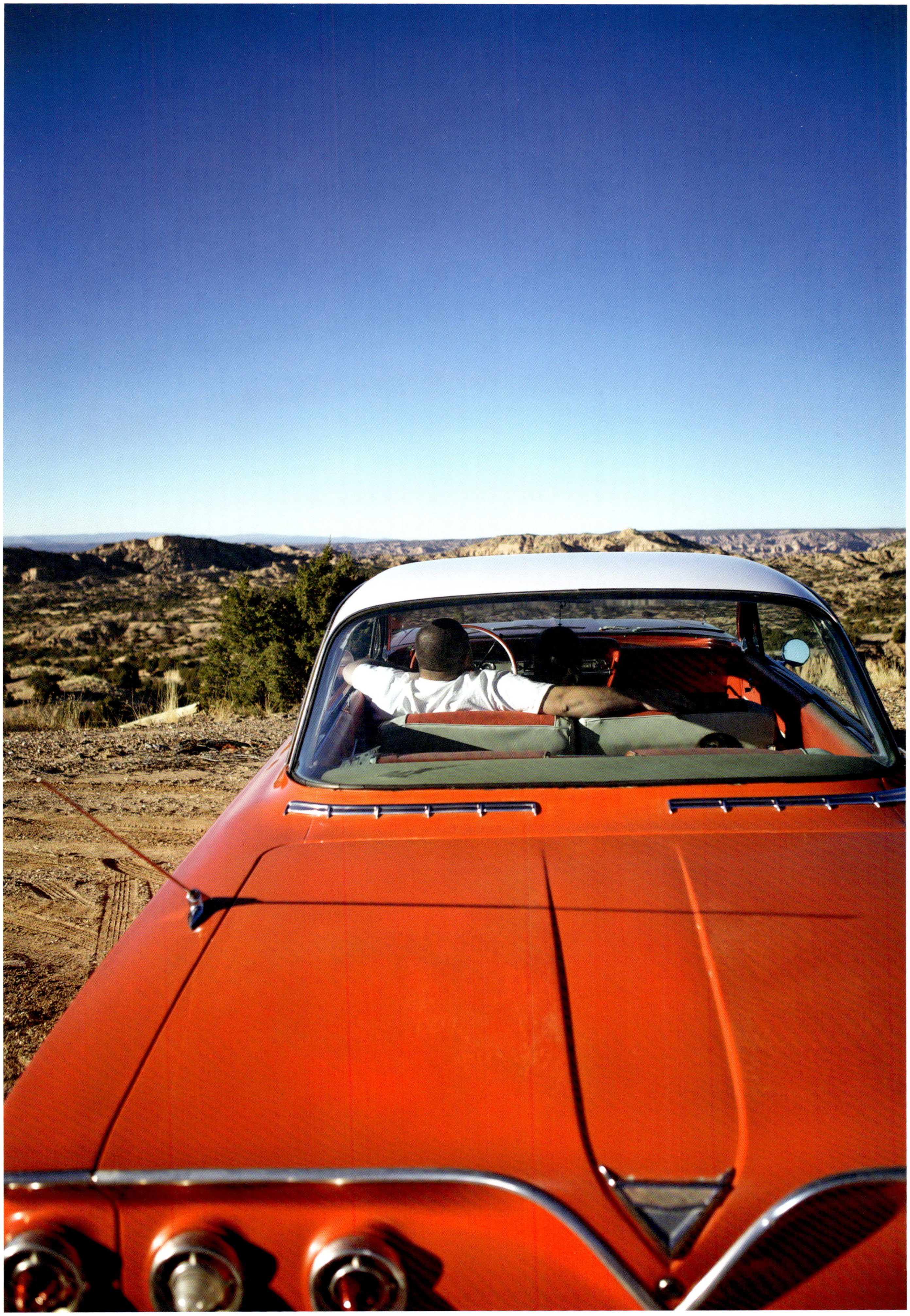

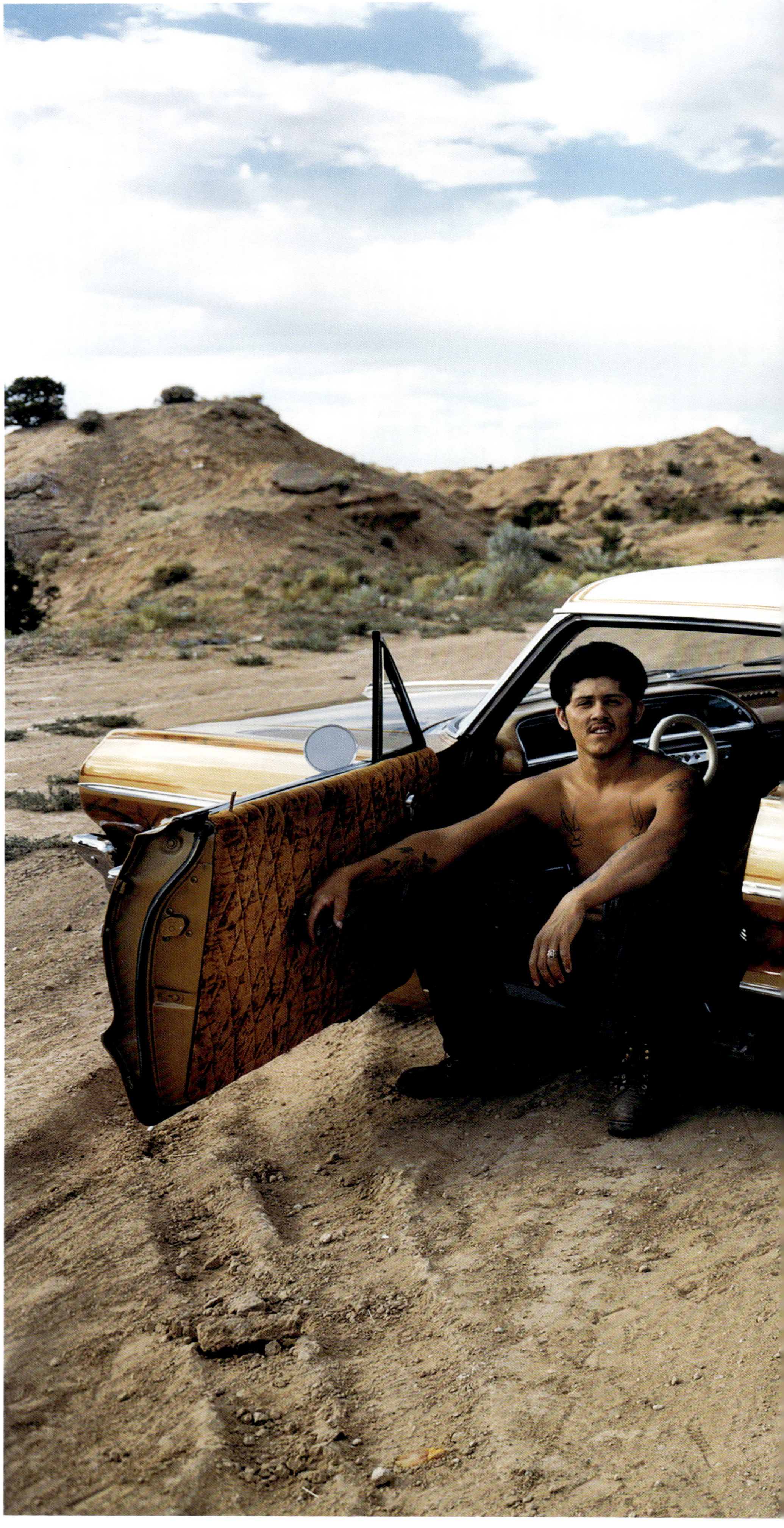

2. Meridel Rubenstein, *Benino Martínez, '64 Chevy*, Chimayó, 1980

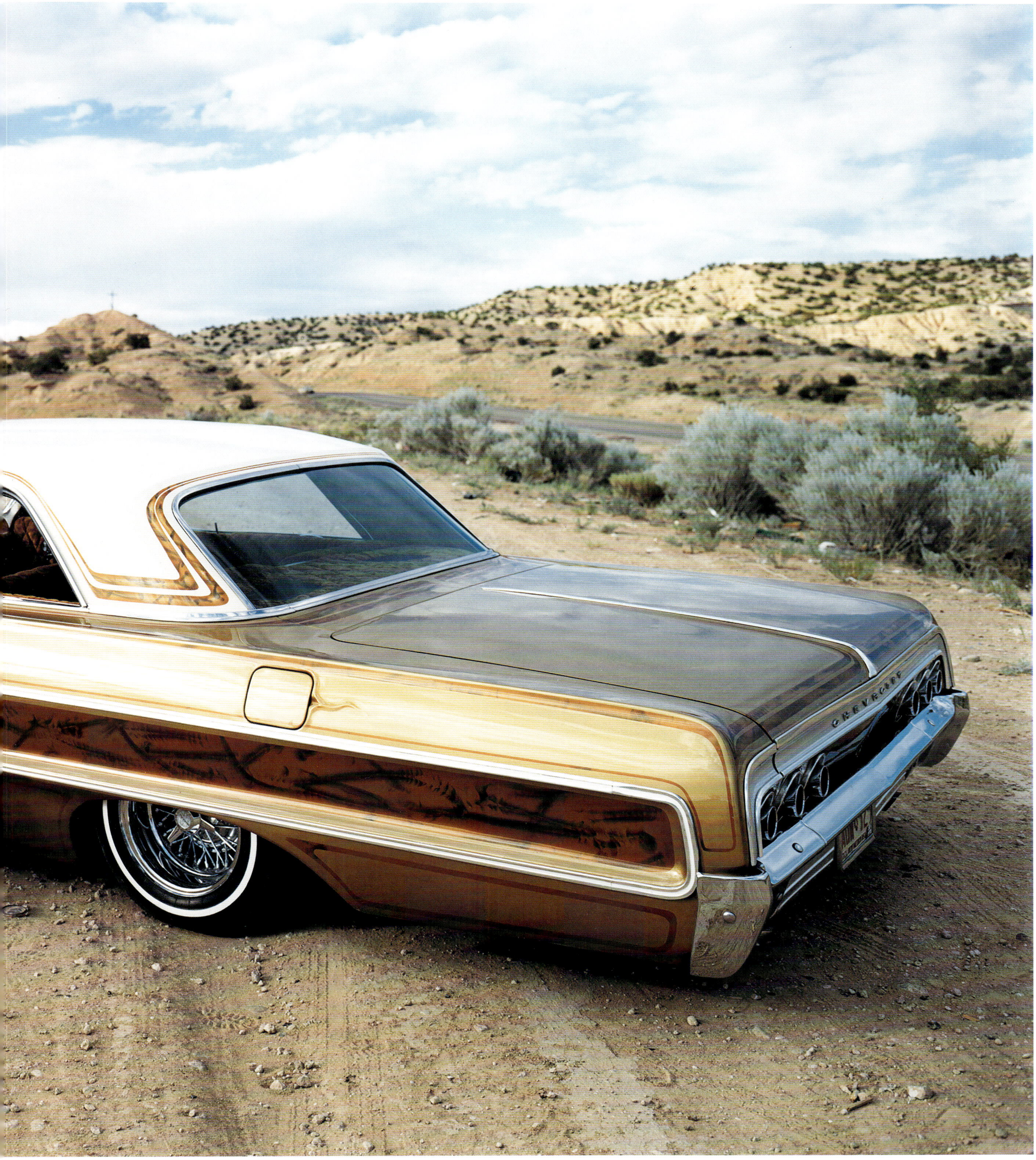

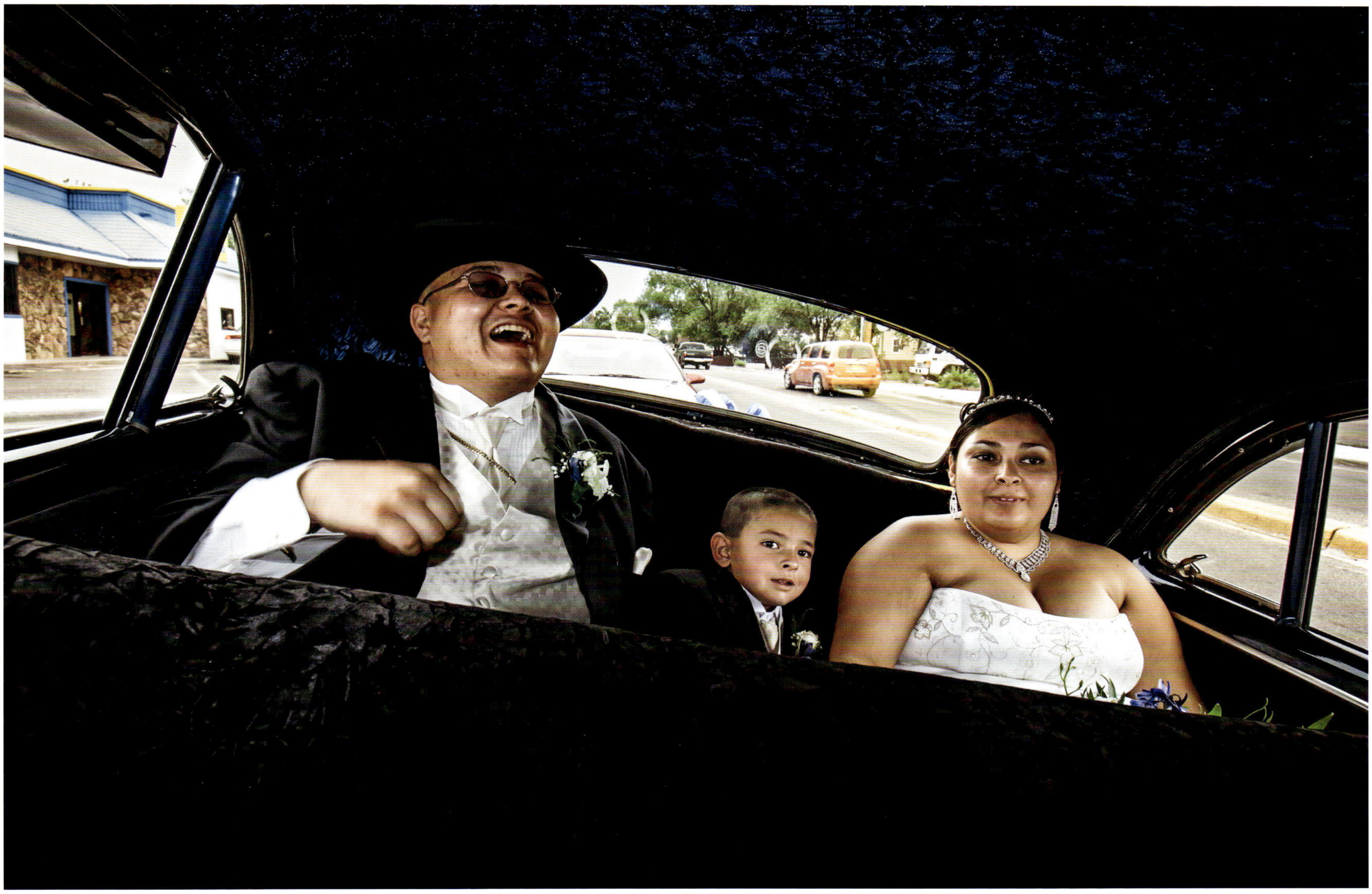

3. Paul Gregory Newman, *The Rolling Wedding Cruise*, Española, 2006

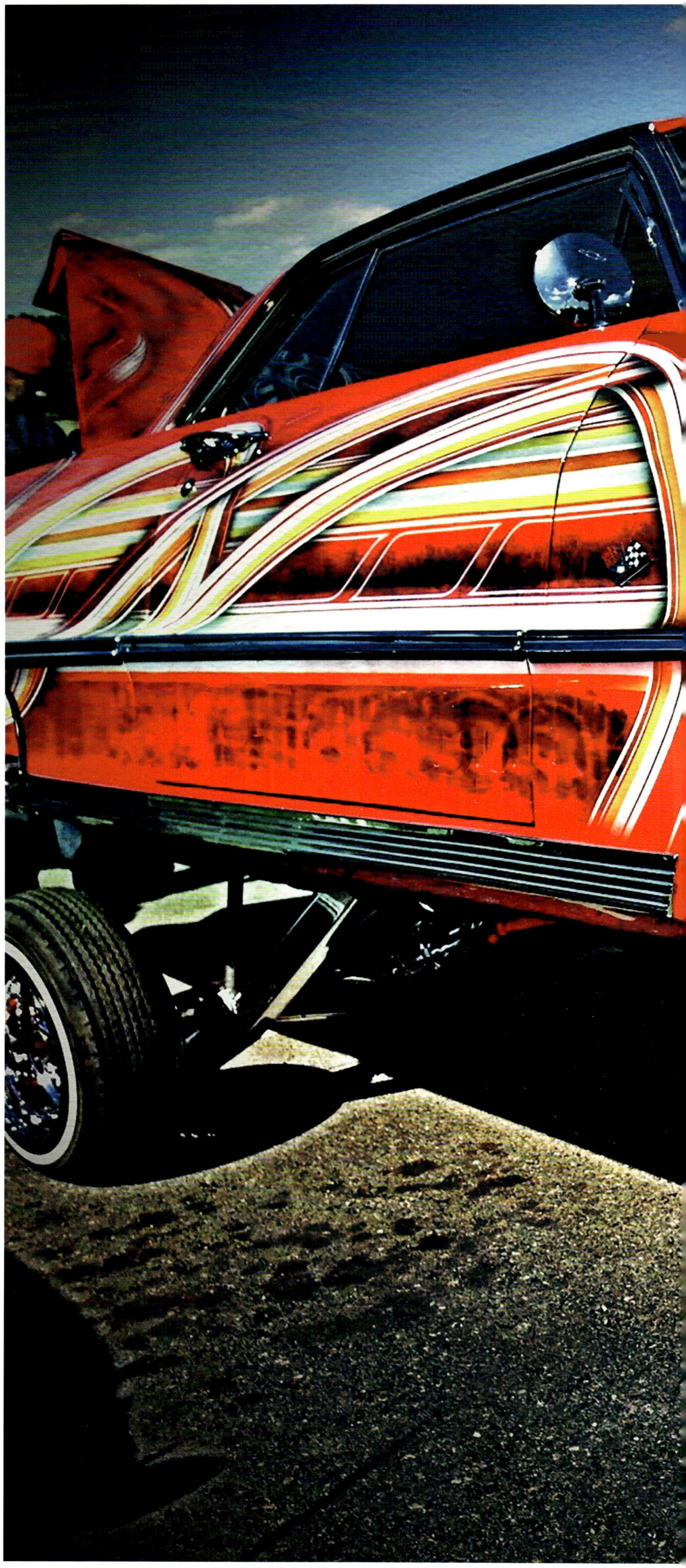

4. Dottie Lopez, *Three Wheel*, 2013

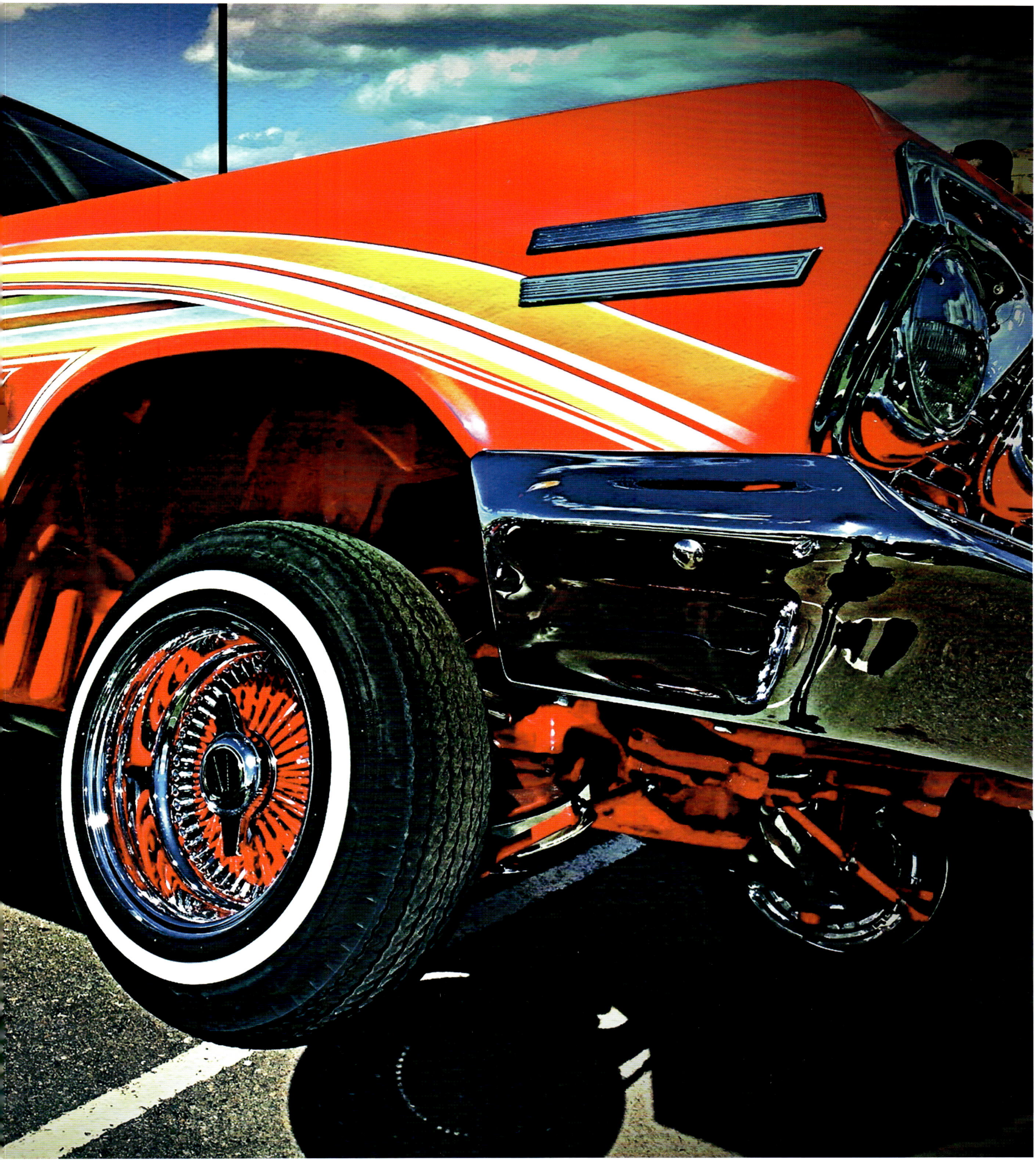

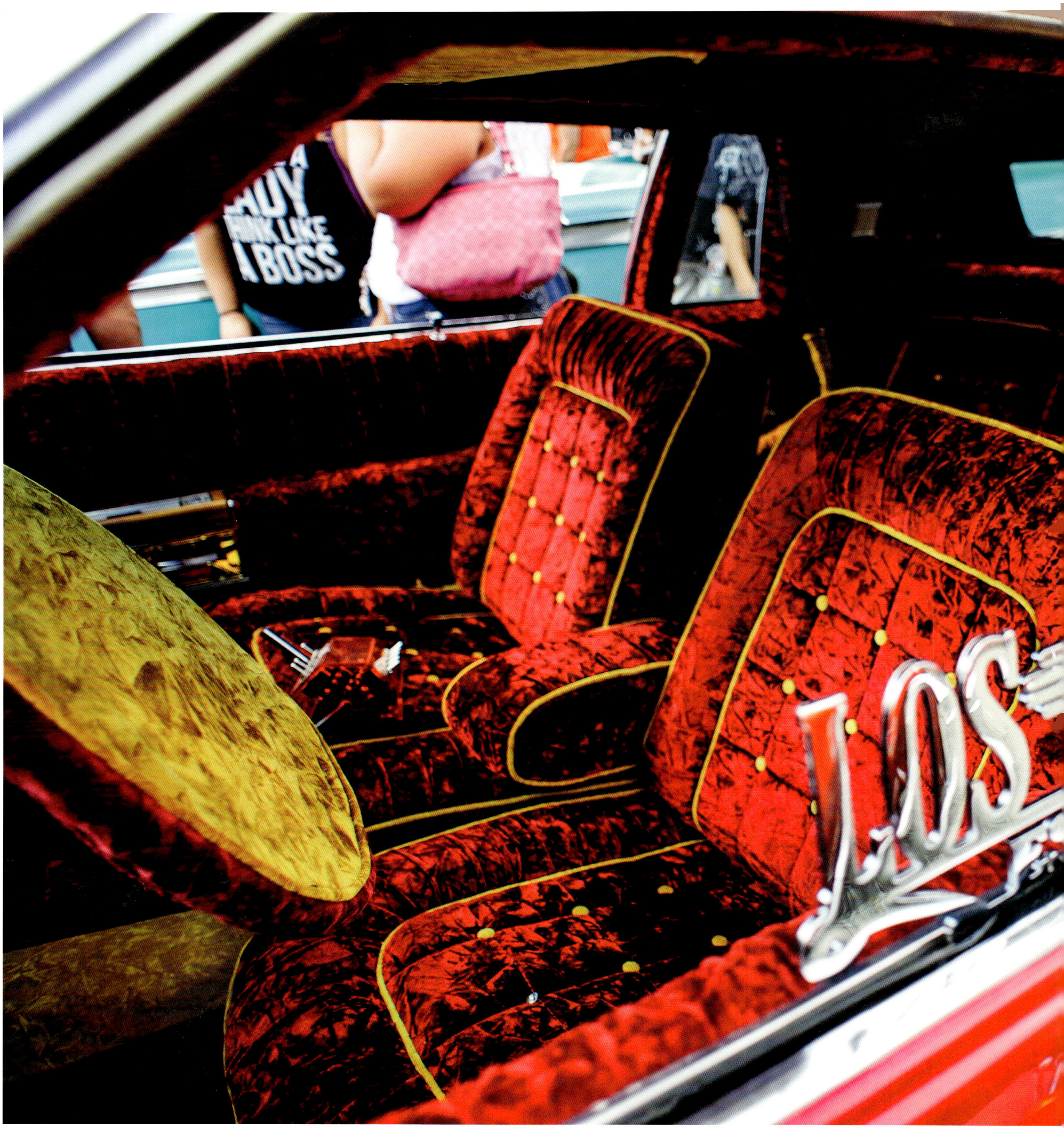

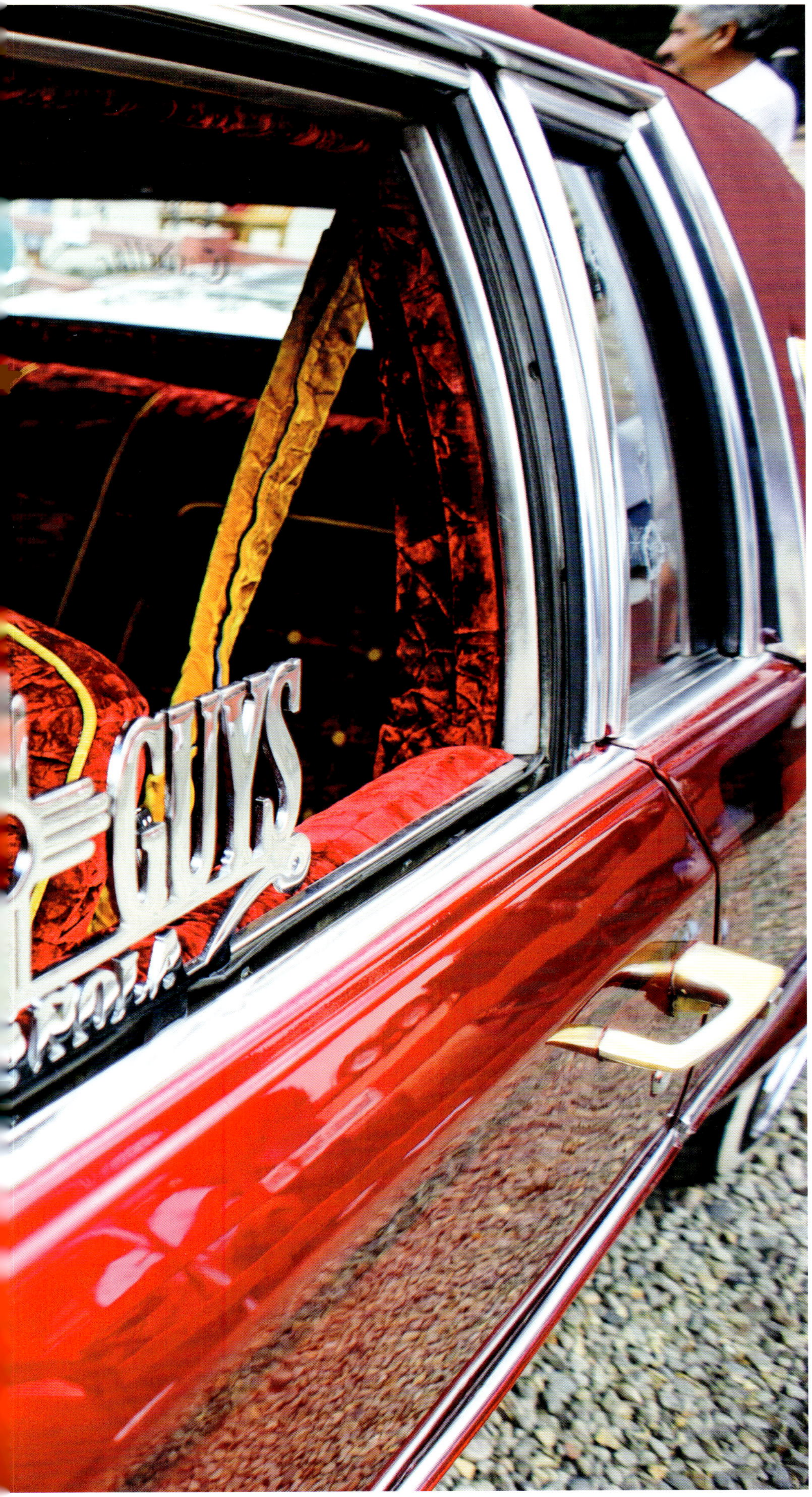

5. Katharine Egli, *Joseph Chacon's 1981 Coupe Deville Daccy,* Tomasita's Second Annual Lowrider and Custom Car Show, 2013

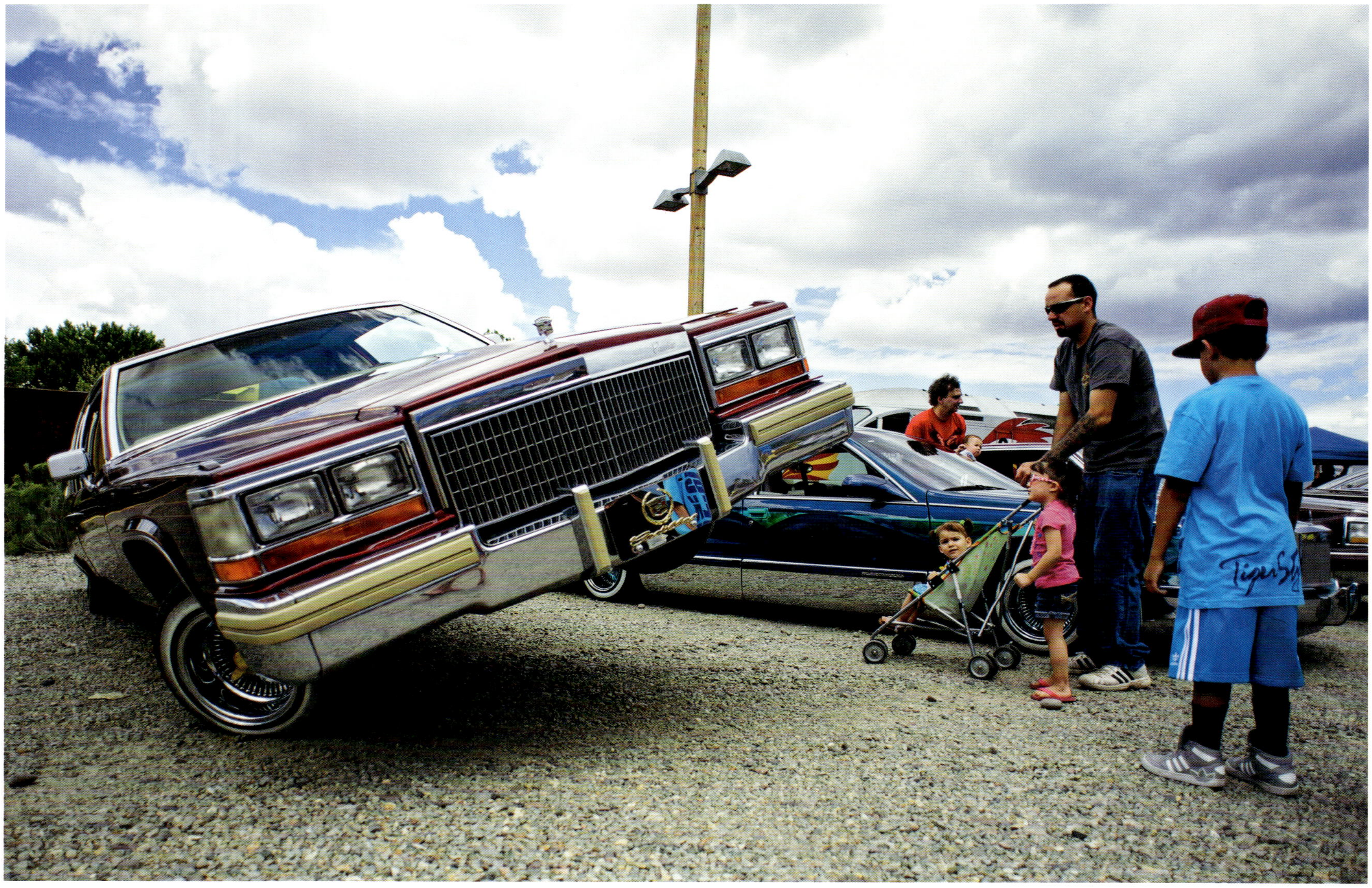

6. Katharine Egli, *Tomasita's Second Annual Lowrider and Custom Car Show*, 2013

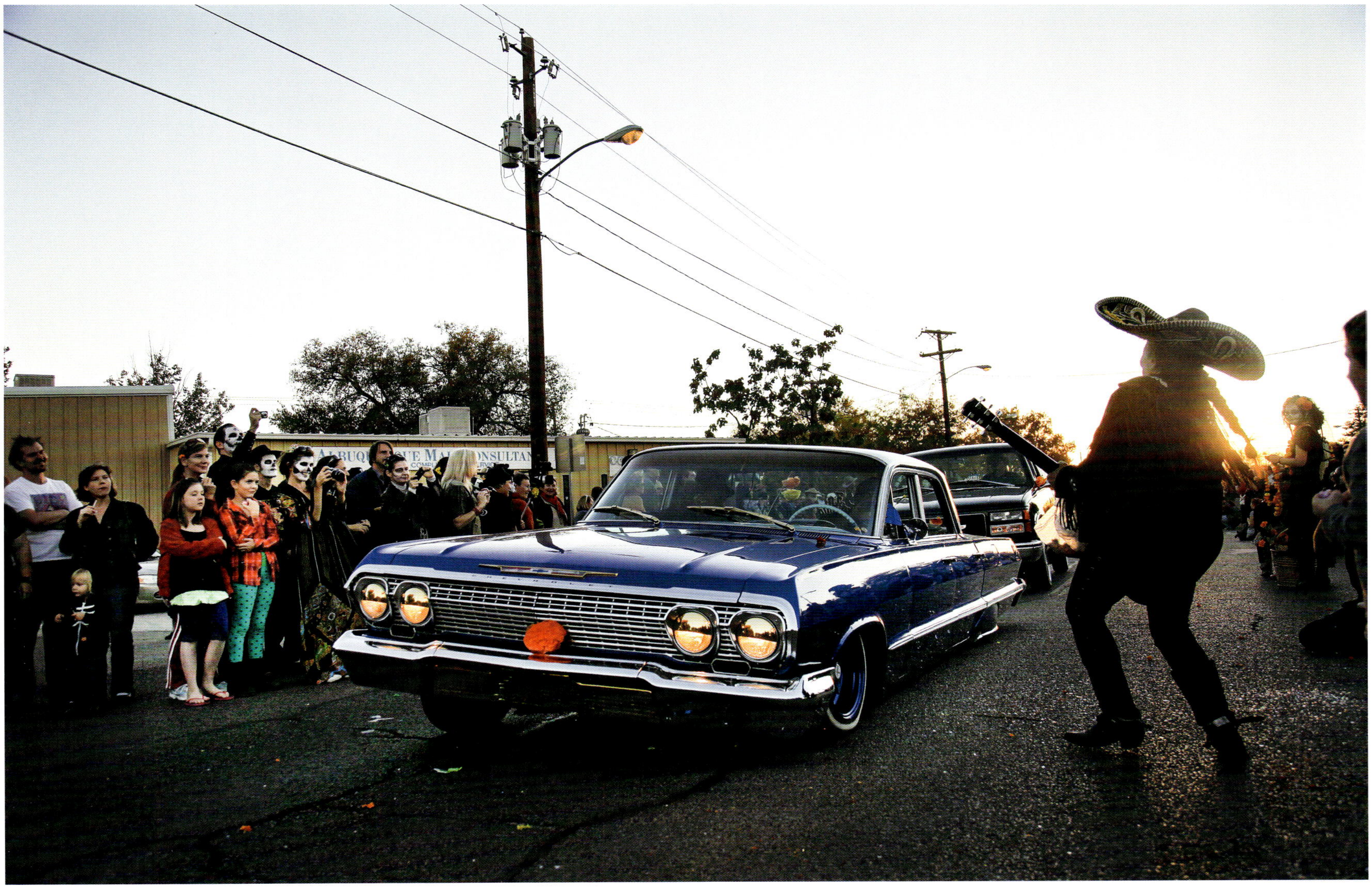

7. Gabriela E. Campos, *Marigold Parade*, 2010

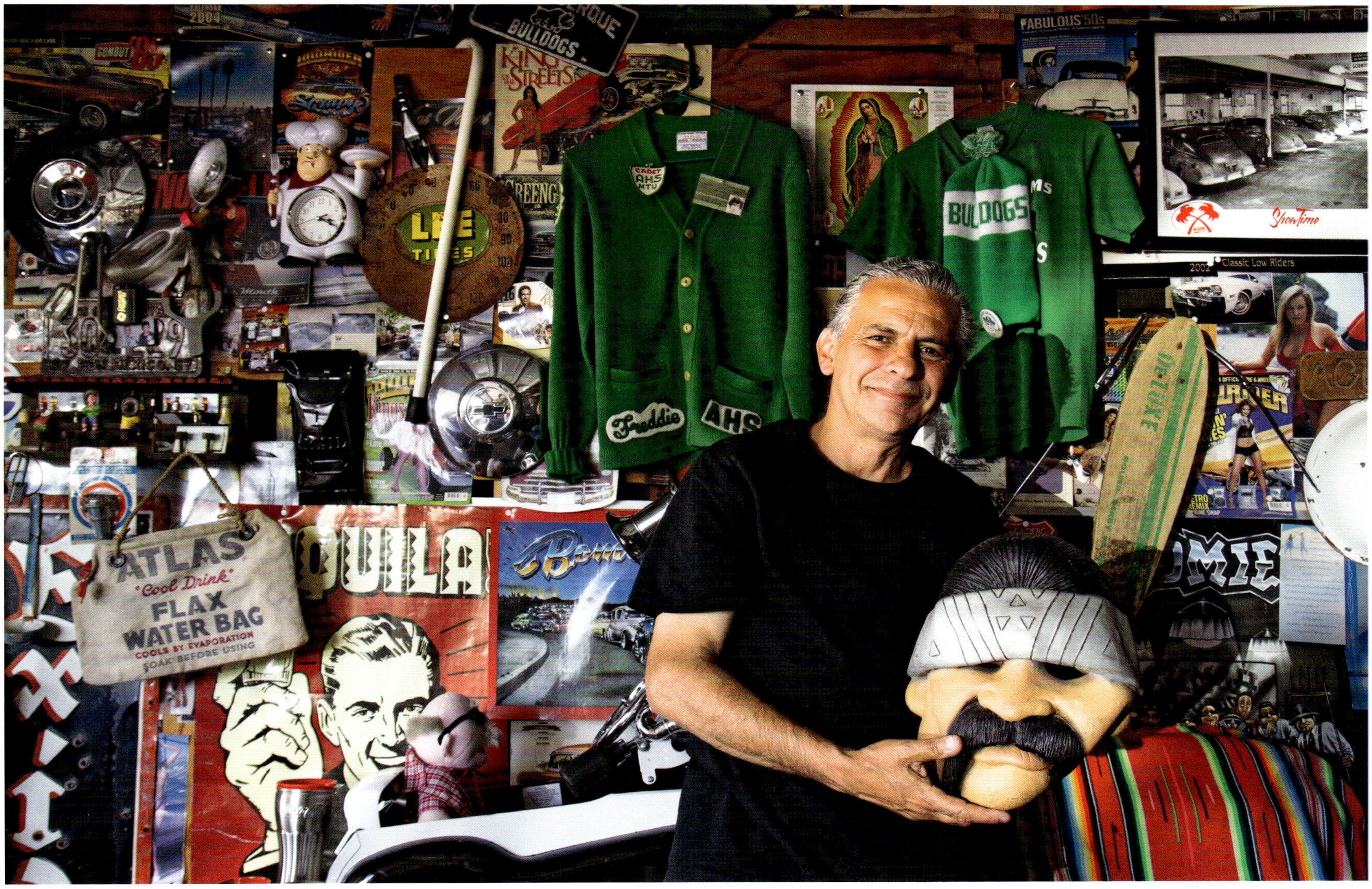

8. Imanol Miranda, *Freddie Gutierrez with Lowrider Memorabilia*, Albuquerque, 2014

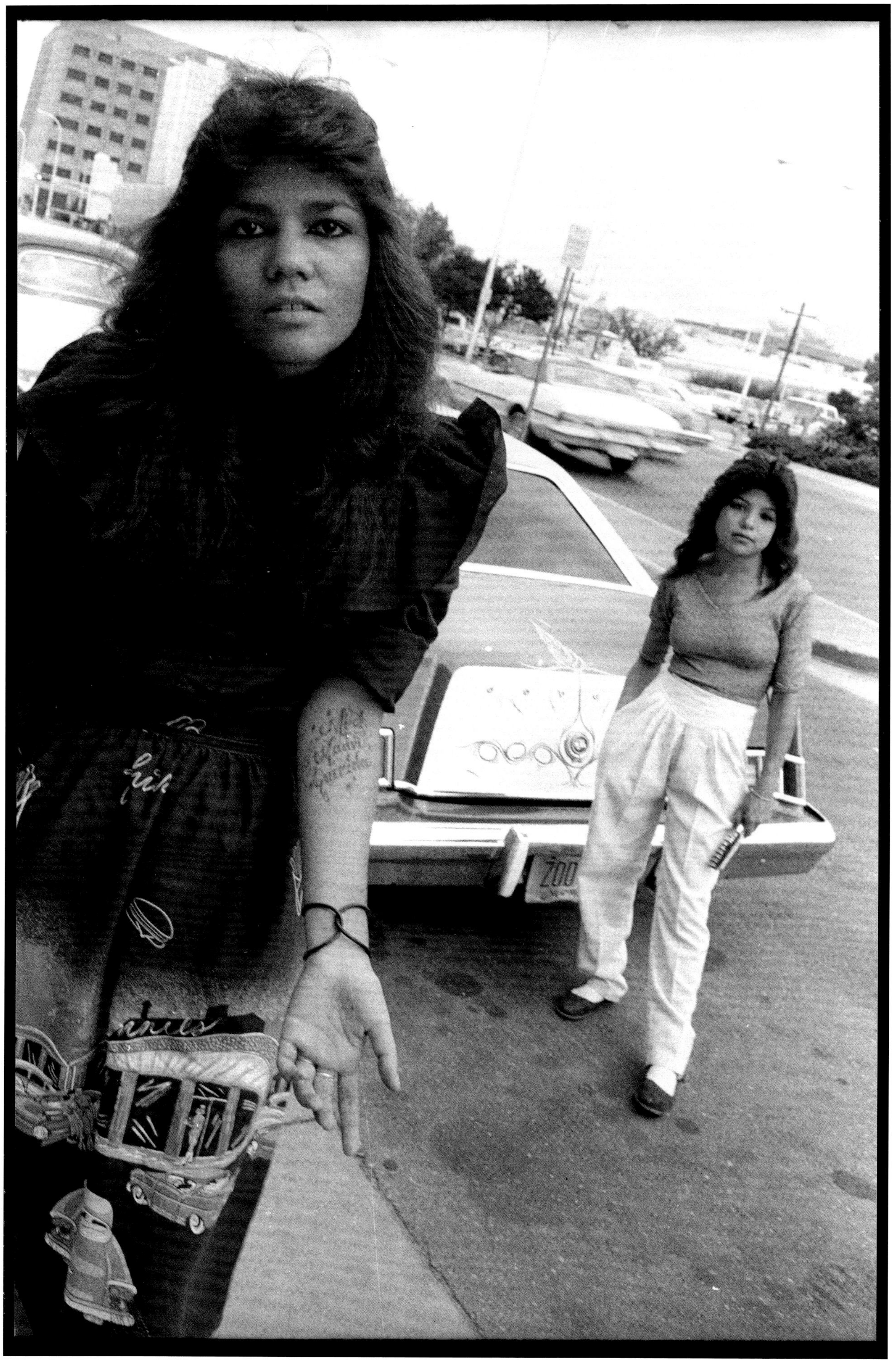

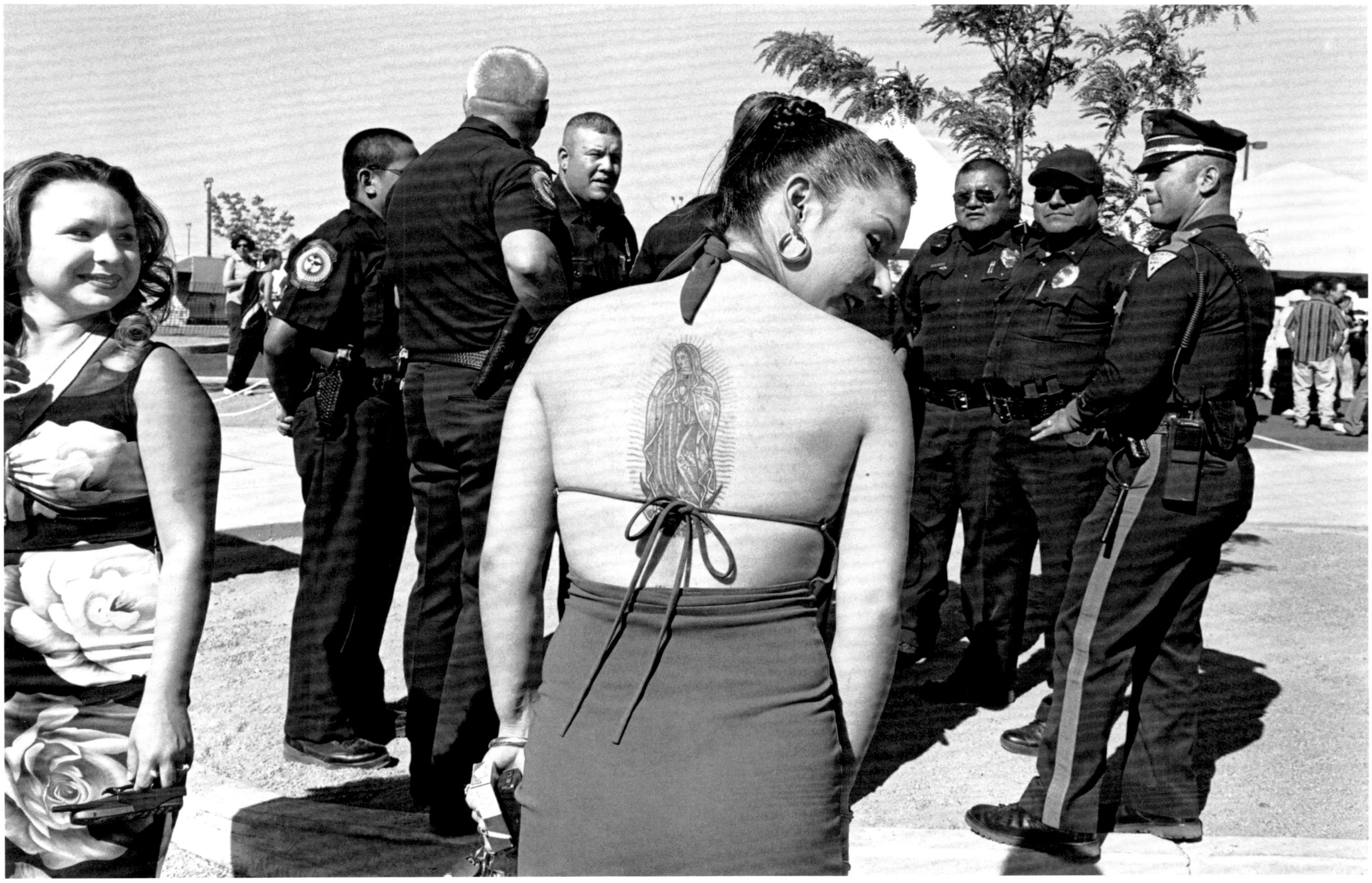

opposite
9. Miguel Gandert, *Home Girls*, Albuquerque Convention Center, 1983

above
10. Norman Mauskopf, *Isleta, New Mexico*, 2002

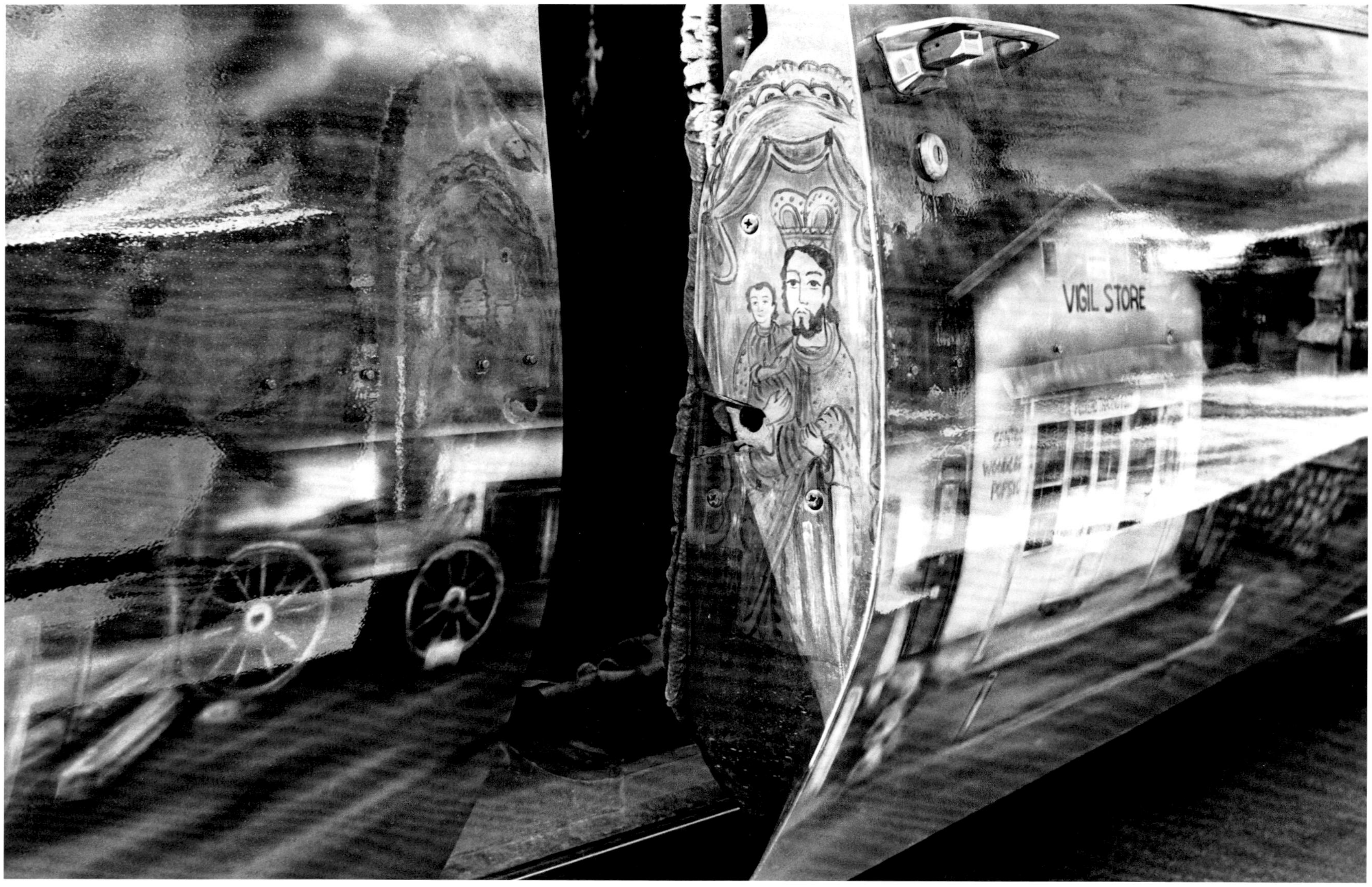

11. Norman Mauskopf, *Chimayó, New Mexico*, 2002

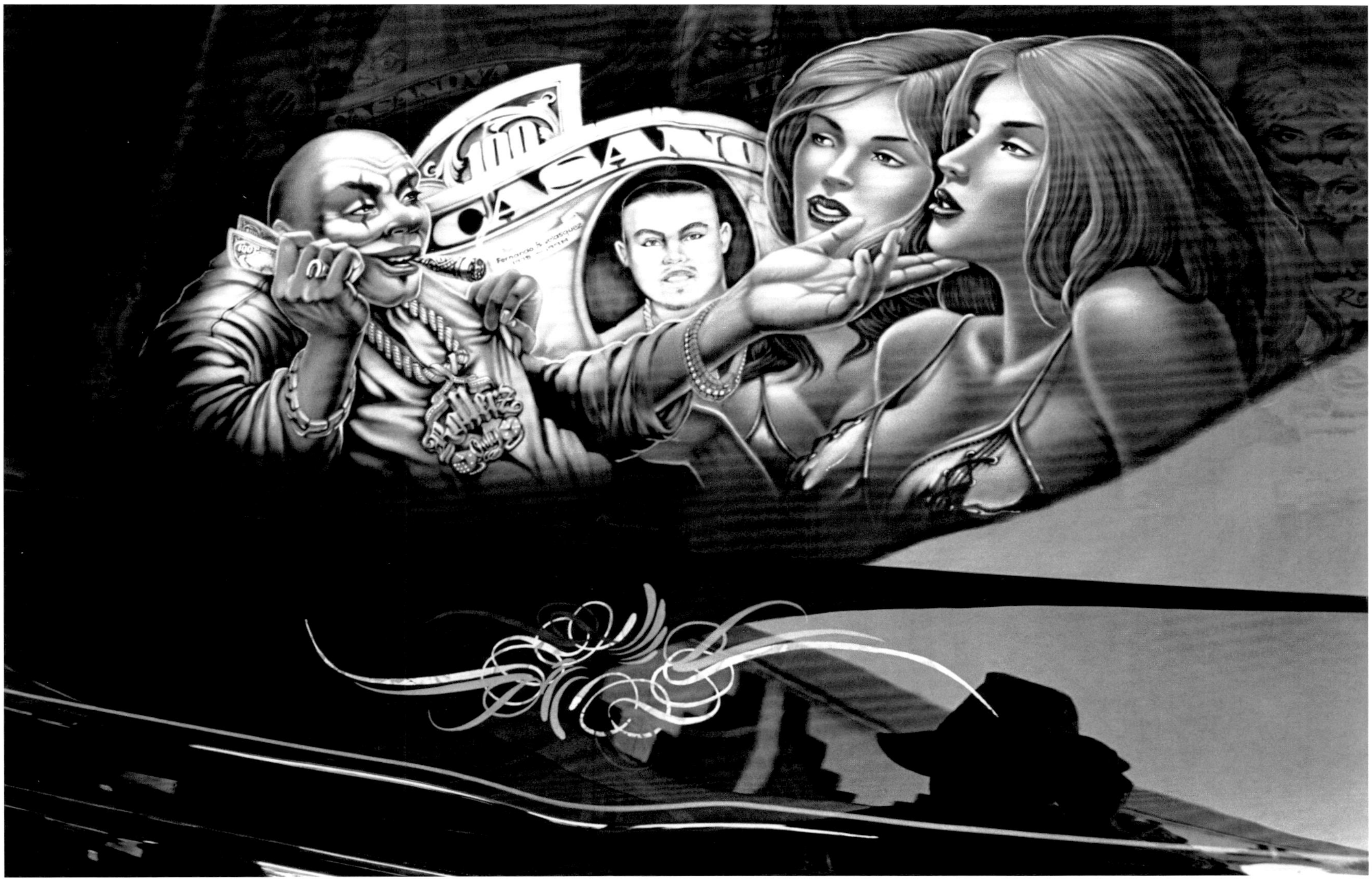

12. Norman Mauskopf, *Isleta, New Mexico*, 2002

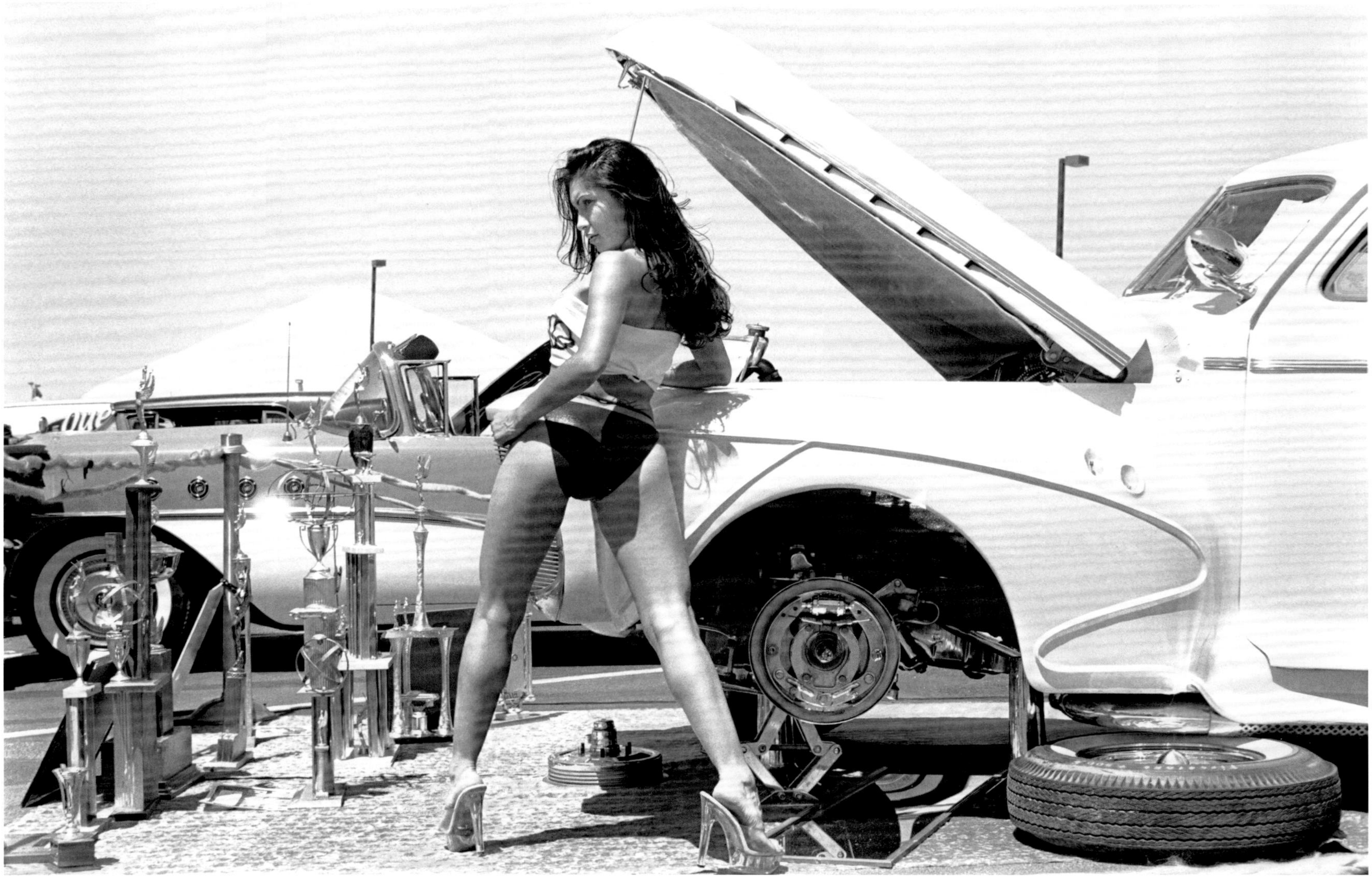

13. Norman Mauskopf, *Isleta, New Mexico*, 2002

14. Elliott McDowell, *Fleetwood, New Mexico*, 1976

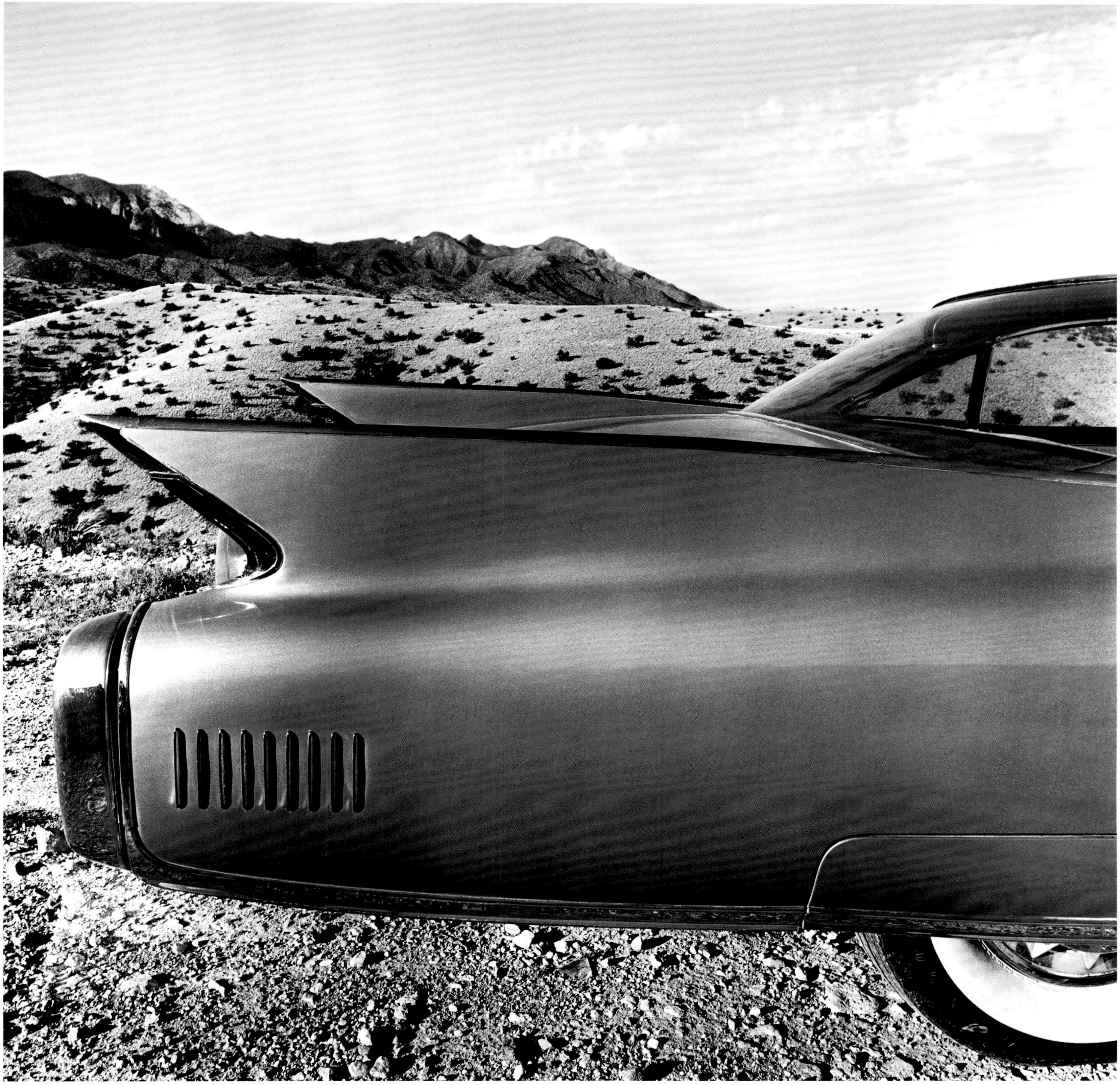

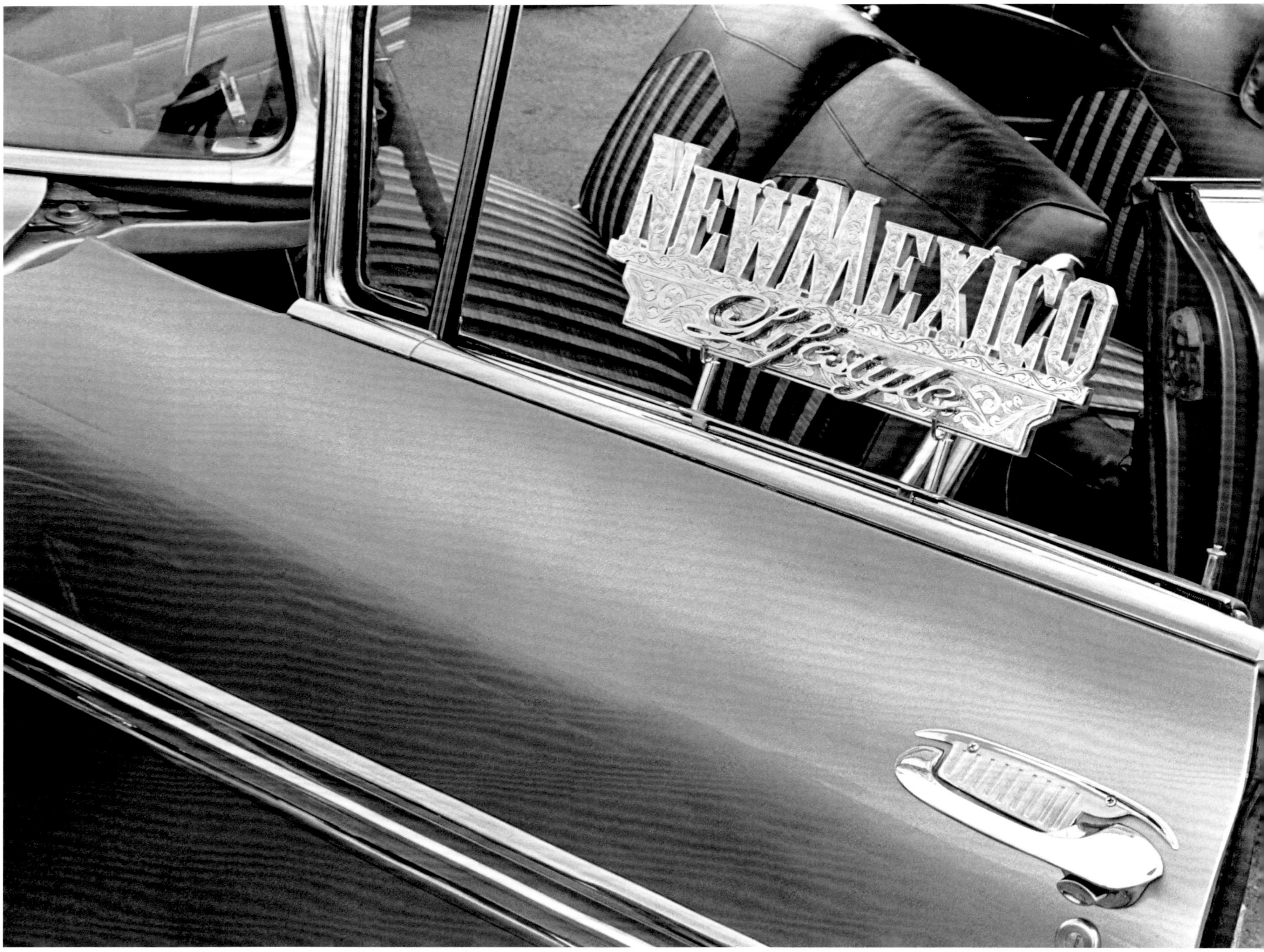

15. Norman Mauskopf, *Santa Fe, New Mexico*, 2009

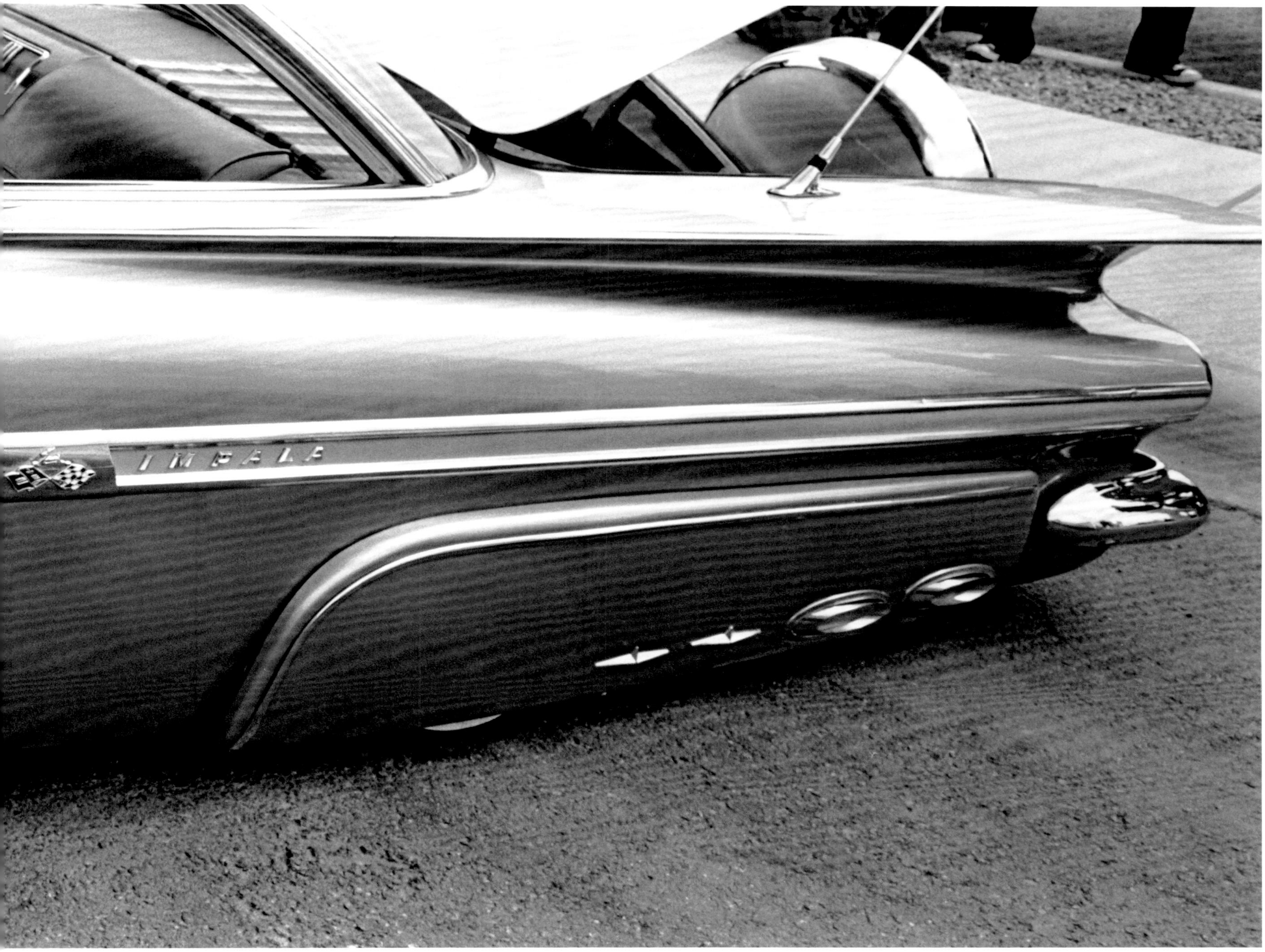
IMPALA

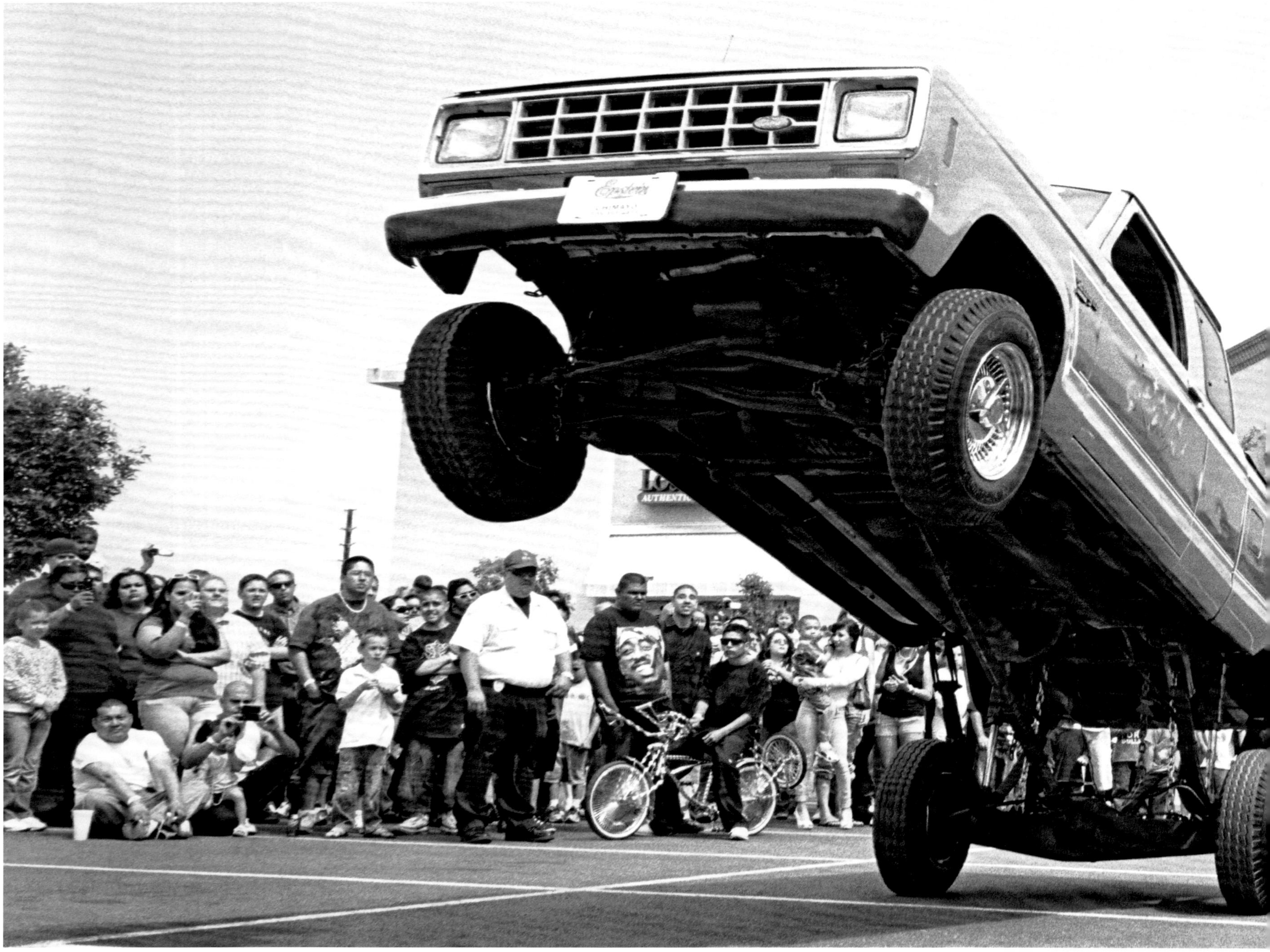

16. Norman Mauskopf, *Santa Fe, New Mexico*, 2009

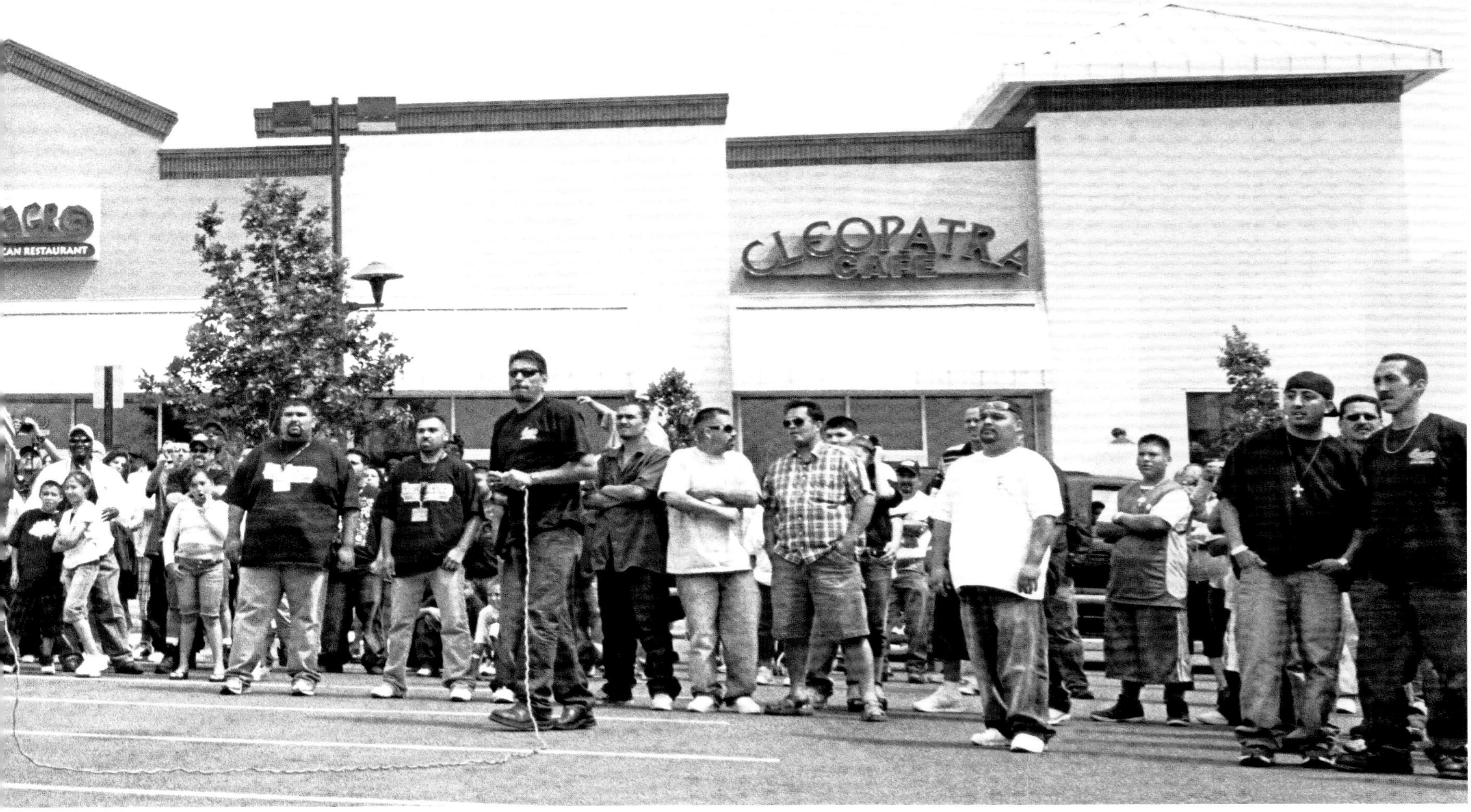
CLEOPATRA
CAFE

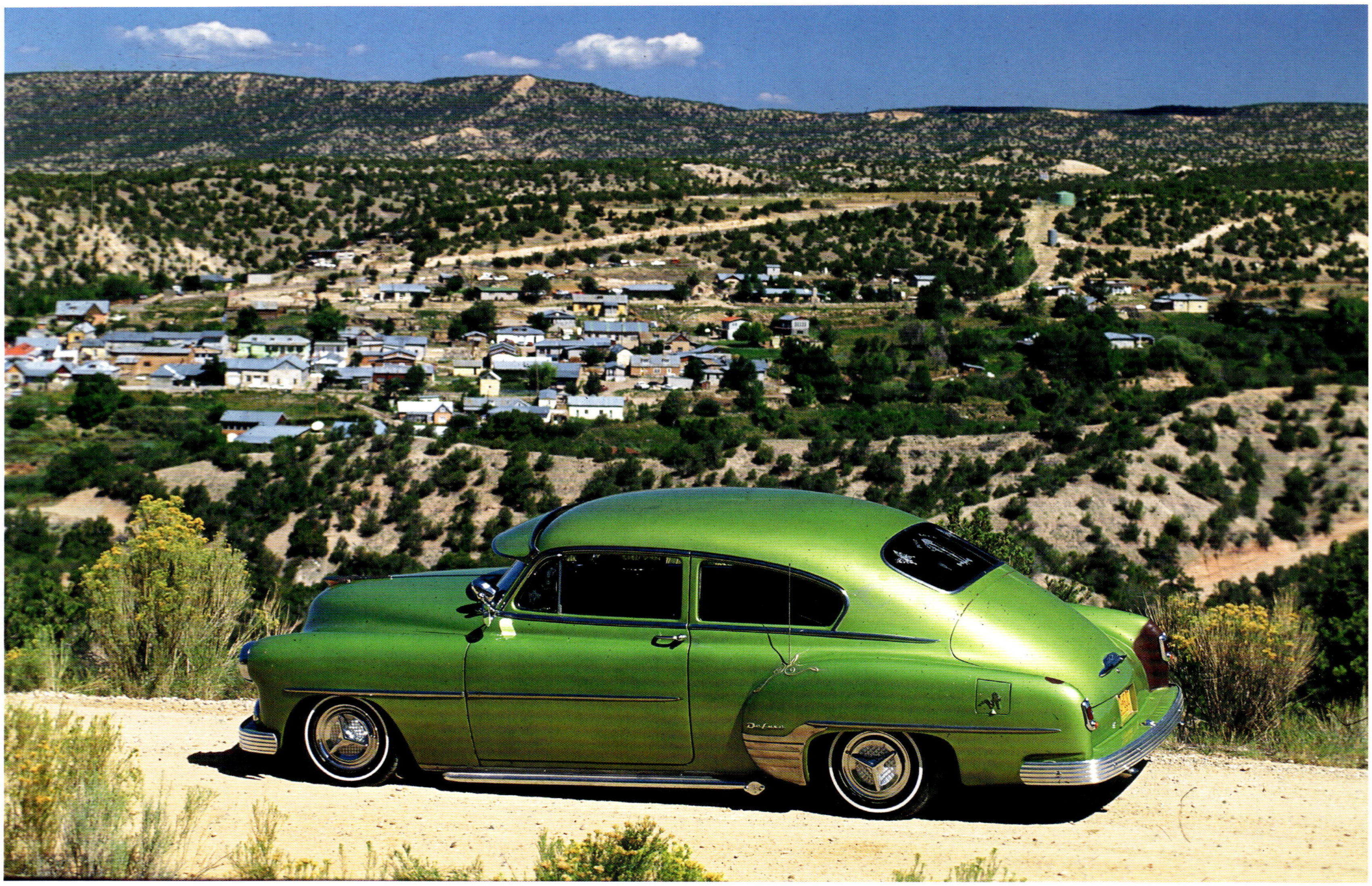

17. Jack Parsons, *'53 Chevrolet Fleetline, Owner Floyd Montoya of Córdova*, 1998

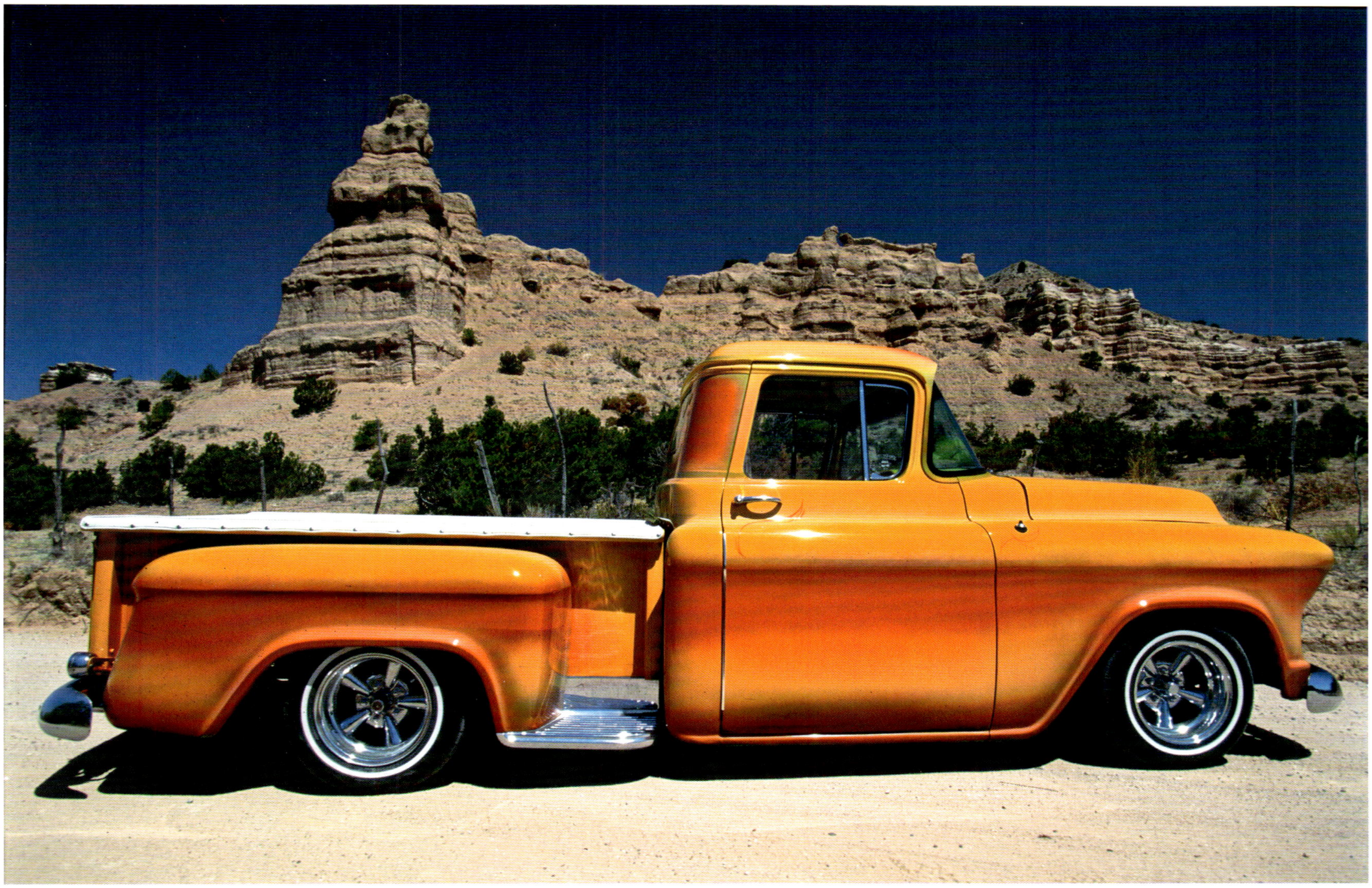

18. Jack Parsons, *'56 Chevrolet Pickup, Owner Joseph Martínez of Chimayó*, 1998

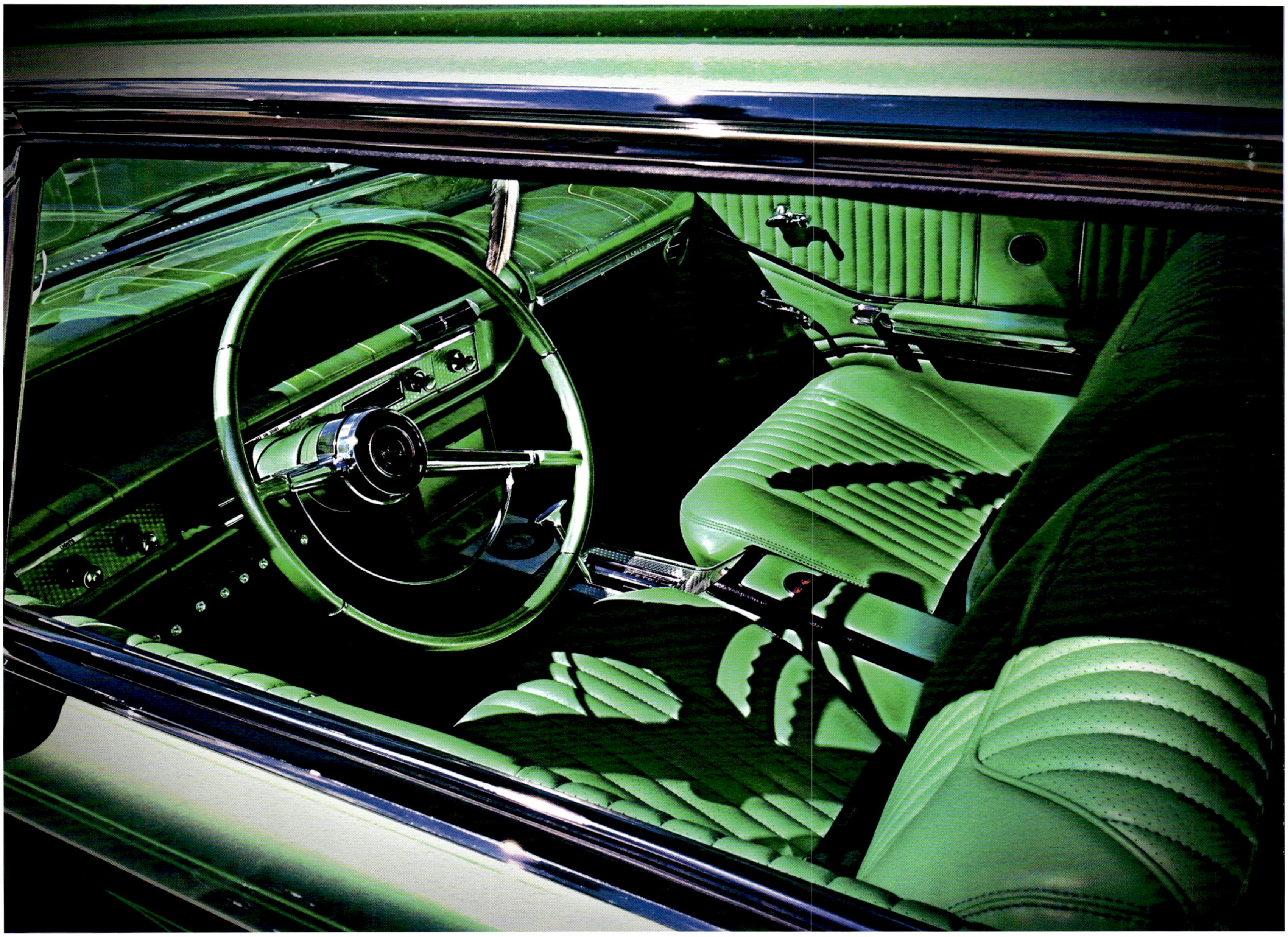

19. Dottie Lopez, *Impala Verde*, April 14, 2013

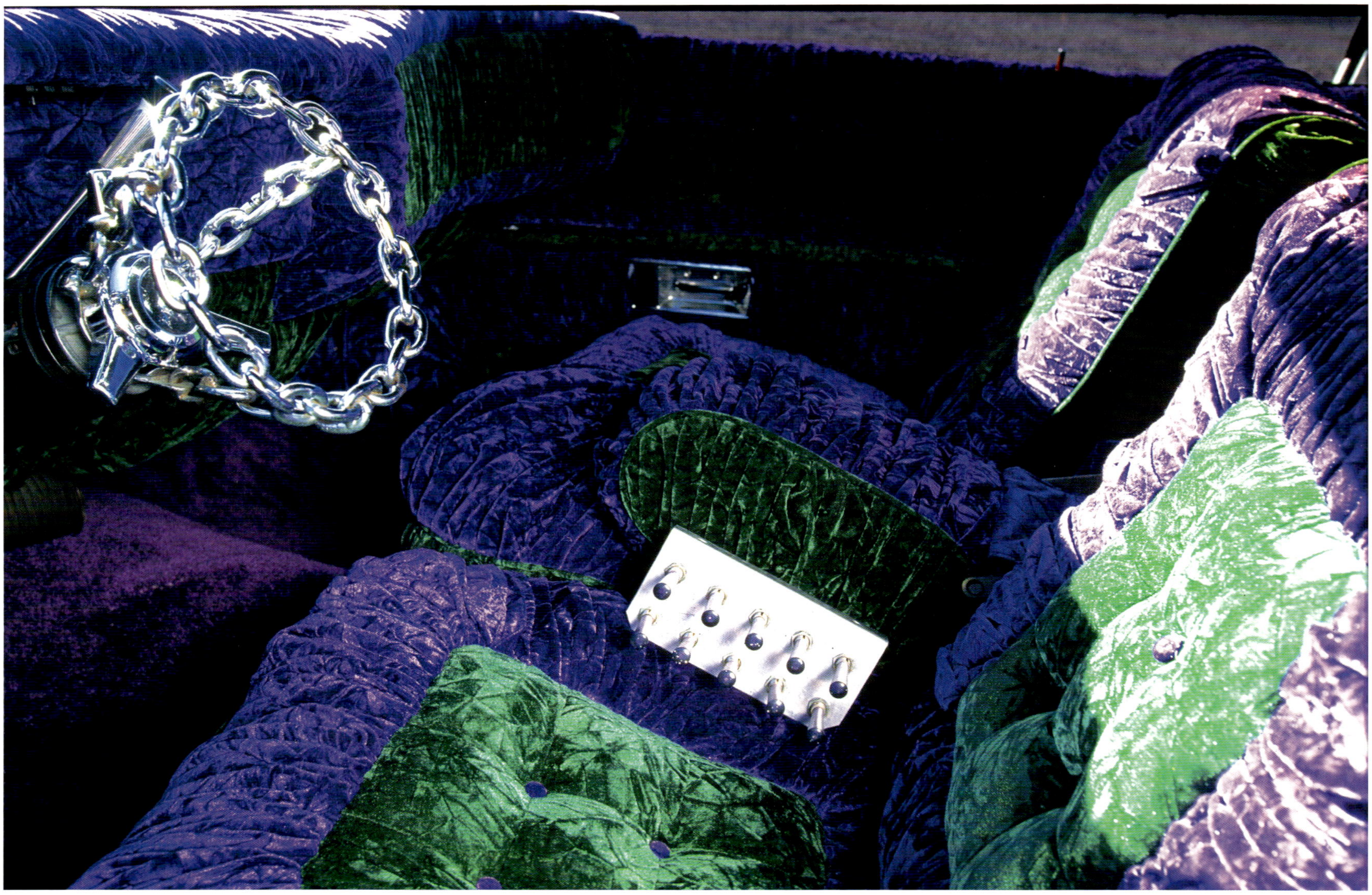

20. Jack Parsons, *'72 Buick Riviera Interior, Owner Adam Garcia of Las Vegas*, 1998

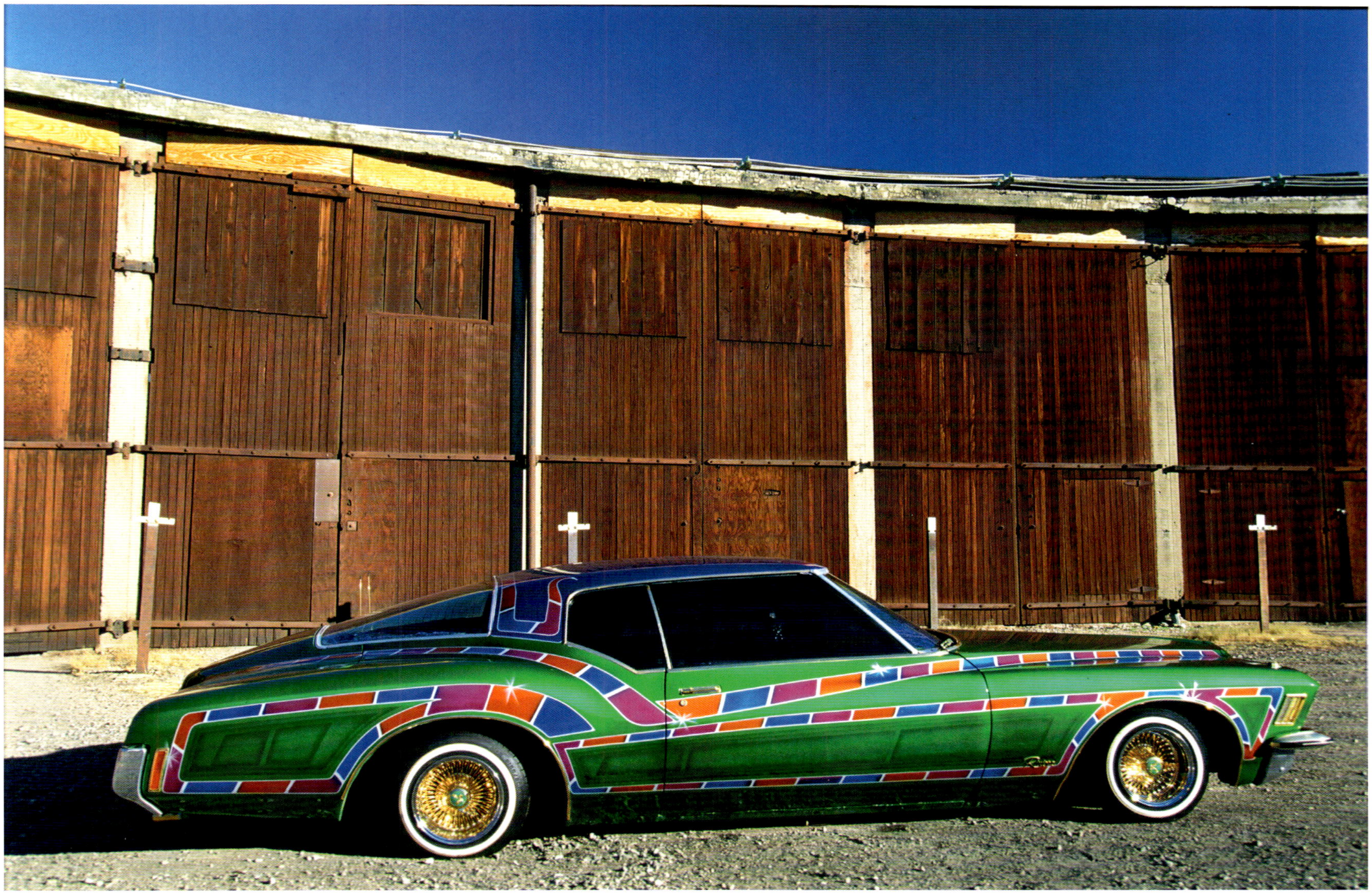

21. Jack Parsons, *'72 Buick Riviera, Owner Adam Garcia of Las Vegas*, 1998

22. Corey Ringo, *A Night on the Town*, 2010

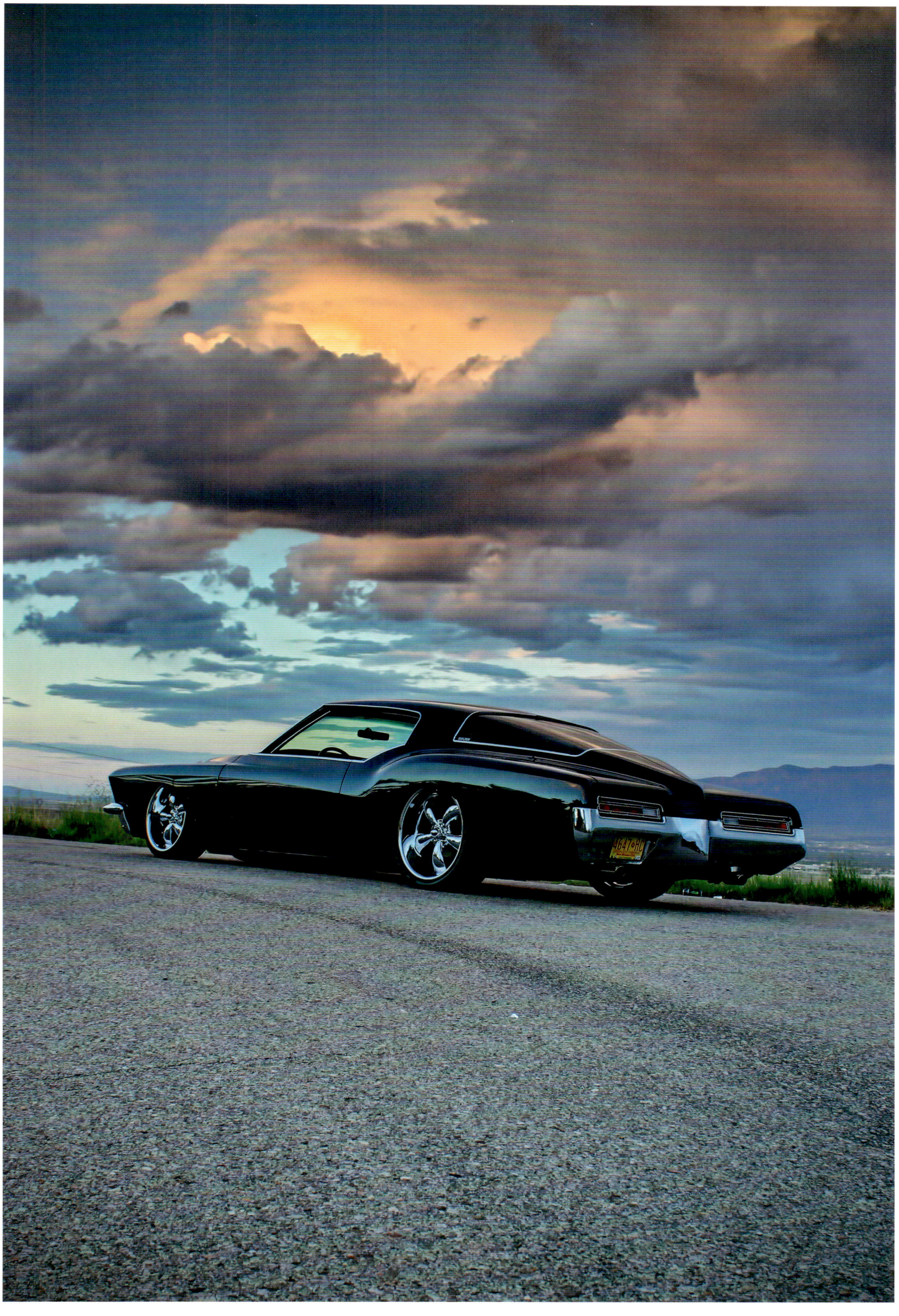

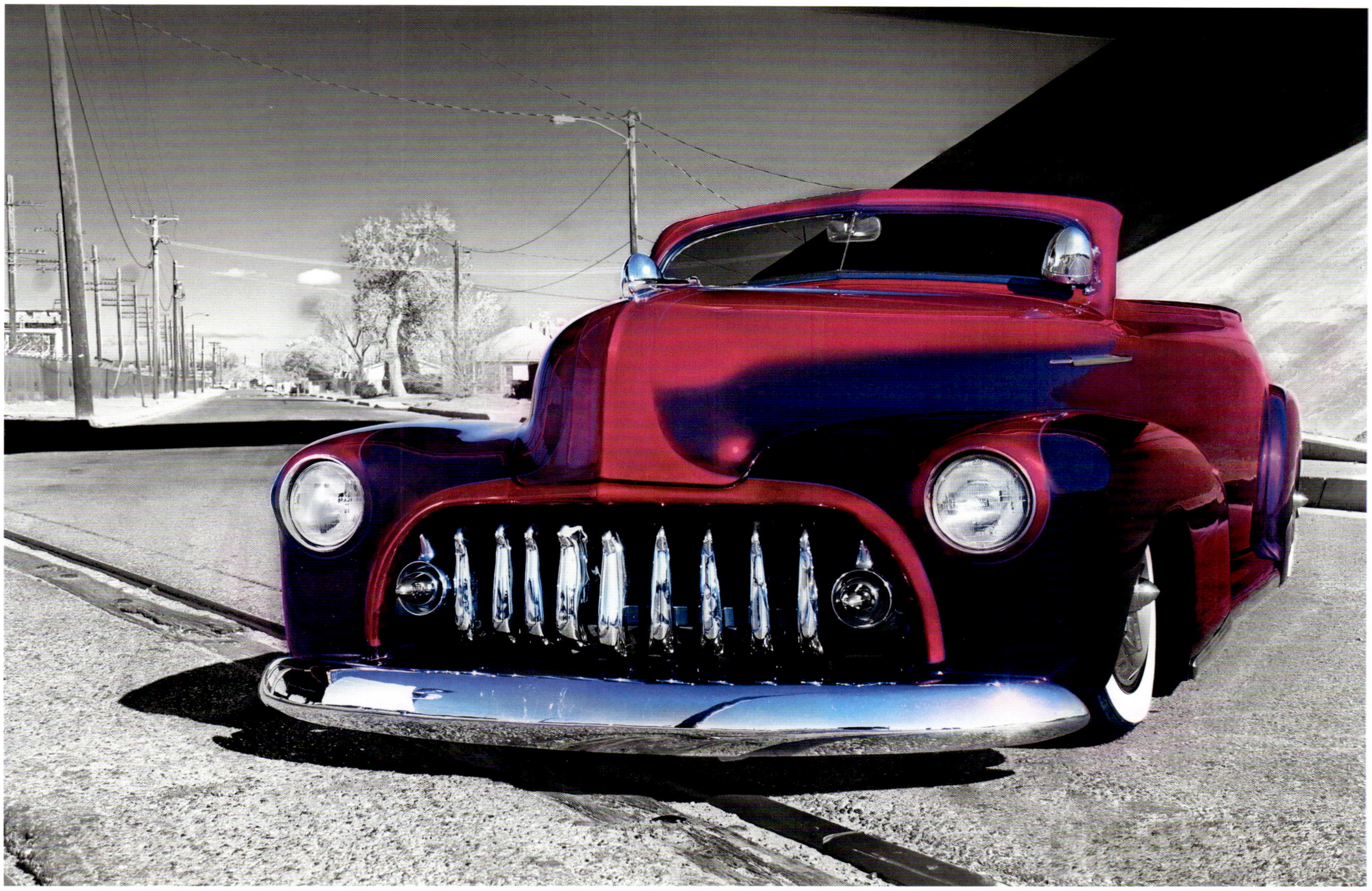

23. Travis Ruiz, *Grill'n Um*, 2011

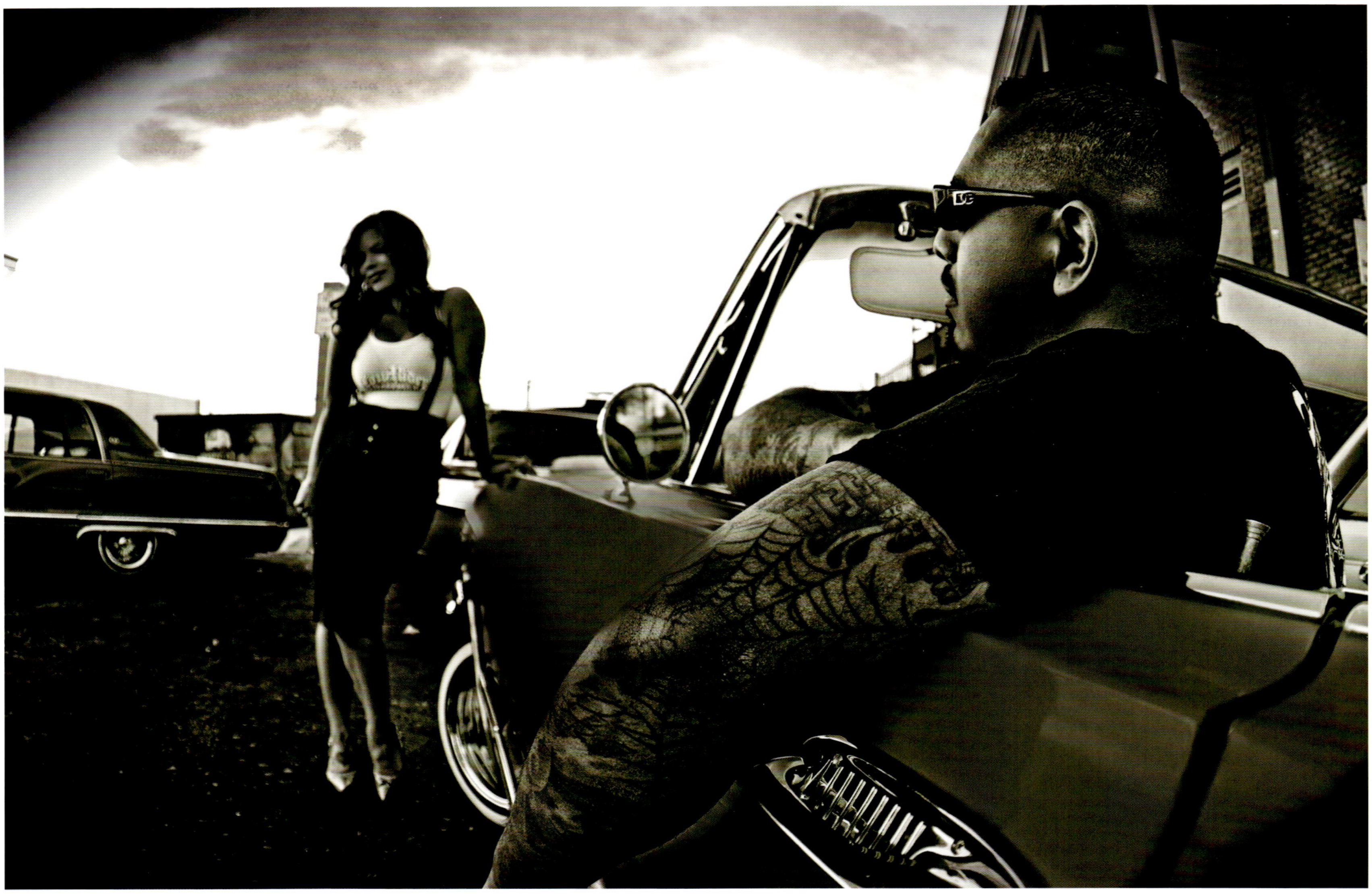

24. Travis Ruiz, *On a Sunday Afternoon*, 2008

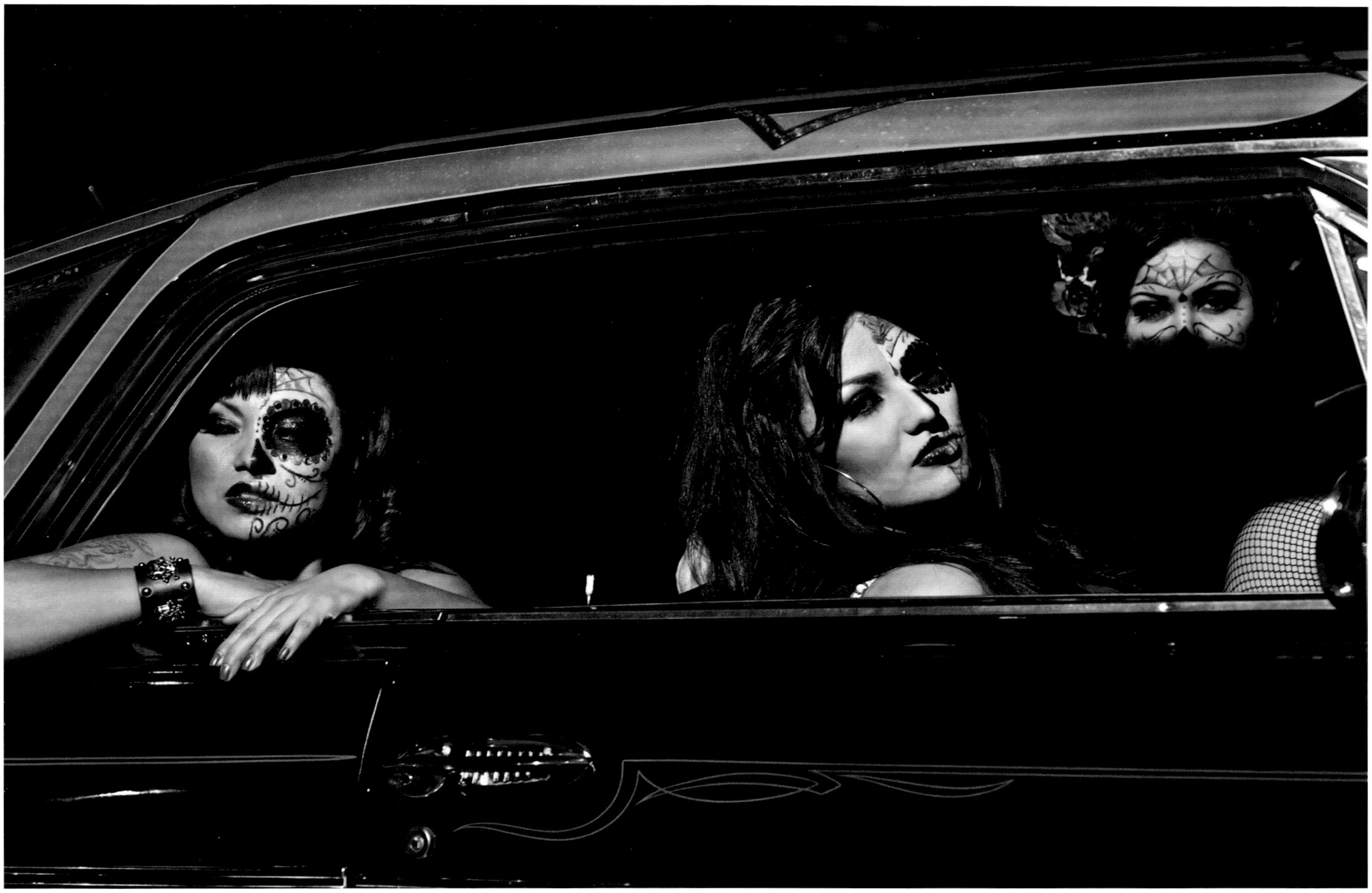

25. Travis Ruiz, *Hermosa Crucero Muerte*, 2010

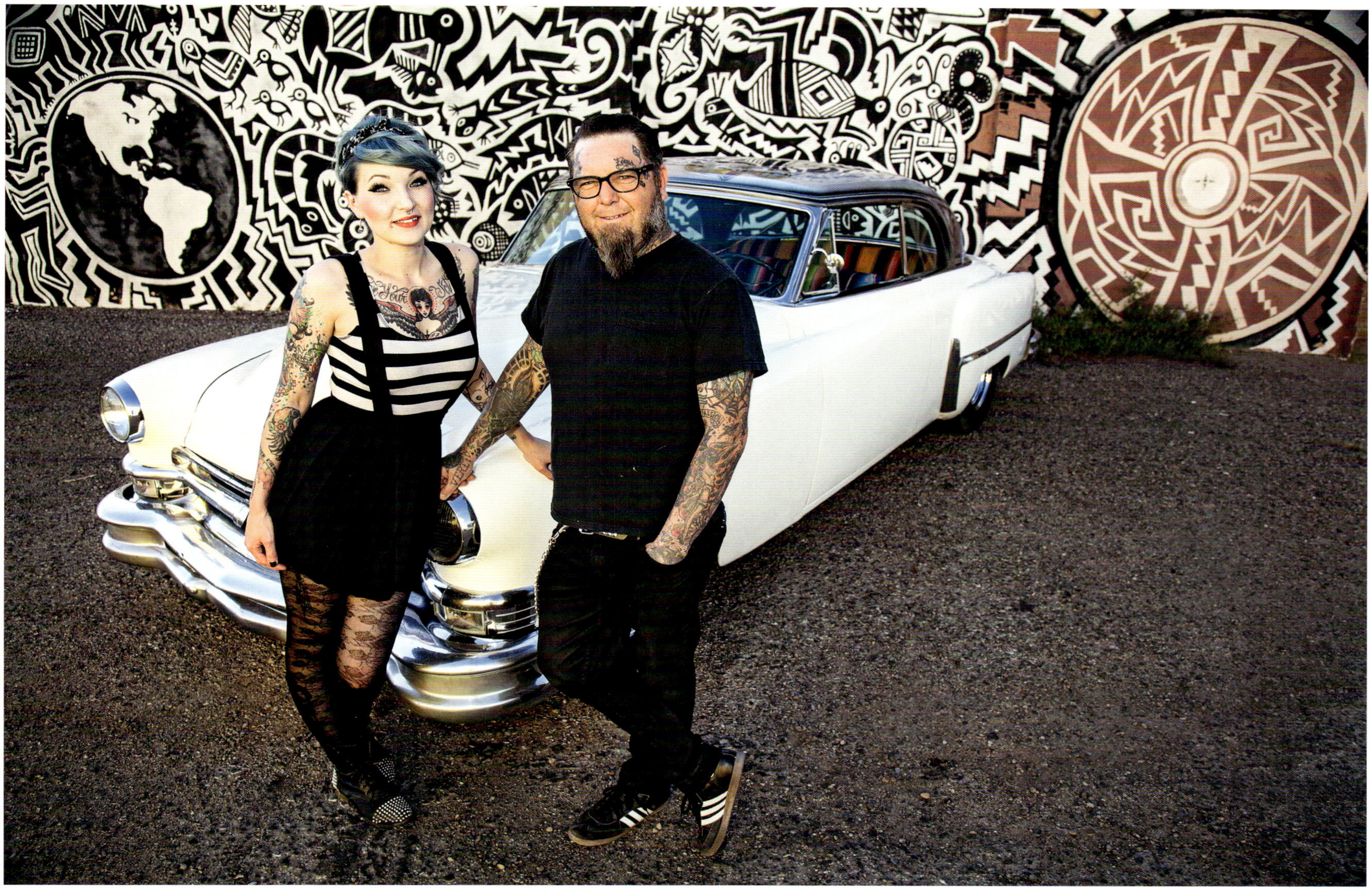

26. Gabriela E. Campos, *Albuquerque Family Portrait*, 2014

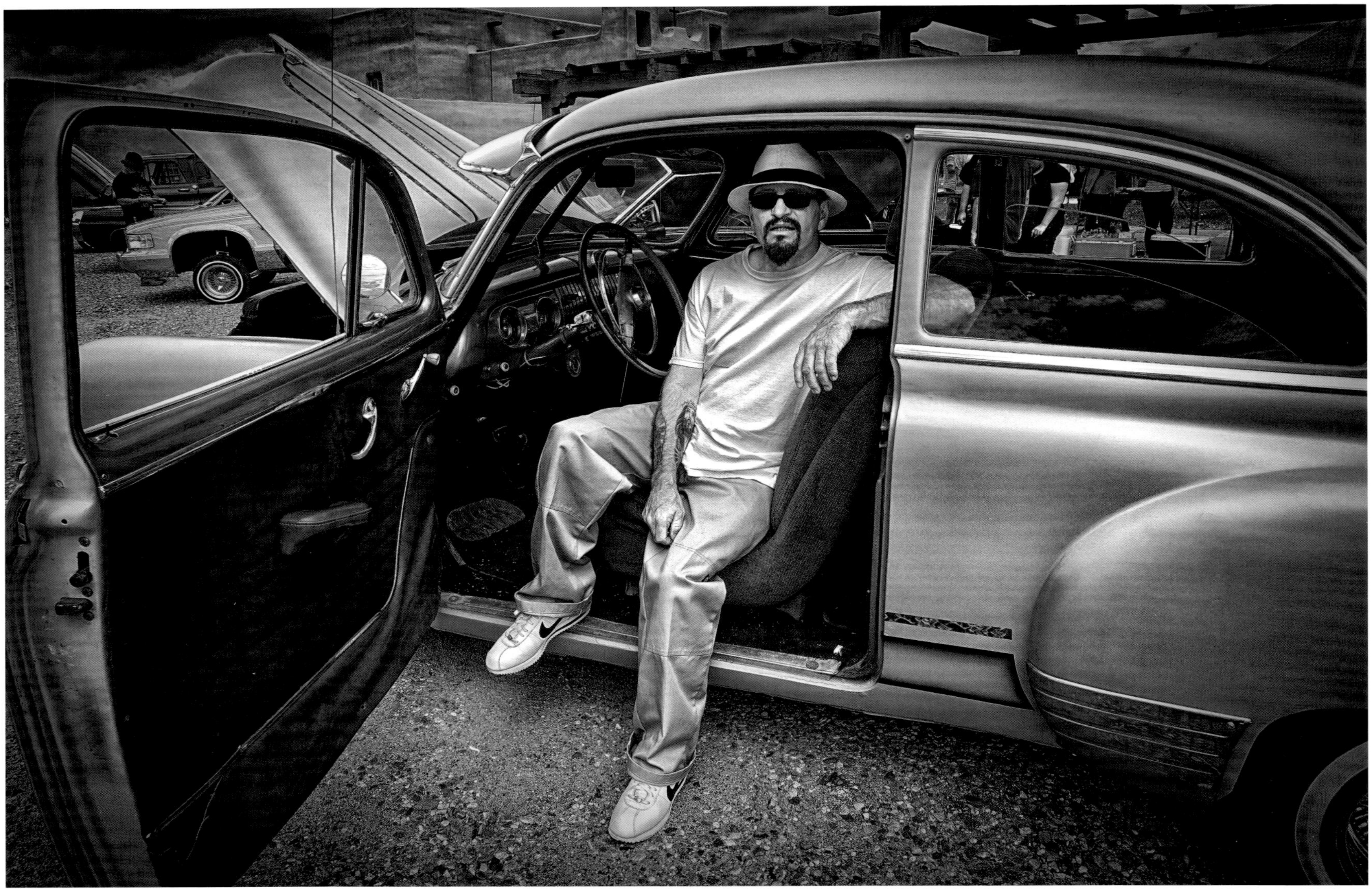

27. Bob Eckert, *Roberto Morales*, Española Plaza, 2015

opposite
28. Bob Eckert, *Joseph Martínez*, Española Plaza, 2015

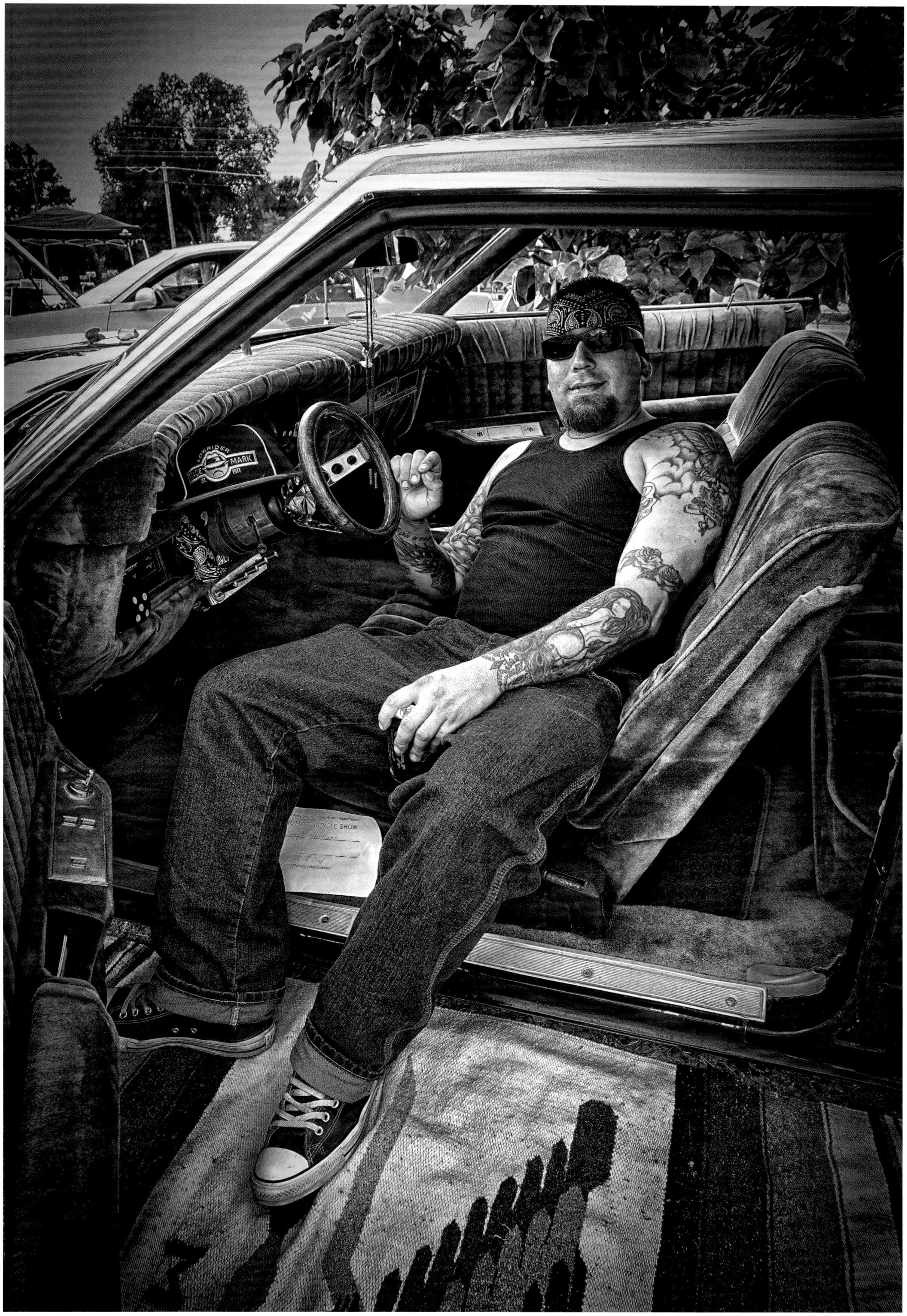
LOWRIDER
MARK

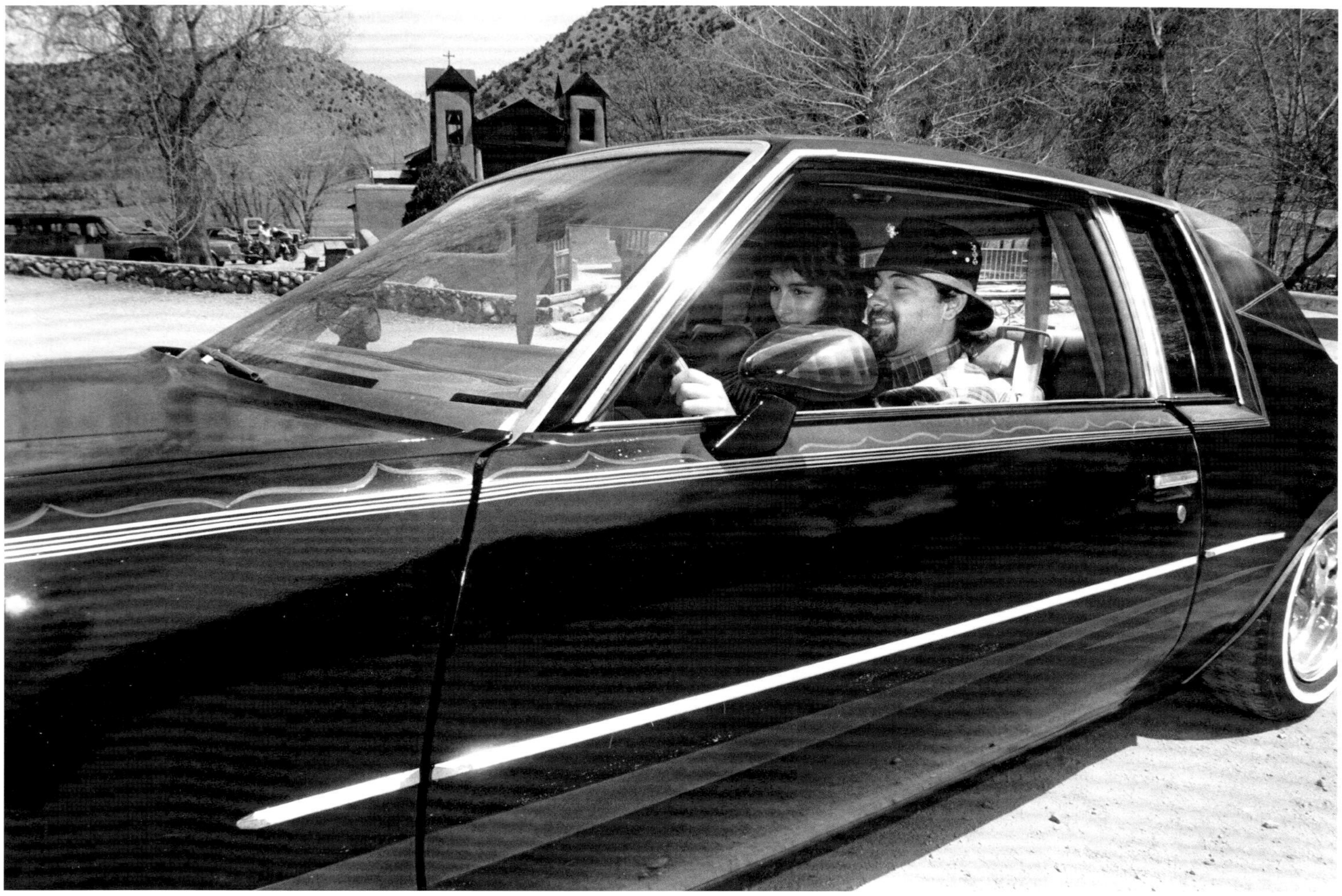

29. Kitty Leaken, *Joan and Arthur Lowlow Medina in Their Lowrider*, ca. 1990

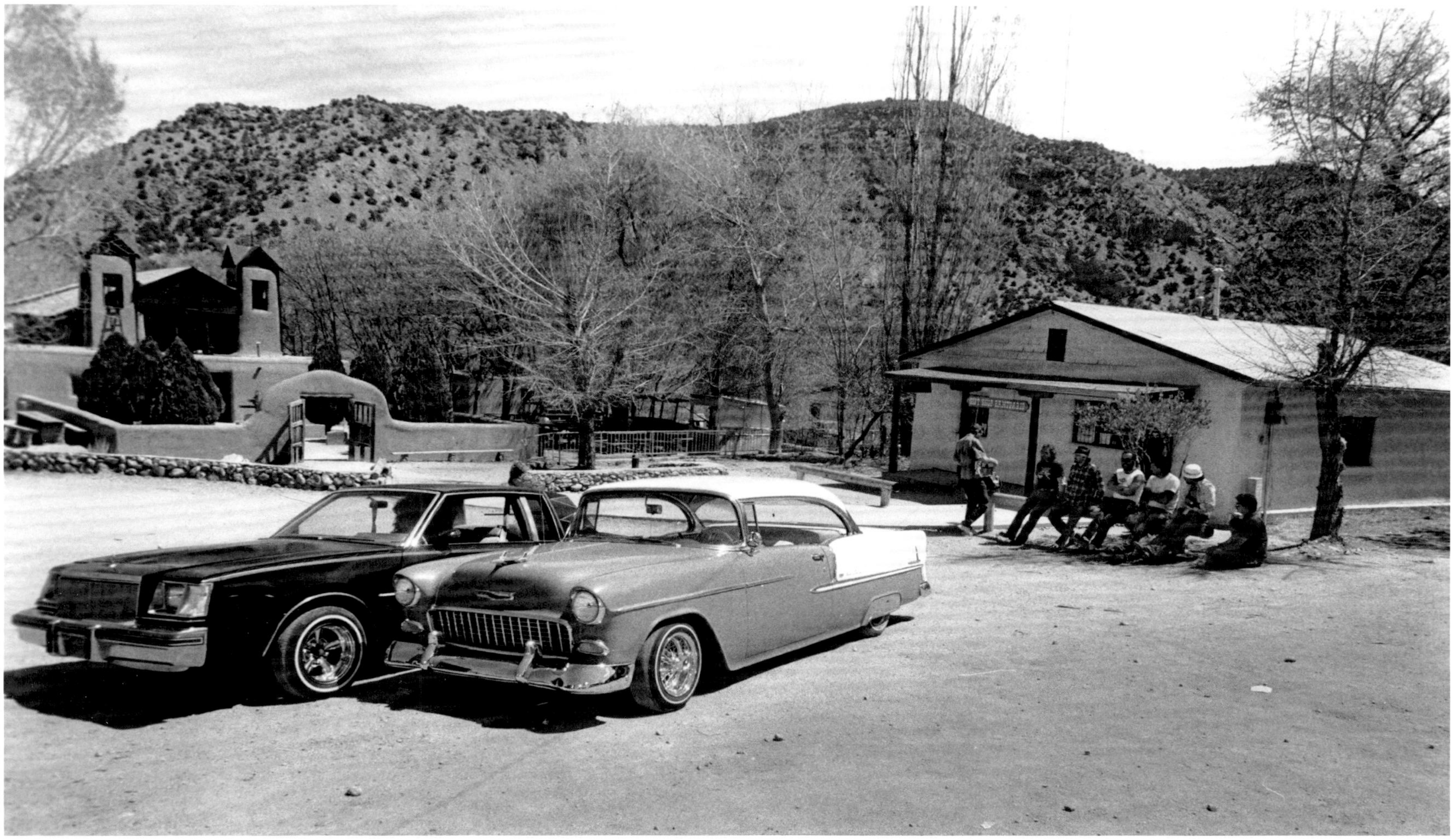

30. Kitty Leaken, *Hanging Out in Chimayó before Cruising to Española*, ca. 1990

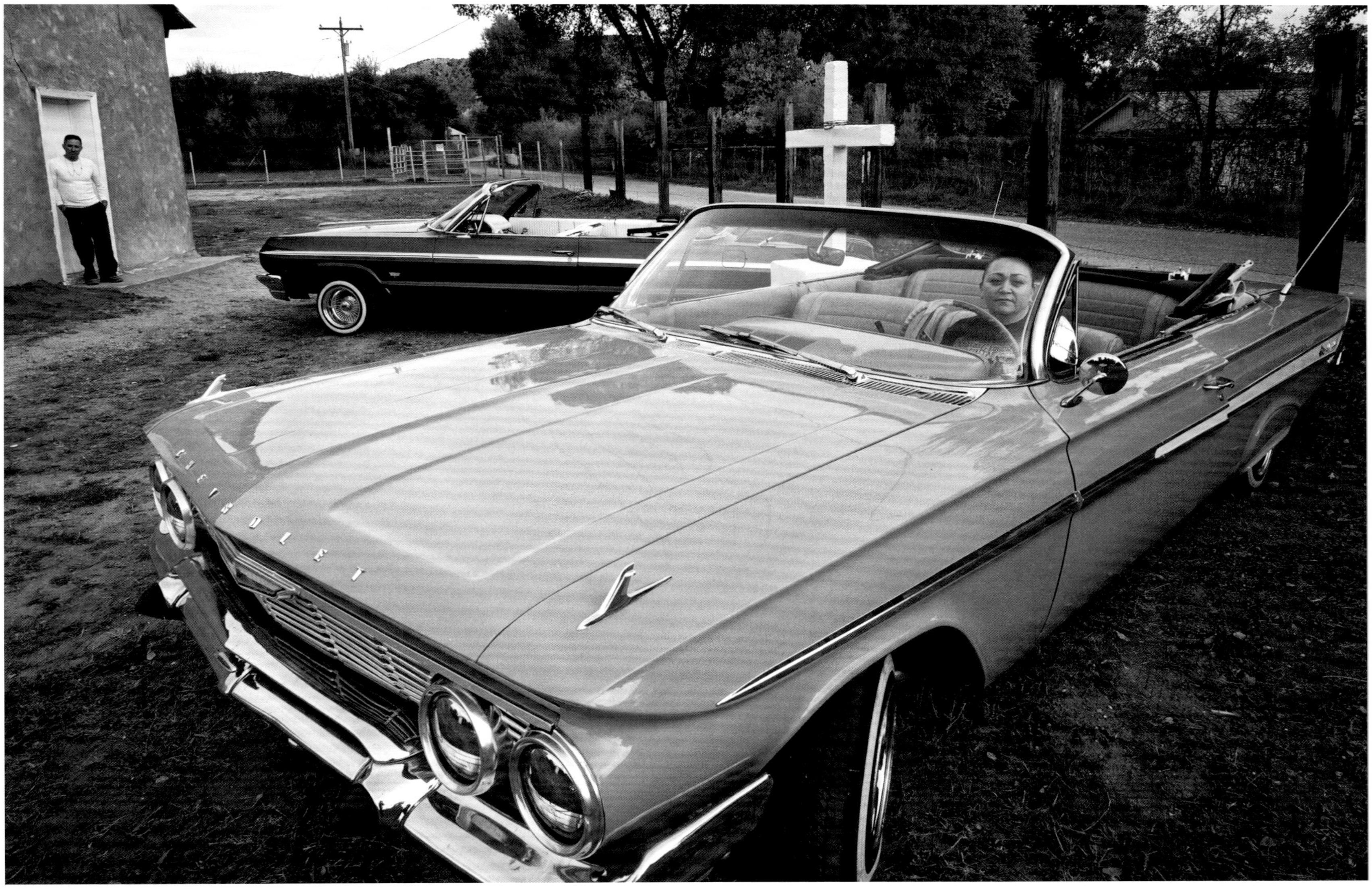

31. Don J. Usner, *Pam Jaramillo in Her '61 Impala at the Los Ranchos Morada, Chimayó*, 2015

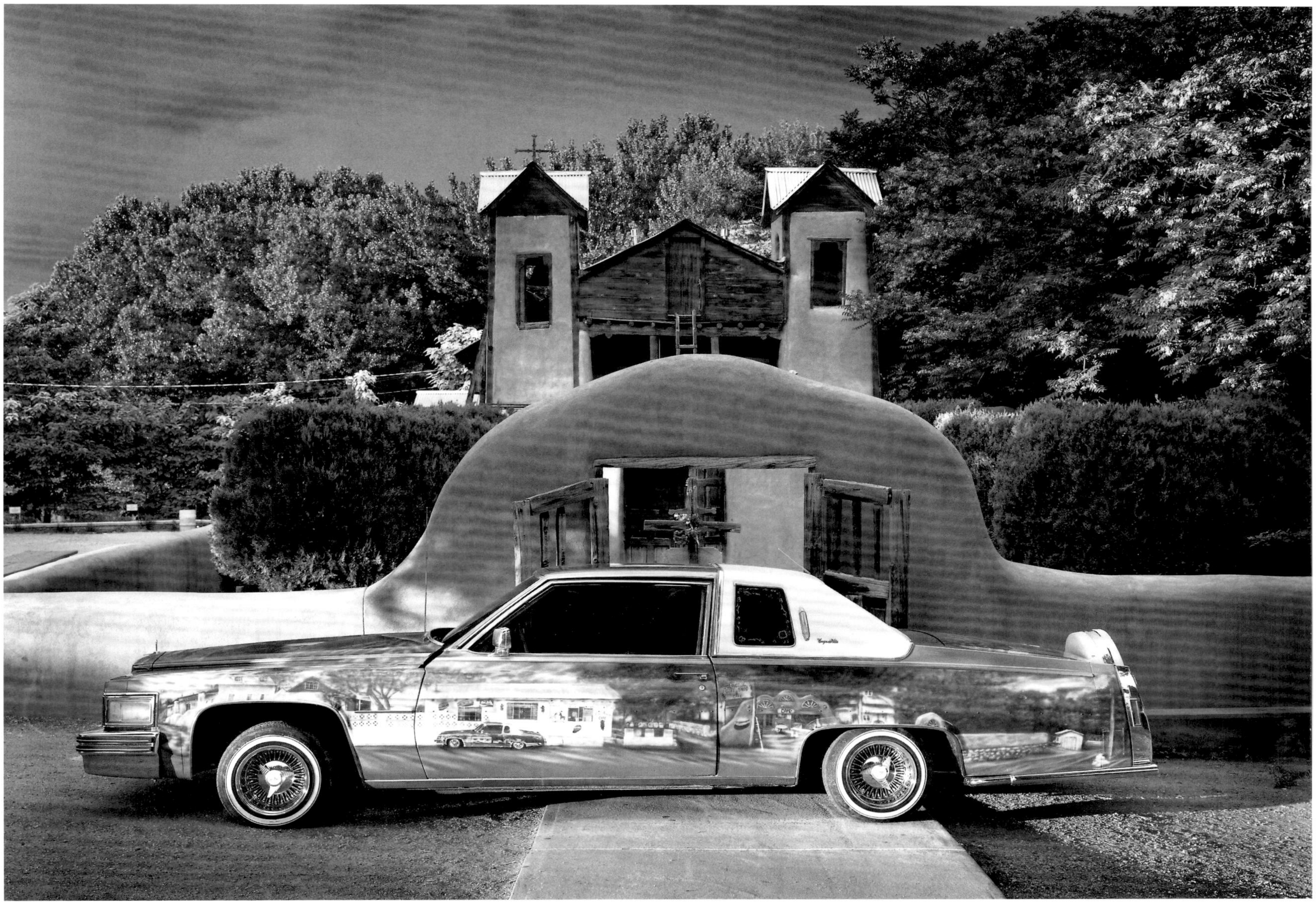

32. Craig Varjabedian, *A Low-rider Cadillac Named "Chimayó,"* 1997

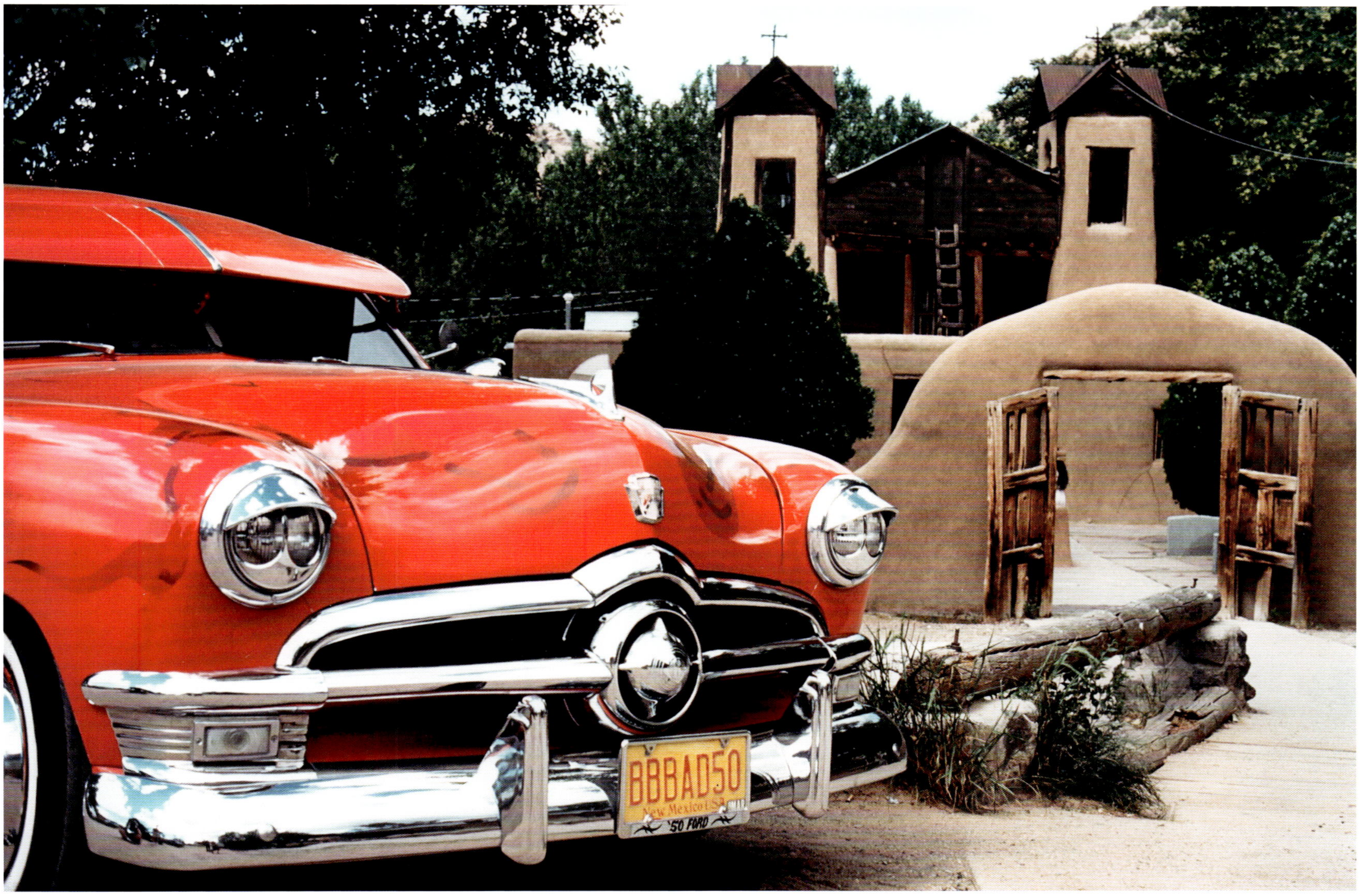

33. Annie Sahlin, *BBBAD50 Owned by Victor Martínez, Chimayó*, 1990

34. Don J. Usner, *Fred Rael in 1967 Impala "Liquid Sunshine,"* Española, 2012

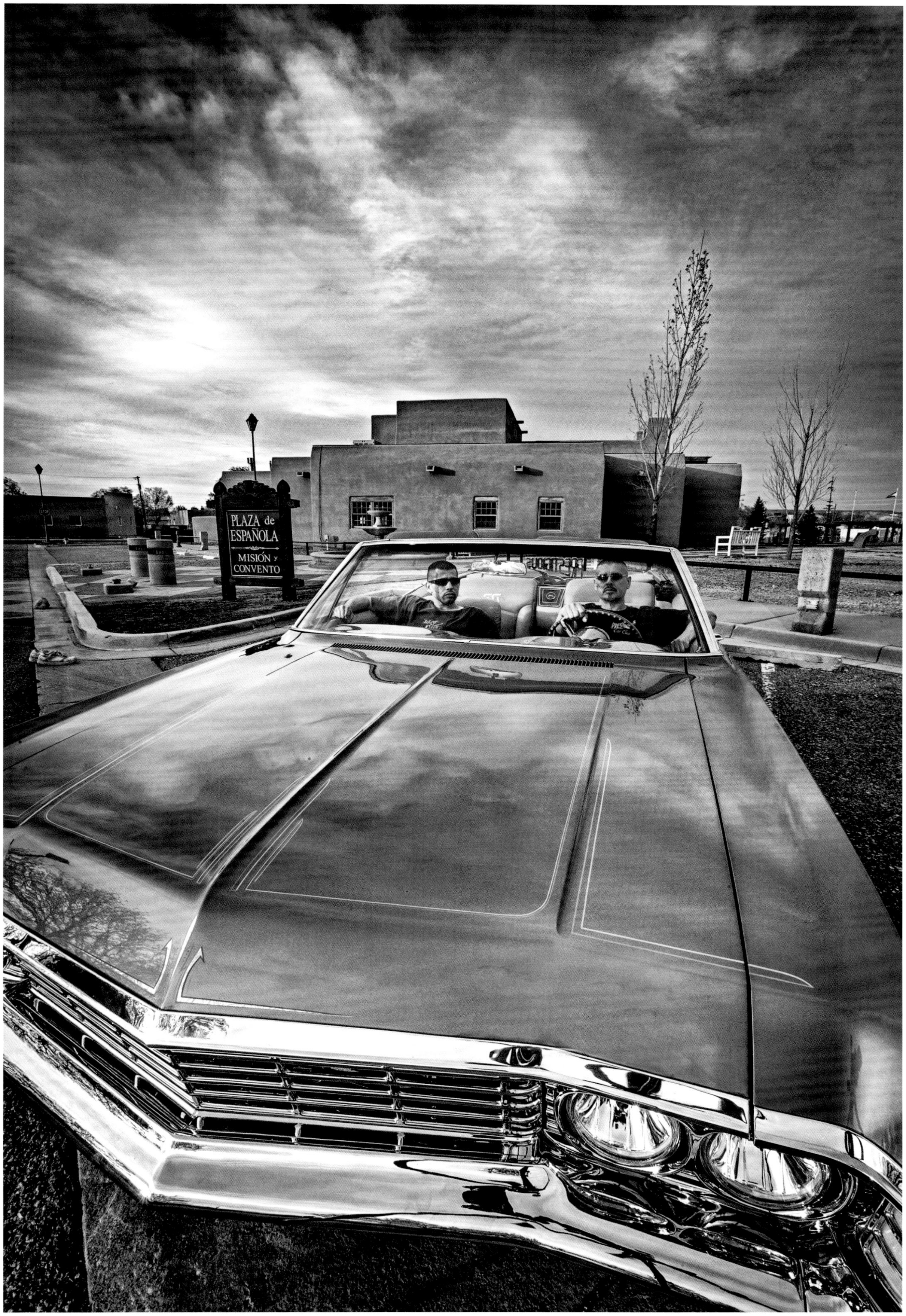
PLAZA de
ESPAÑOLA
MISIÓN y
CONVENTO

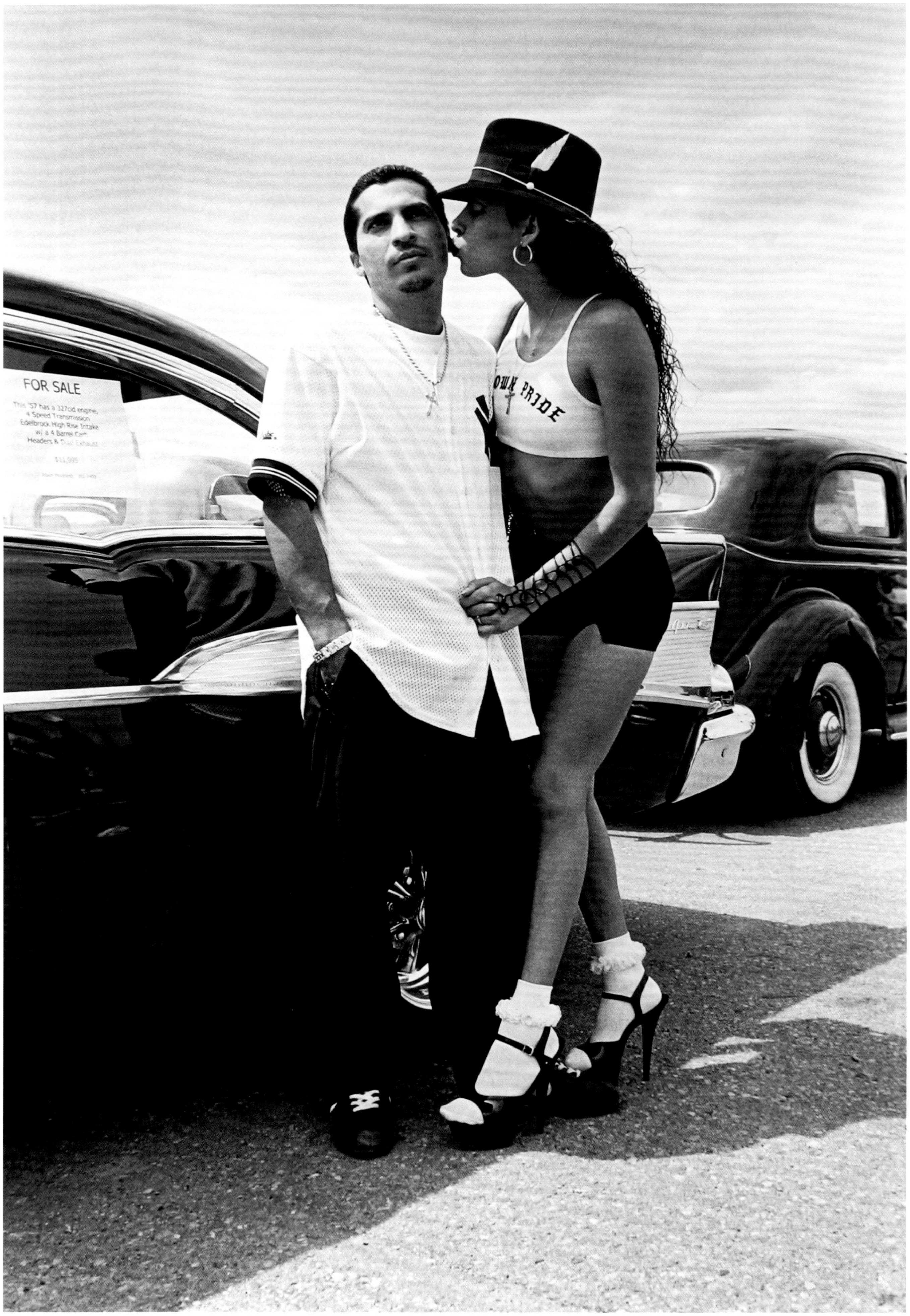
FOR SALE
This '57 has a 327cid engine,
4 Speed Transmission
Edelbrock High Rise Intake
w/ a 4 Barrel Carb
PRIDE

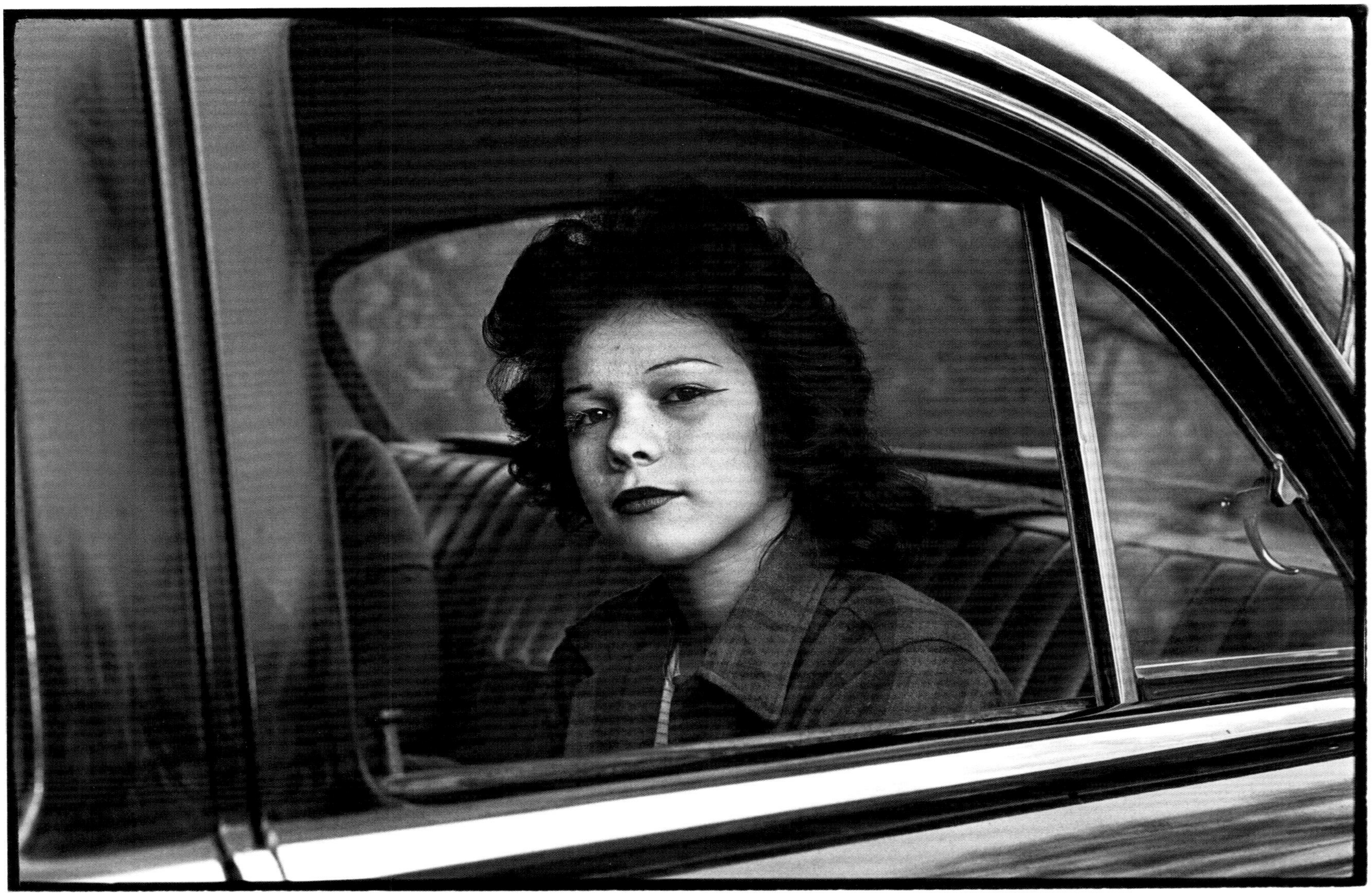

opposite
35. Norman Mauskopf, *Española, New Mexico*, 2001

above
36. Kevin Bubriski, *San Gabriel Park, Albuquerque*, 1983

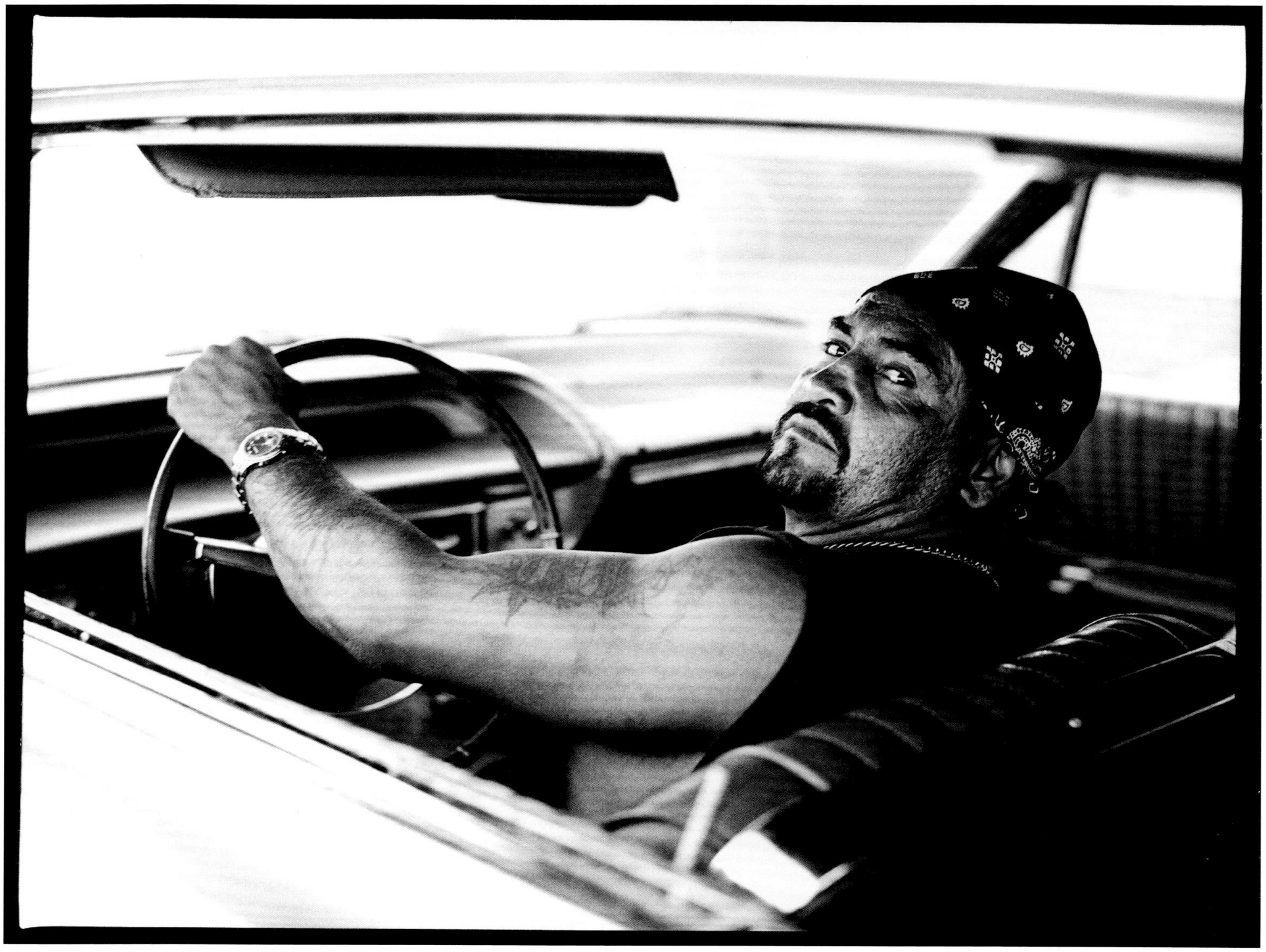

37. Hunter Barnes, *Patrick*, 2003

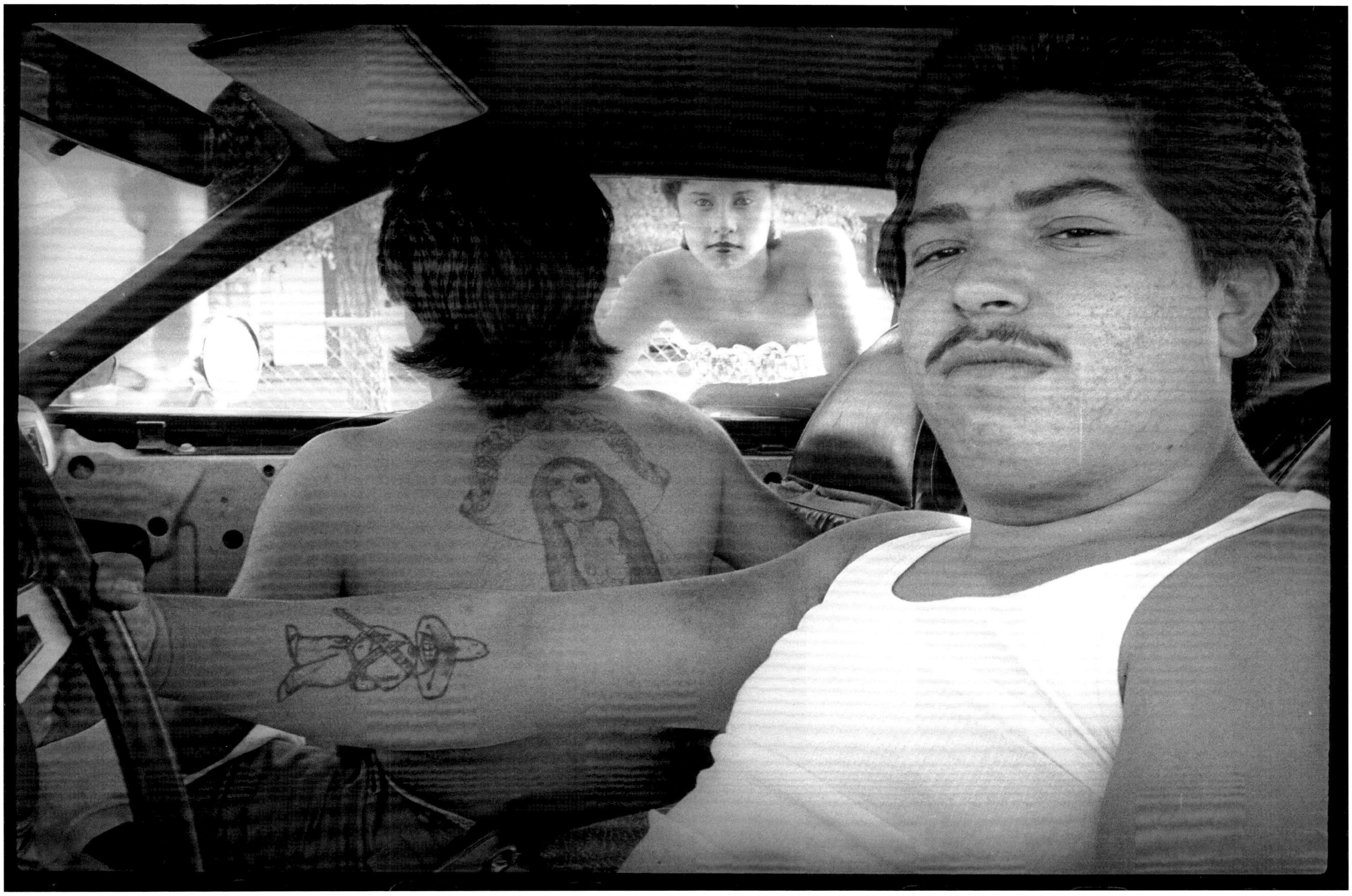

38. Miguel Gandert, *Melissa Armijo, Eloy Montoya, and Richard "El Wino,"* Madrid, 1983

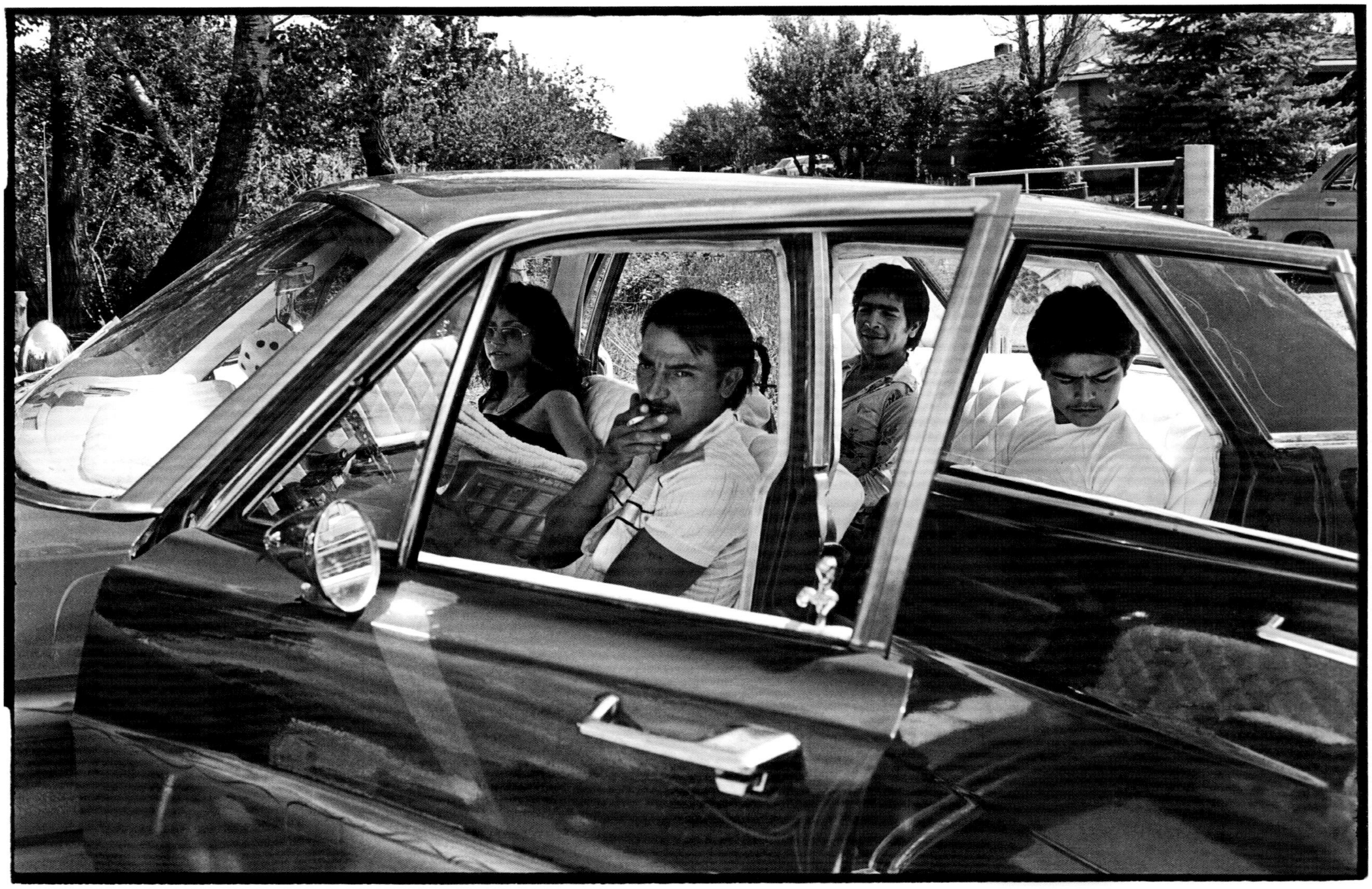

39. Kevin Bubriski, *El Rito Fiesta Parade*, 1981

opposite
40. Sam Adams, *Lowrider Car Show*, Española, 2000

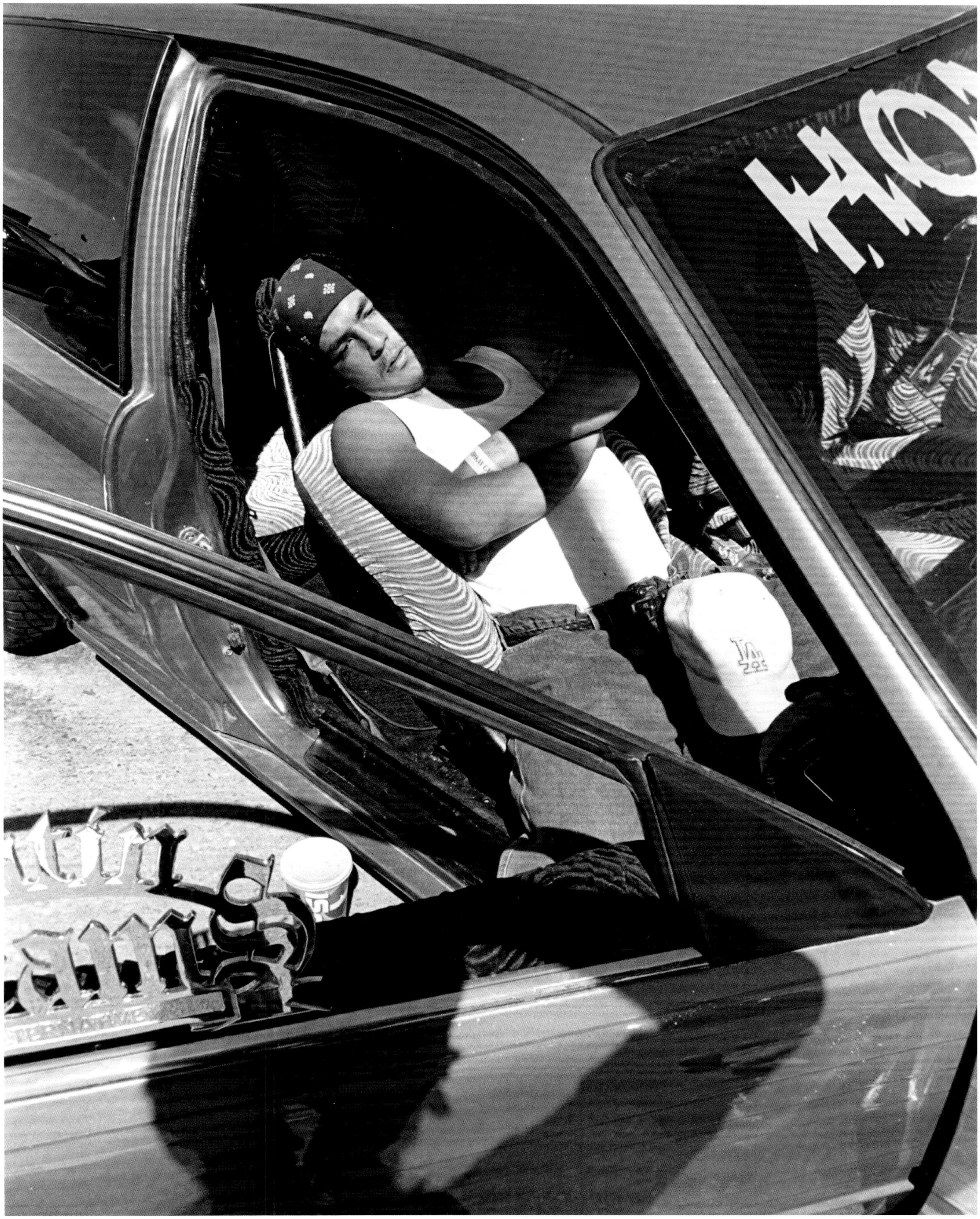

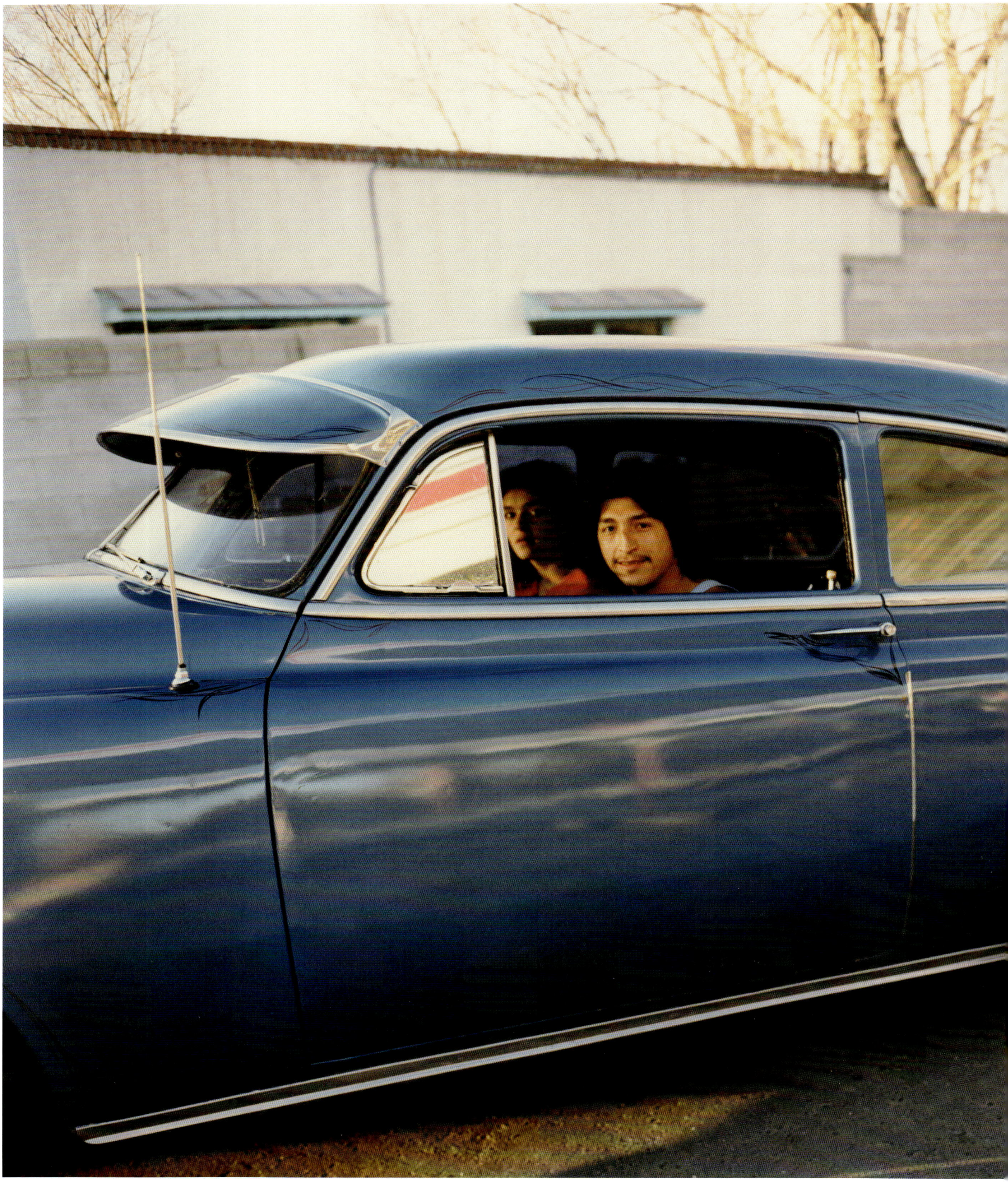

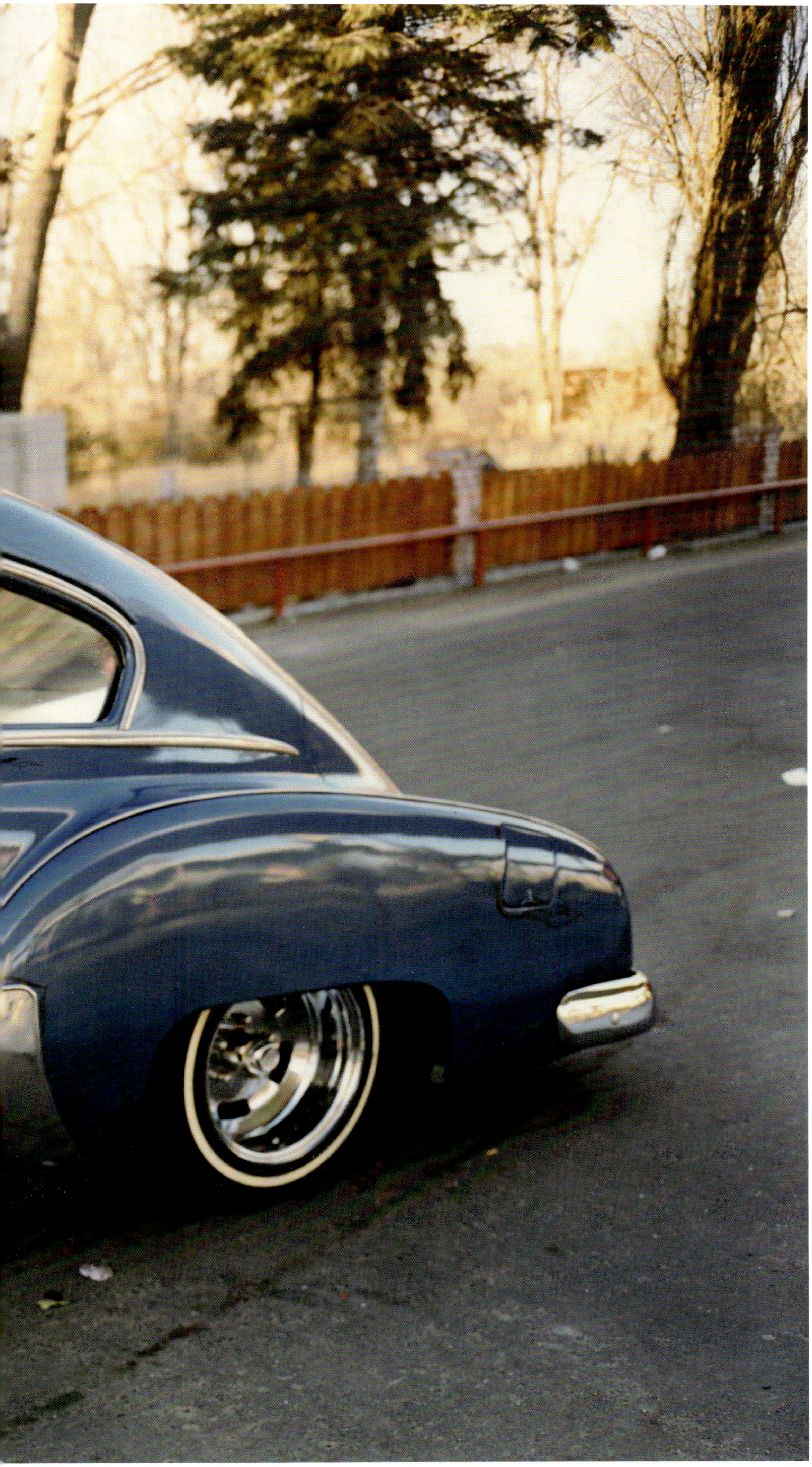

41. Meridel Rubenstein, *Donaldo Valdez*, New Mexico, 1980

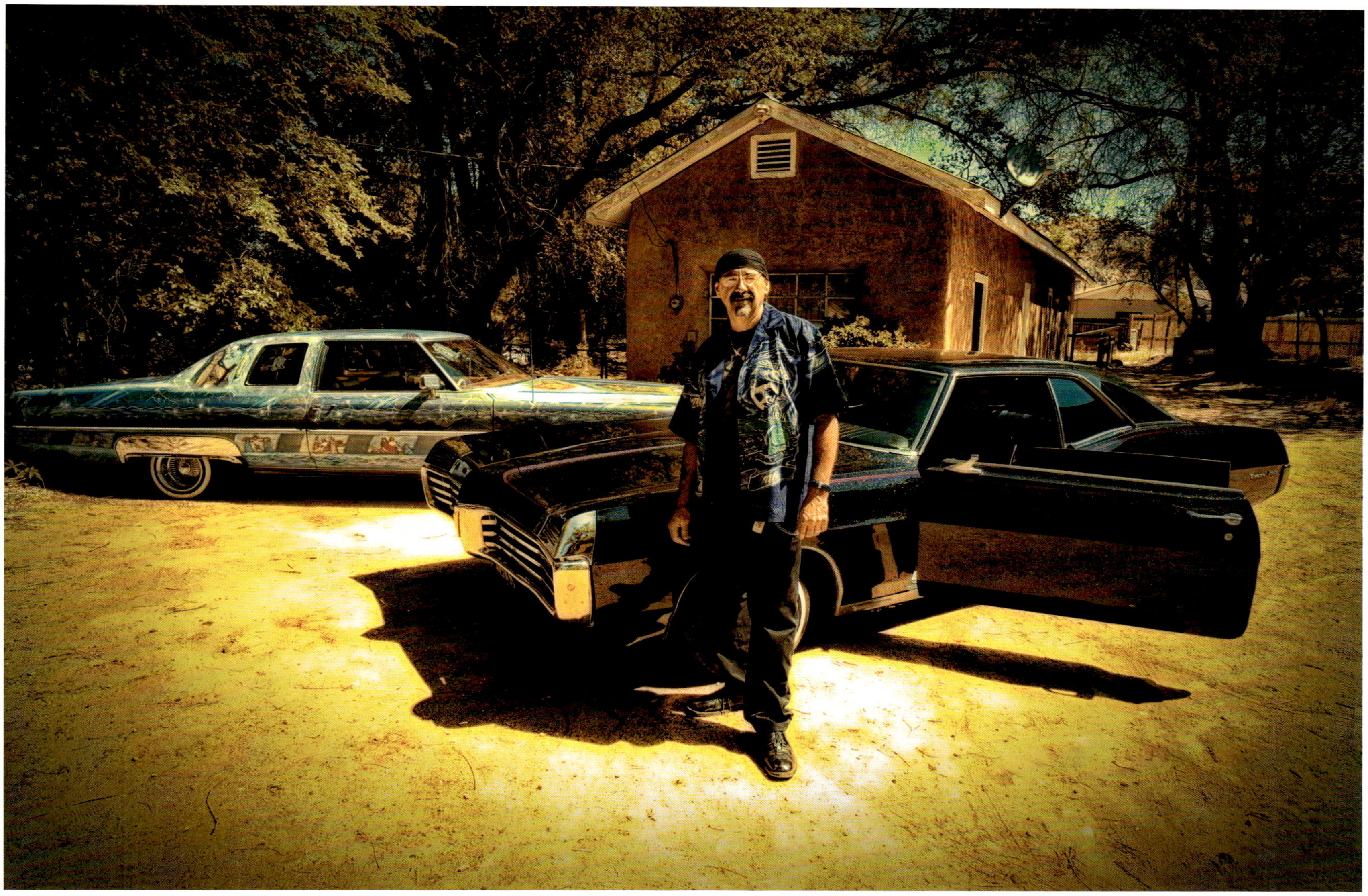

42. Bob Eckert, *Arthur "Lowlow" Medina with Muralized 1976 Cadillac Coupe DeVille and 1967 Pontiac Grand Prix*, Chimayó, 2012

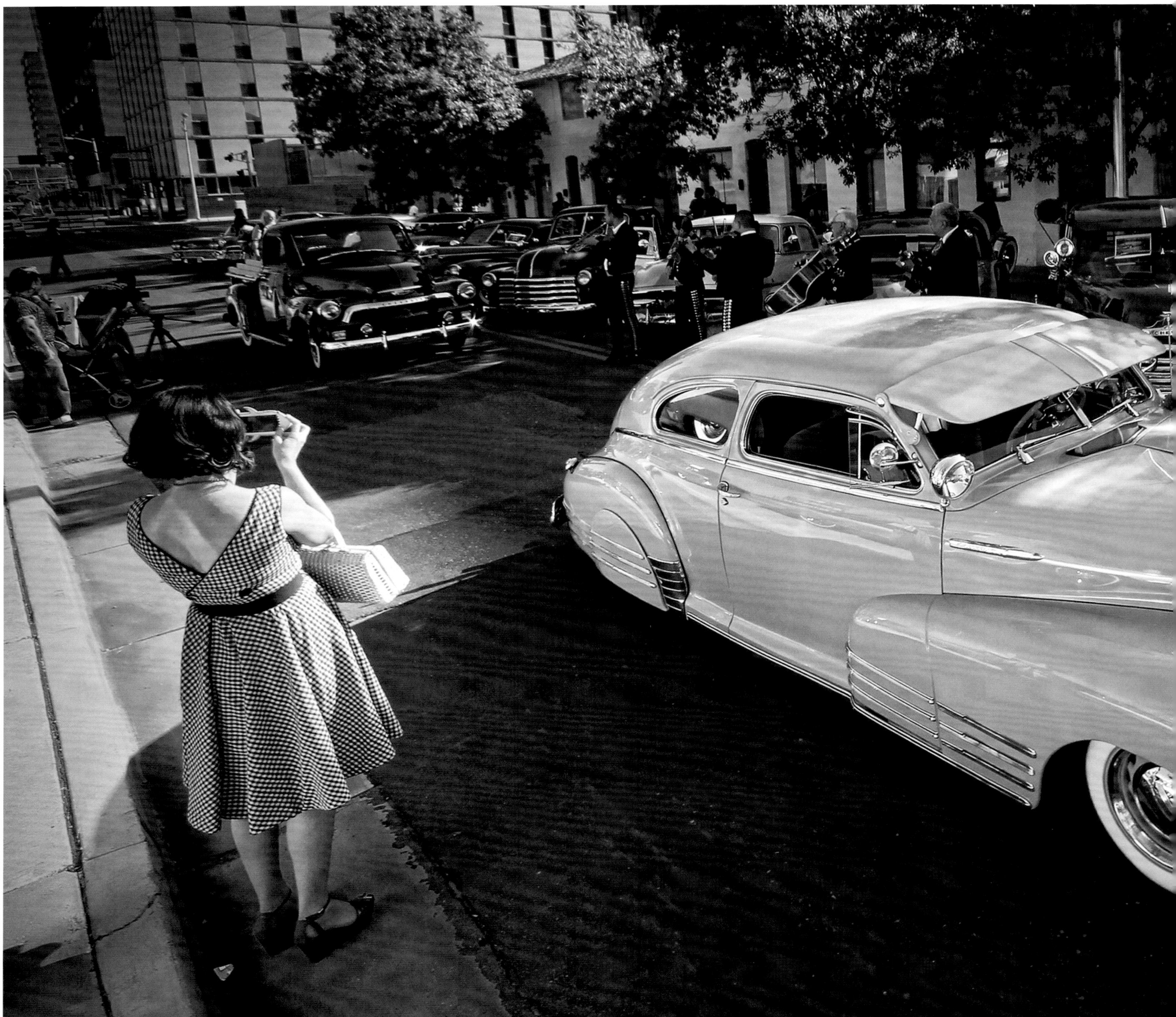

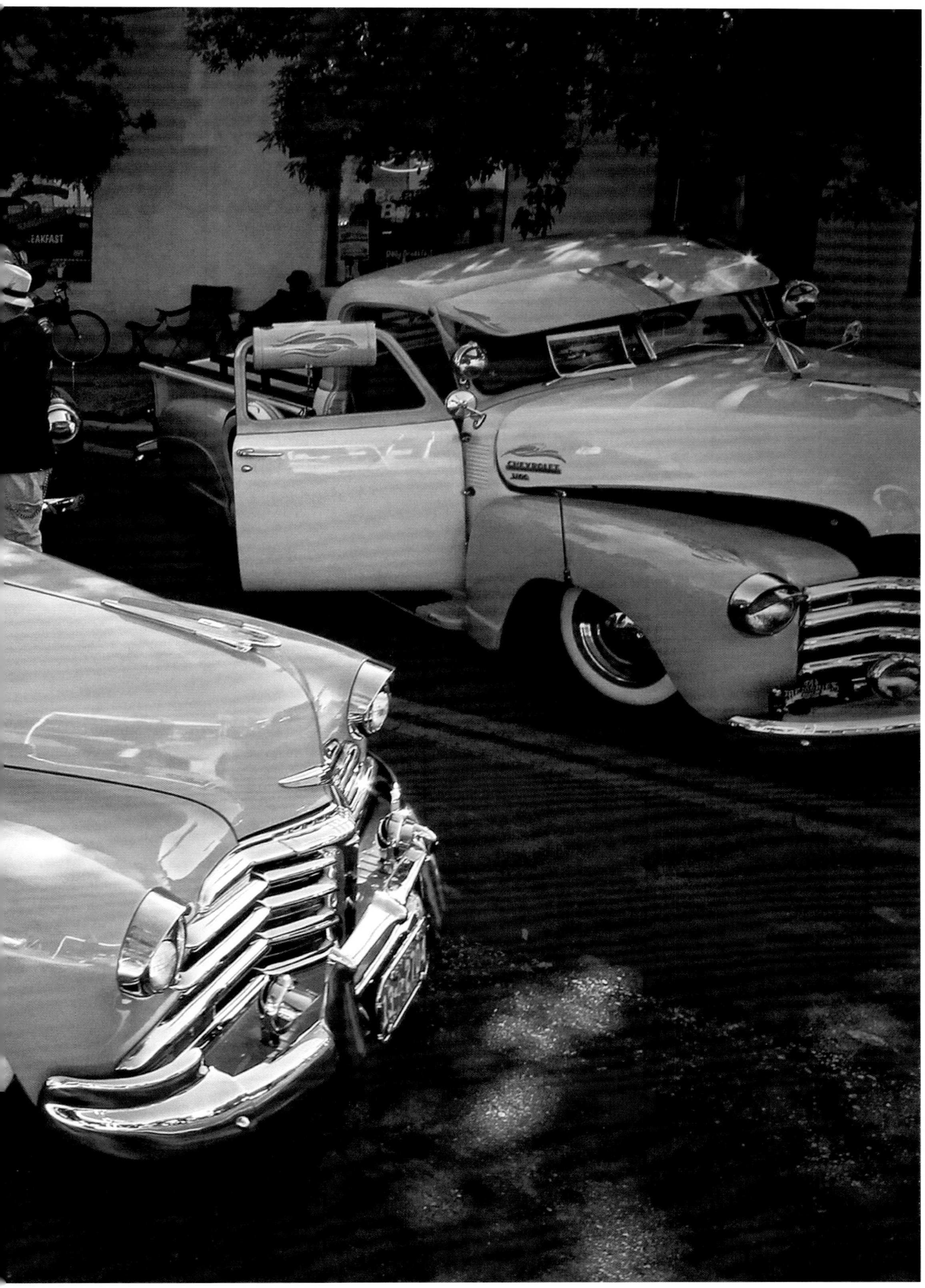

43. Corey Ringo, *Mariachis and Bombas*, Albuquerque, 2015

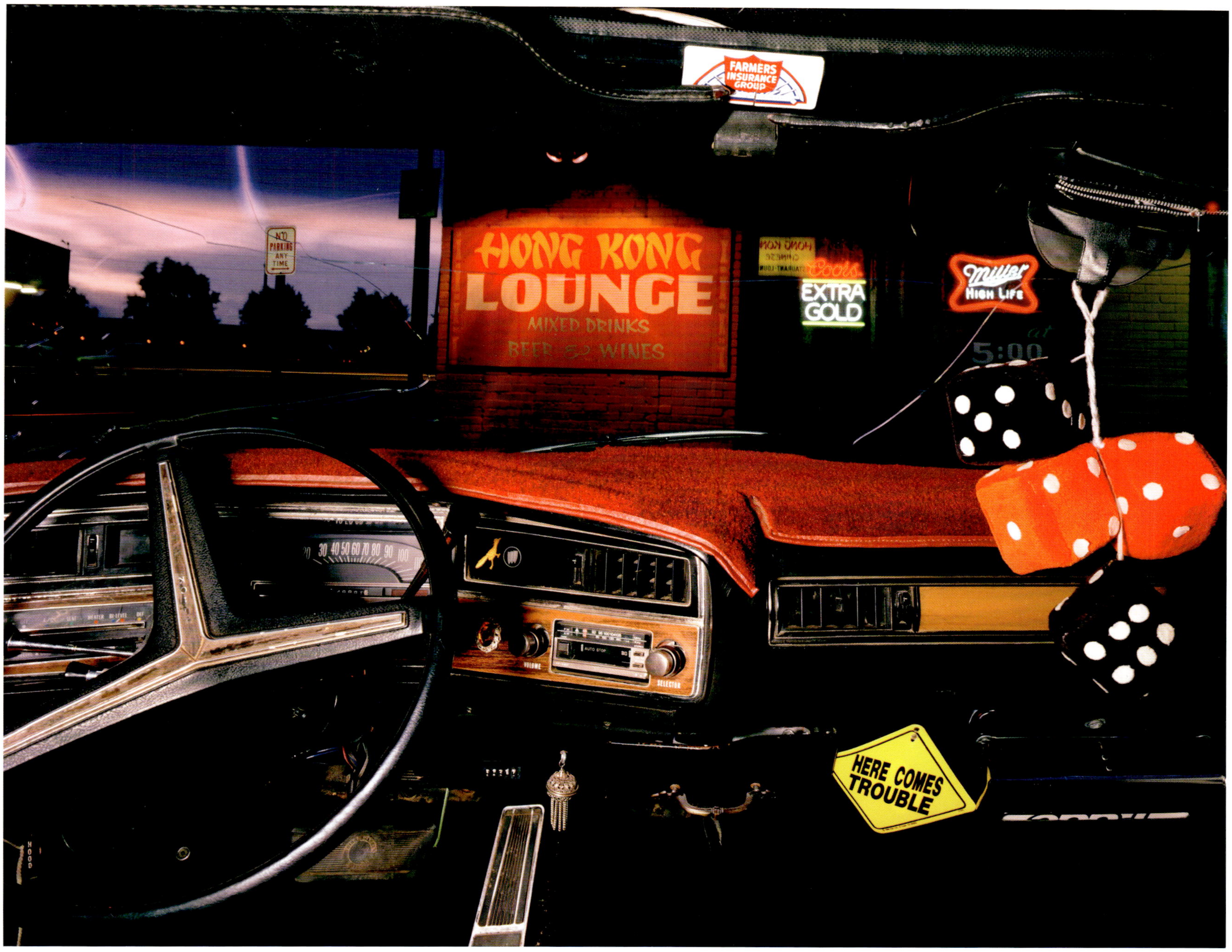

44. Alex Harris, *Hong Kong Lounge, Las Vegas, New Mexico, Looking North from Richard Lucero's 1972 Buick Centurion*, 1987

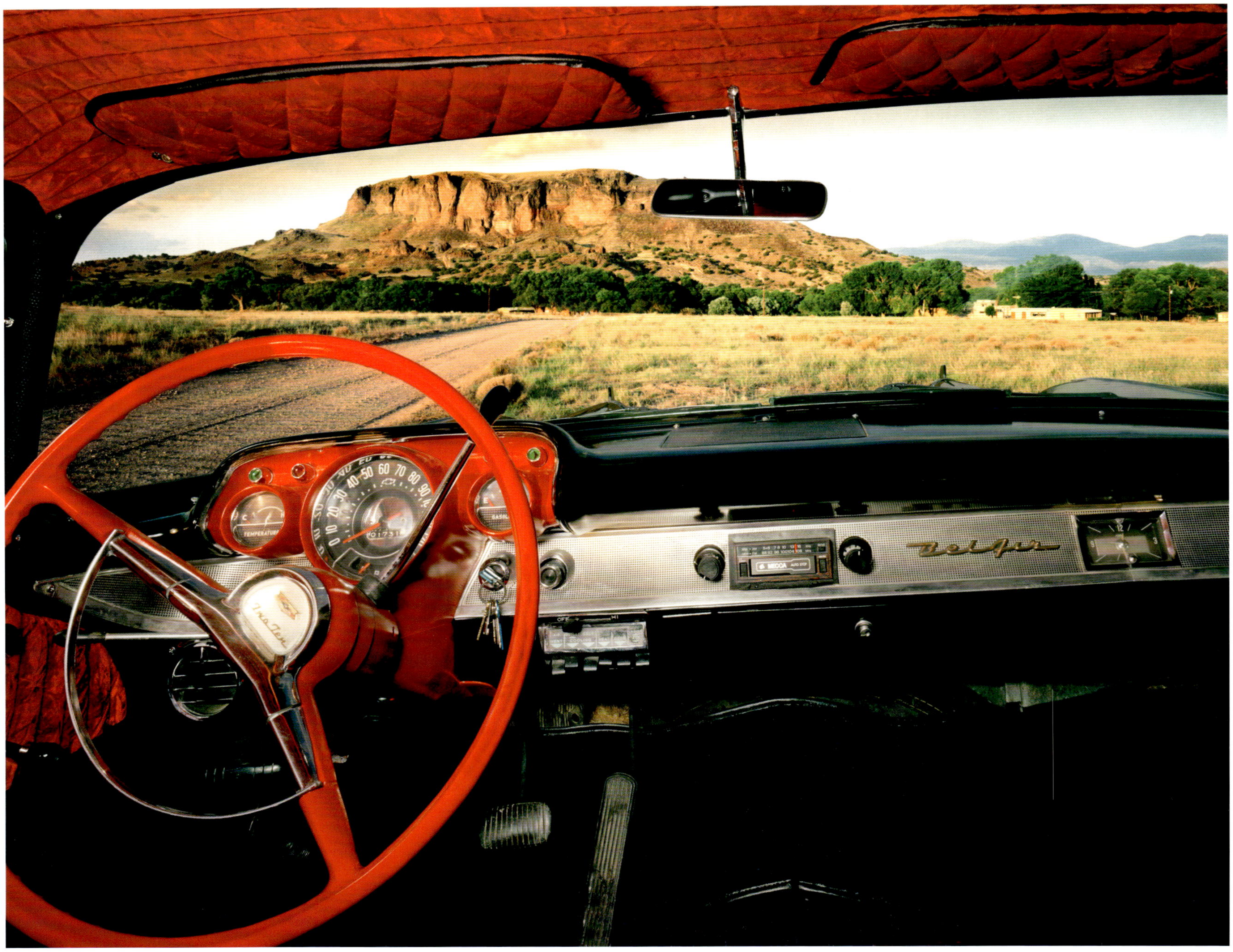

45. Alex Harris, *Black Mesa, Looking East from Fred Cata's 1957 Chevrolet Belair*, 1987

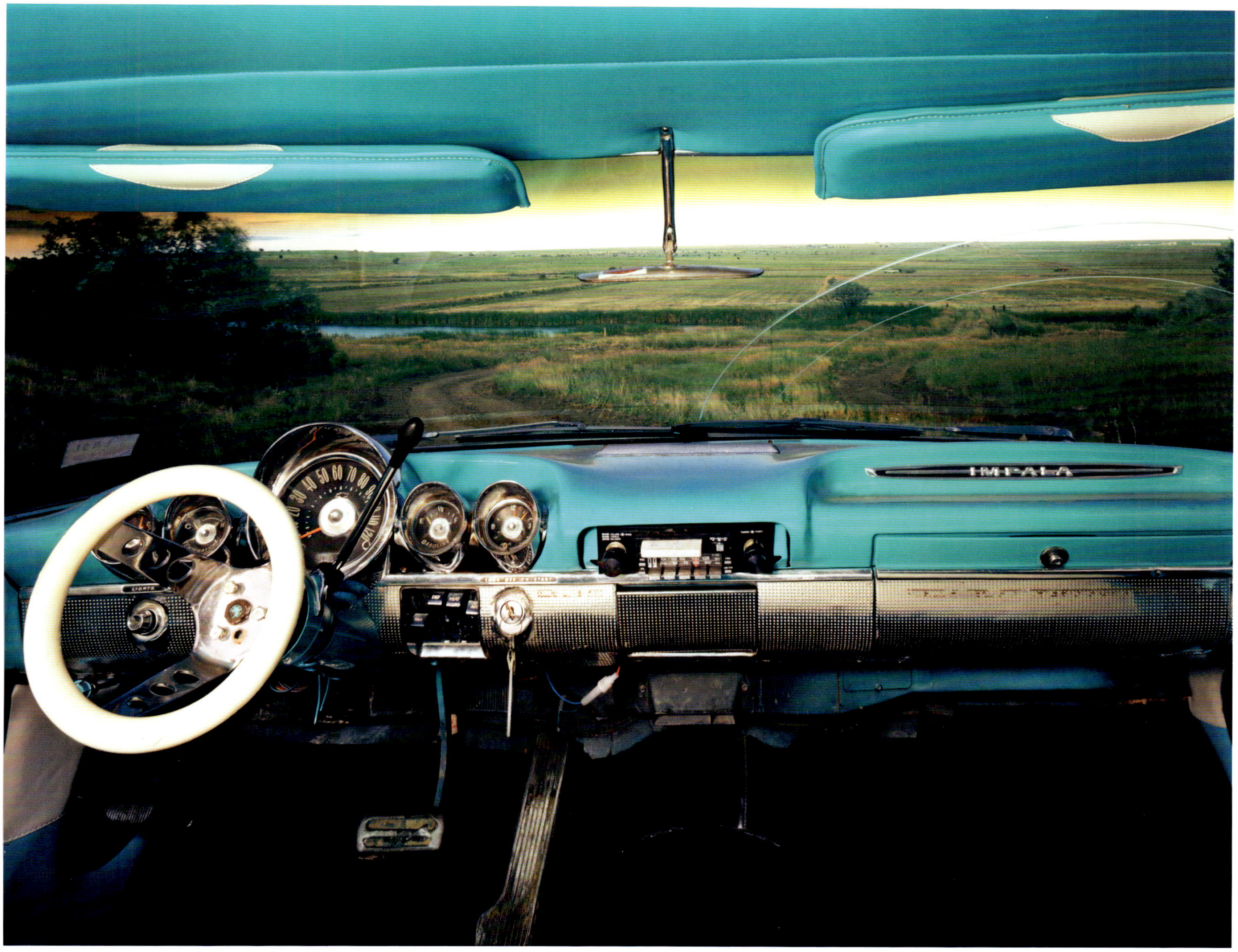

46. Alex Harris, *Las Vegas, New Mexico, Looking East from Myles Sweeney's 1960 Chevrolet Impala*, 1987

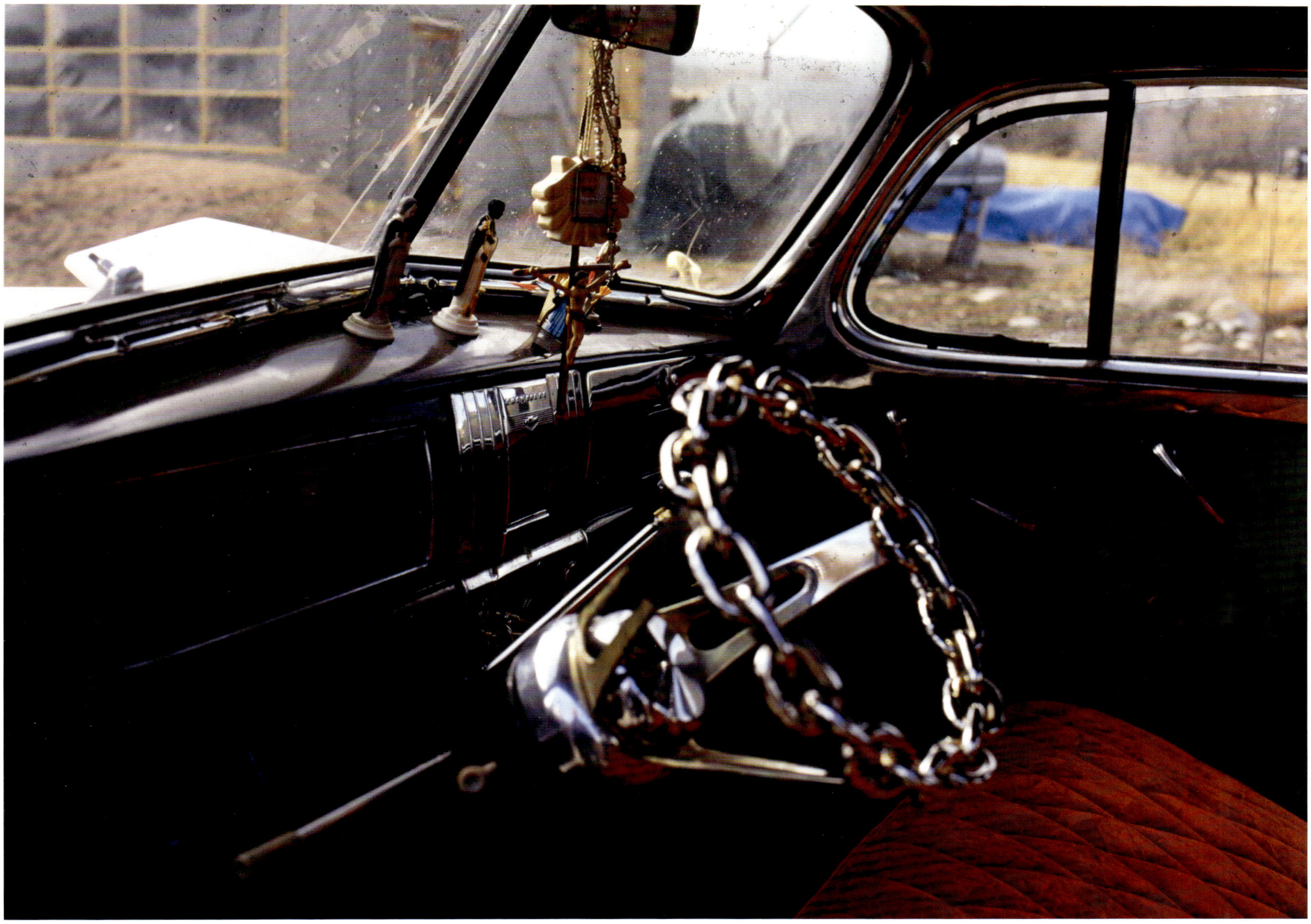

47. Siegfried Halus, *Lowrider Dashboard Shrine*, El Rito, New Mexico, 1998

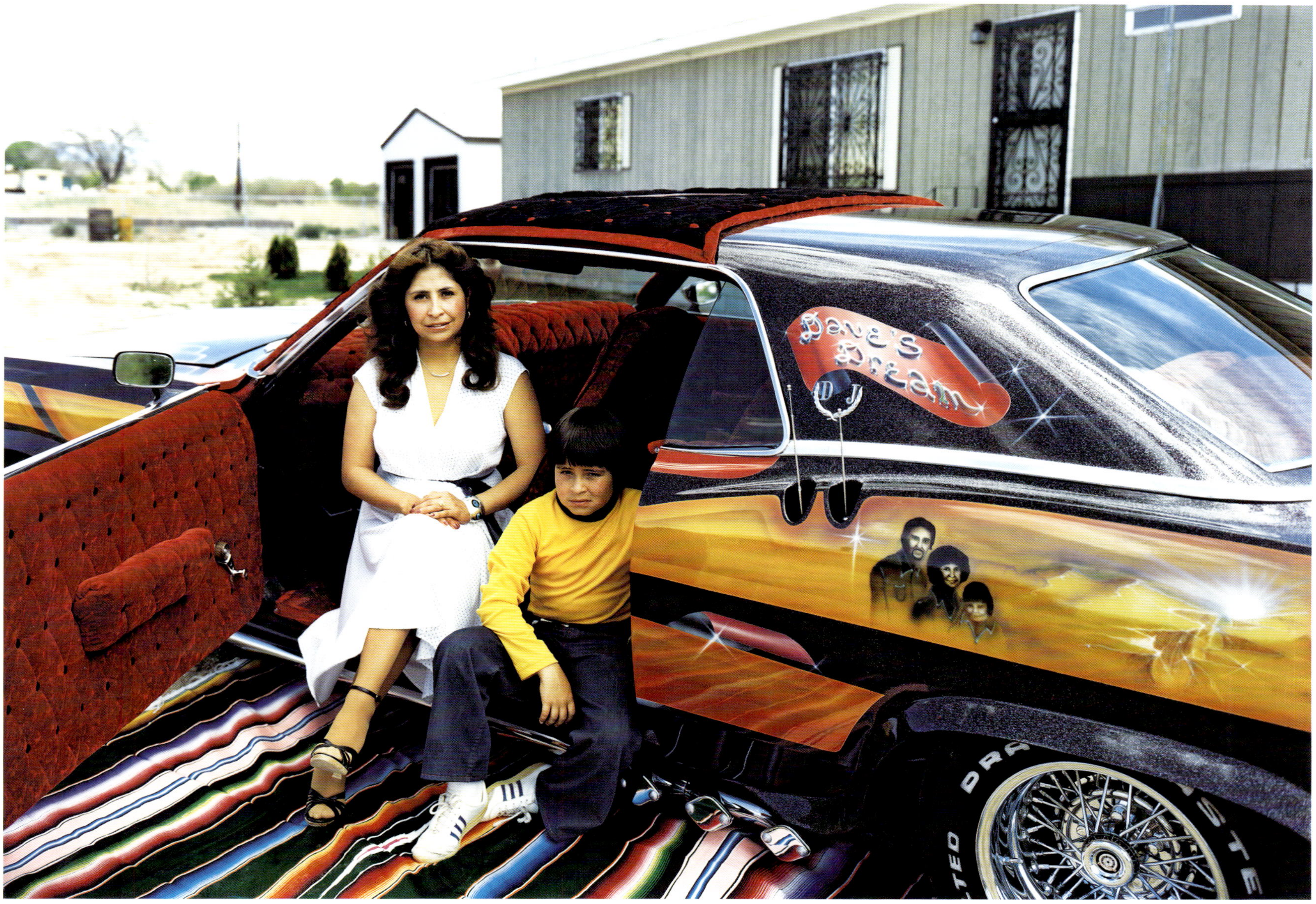

48. Meridel Rubenstein, *Irene Maria and Dave Jaramillo Jr. in "Dave's Dream" (1960 Ford LTD)*, San Juan, 1980

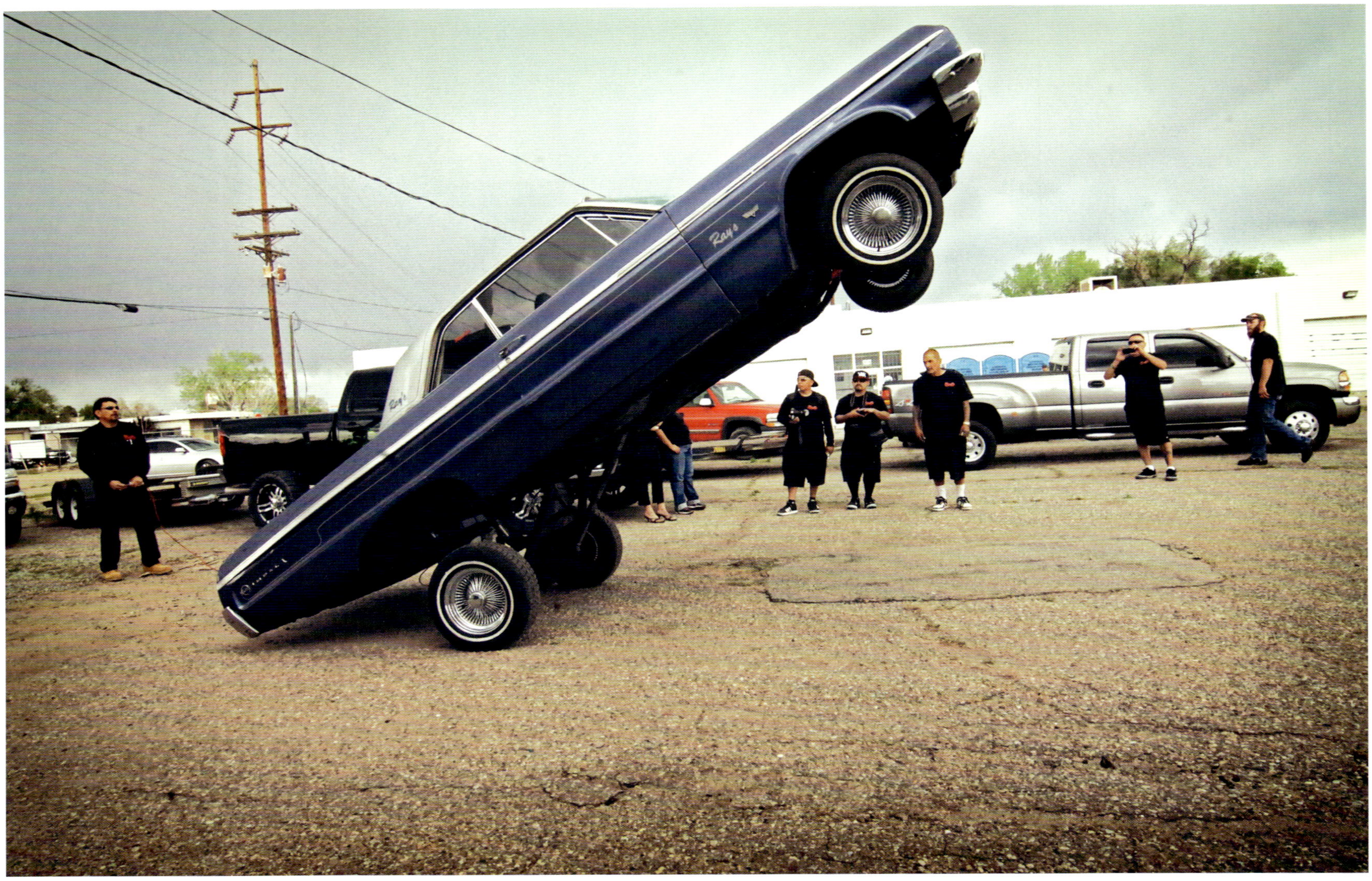

49. Bob Eckert, *Car Hopping*, Española, 2014

opposite
50. Travis Ruiz, *Houston We Have a Problem*, 2009

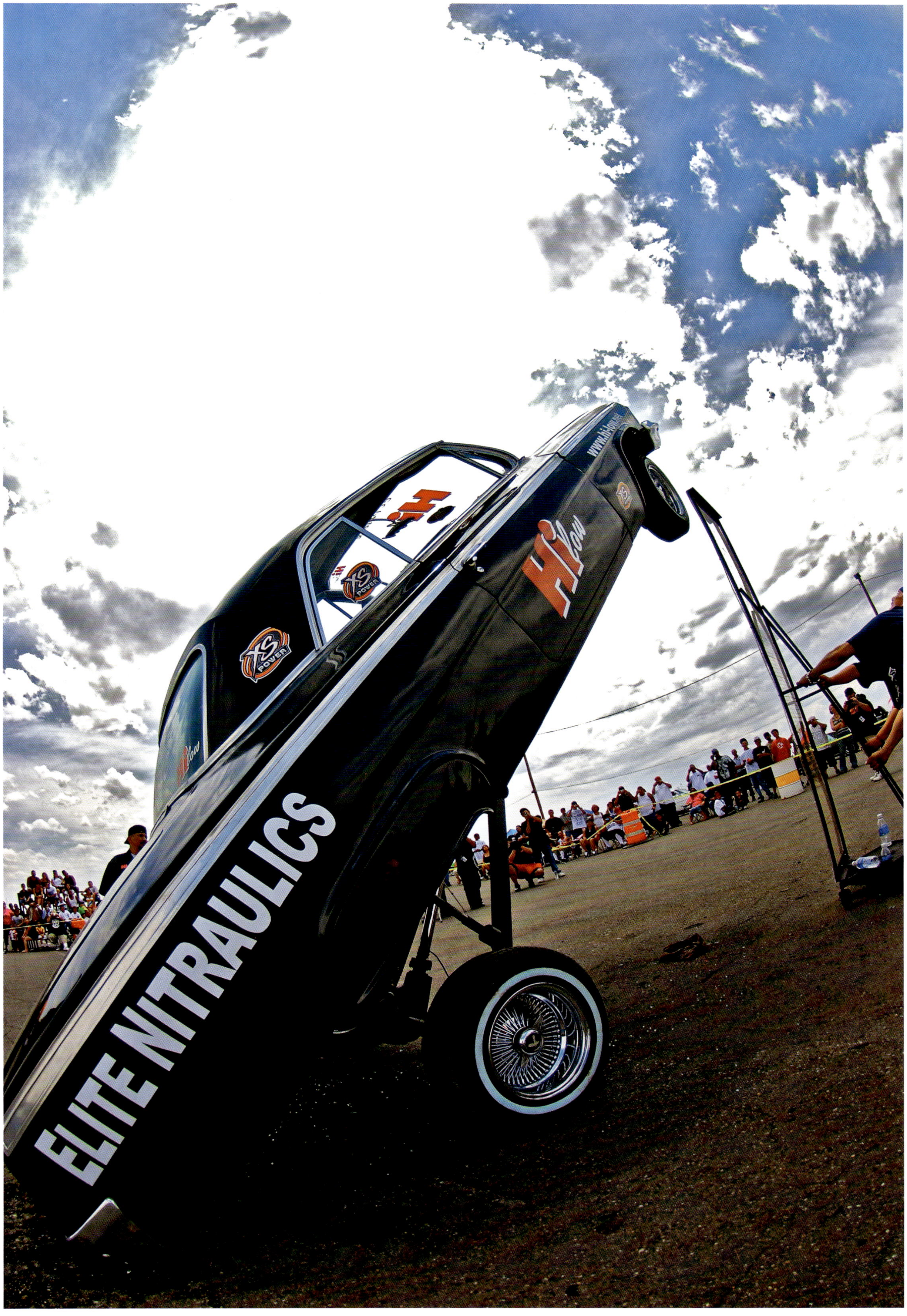
ELITE NITRAULICS

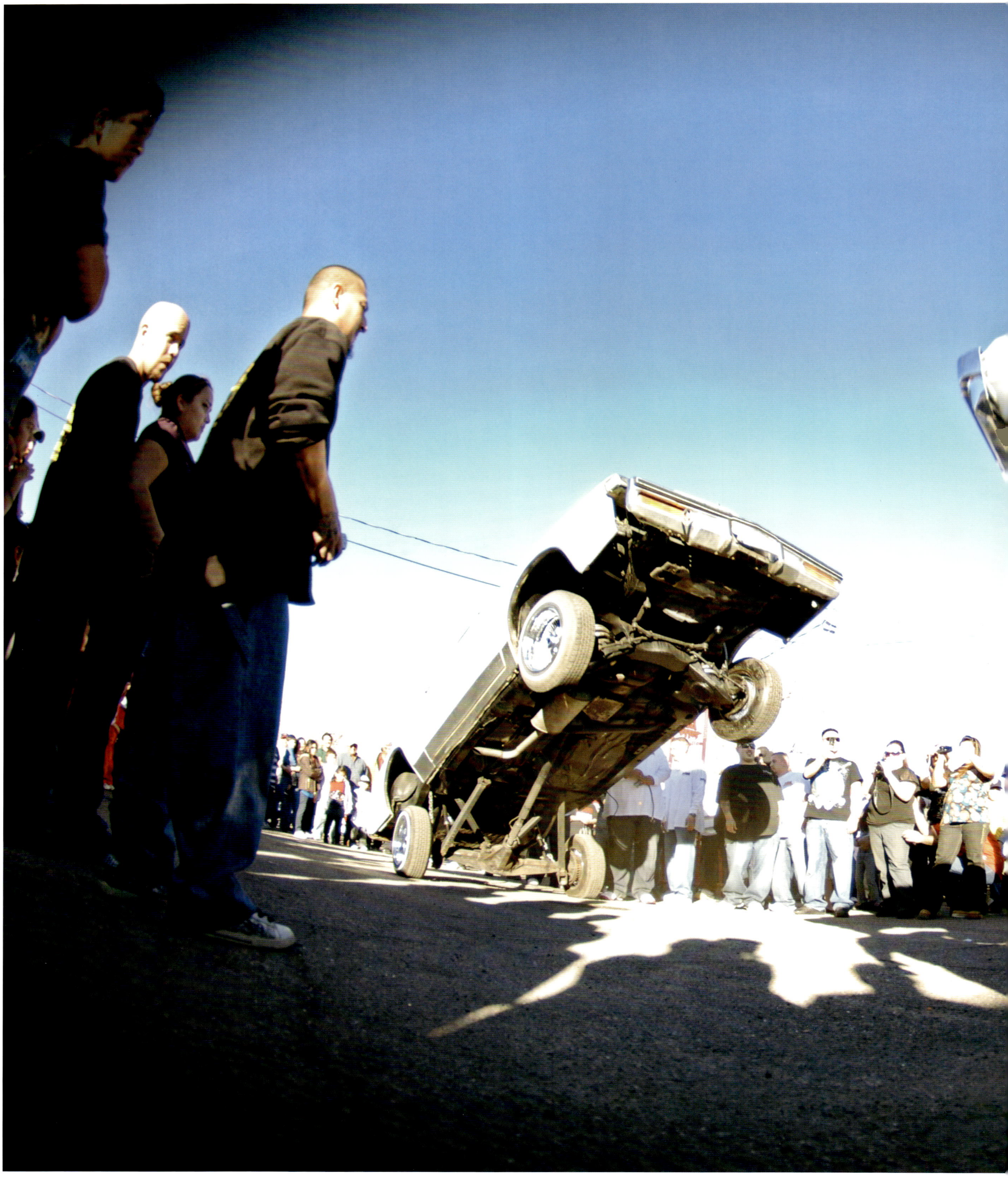

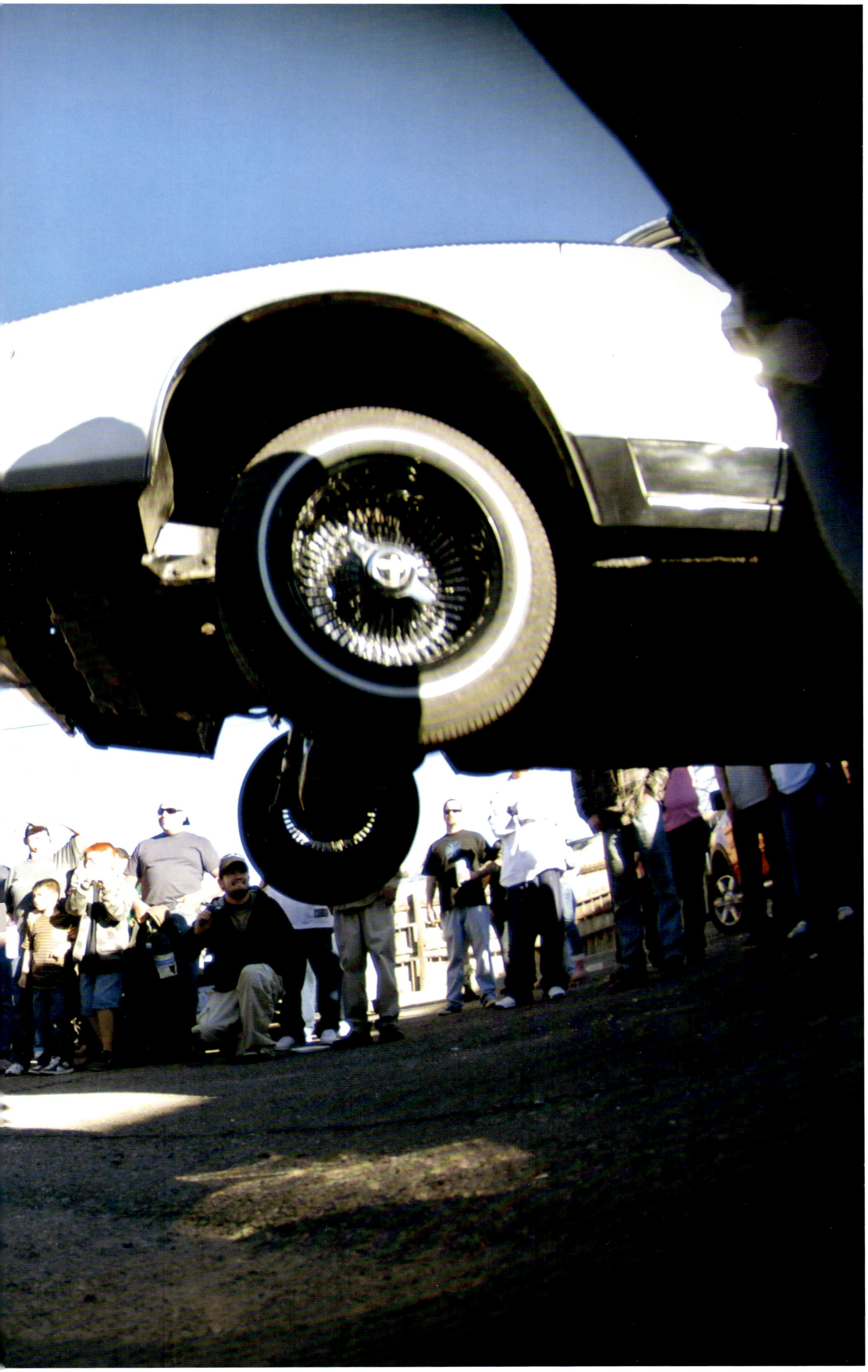

51. Travis Ruiz, *Nose'd Up*, 2009

52. Don J. Usner, *Randy Martínez Mural*, Española, 2012

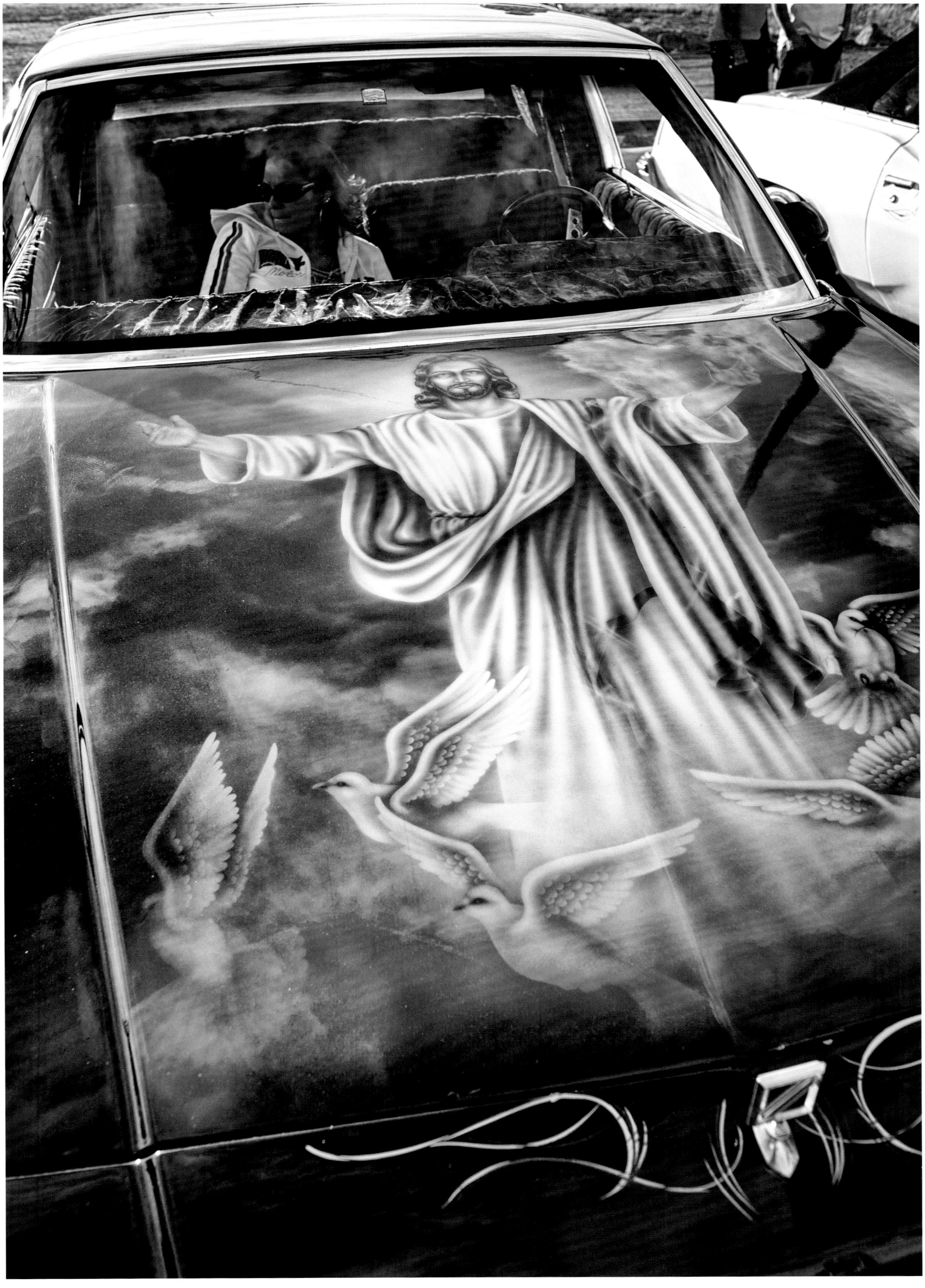

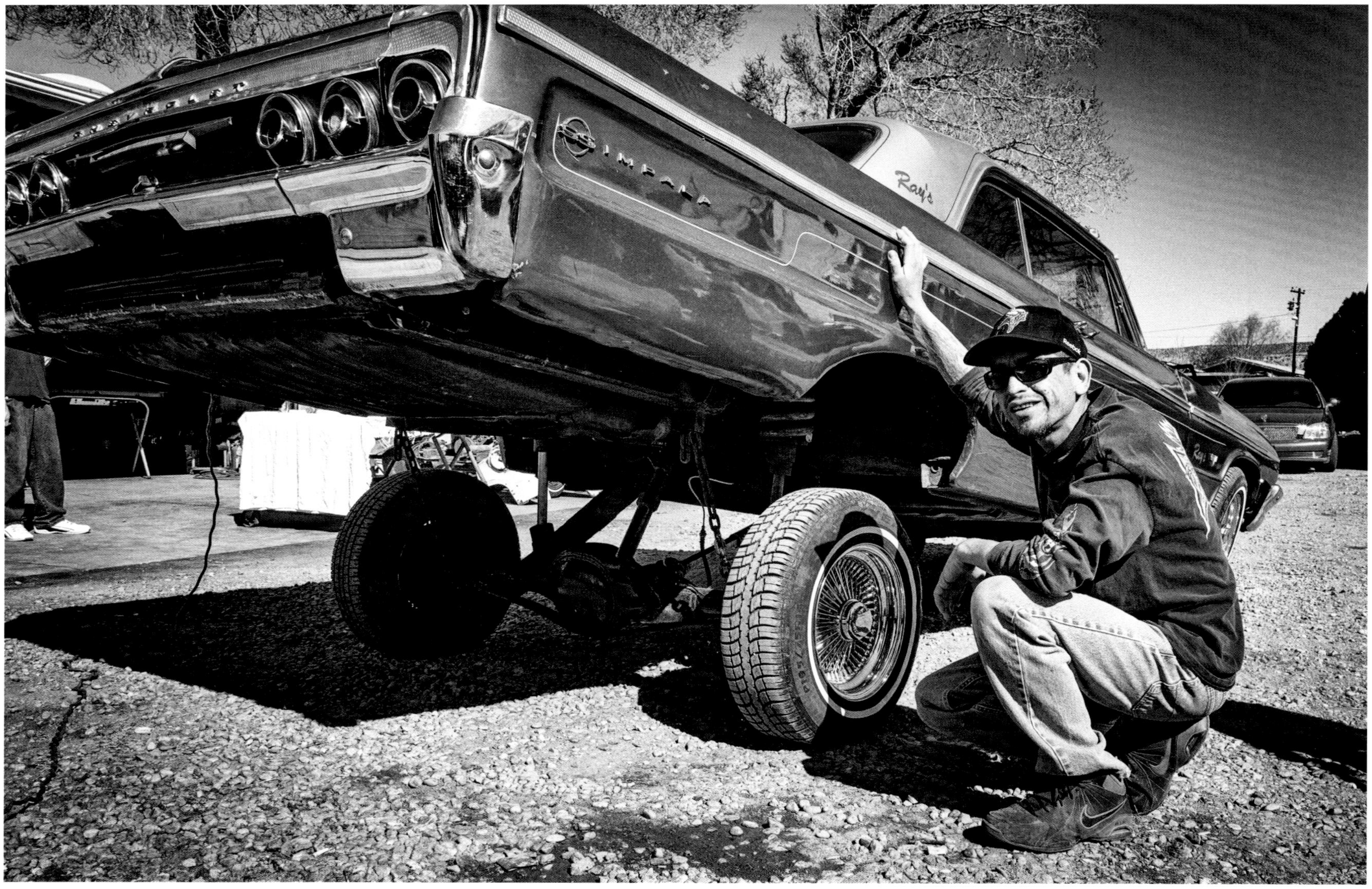

53. Don J. Usner, *Larry Martínez with Eppie's 1964 Impala, Ray's Garage,* Chimayó, 2012

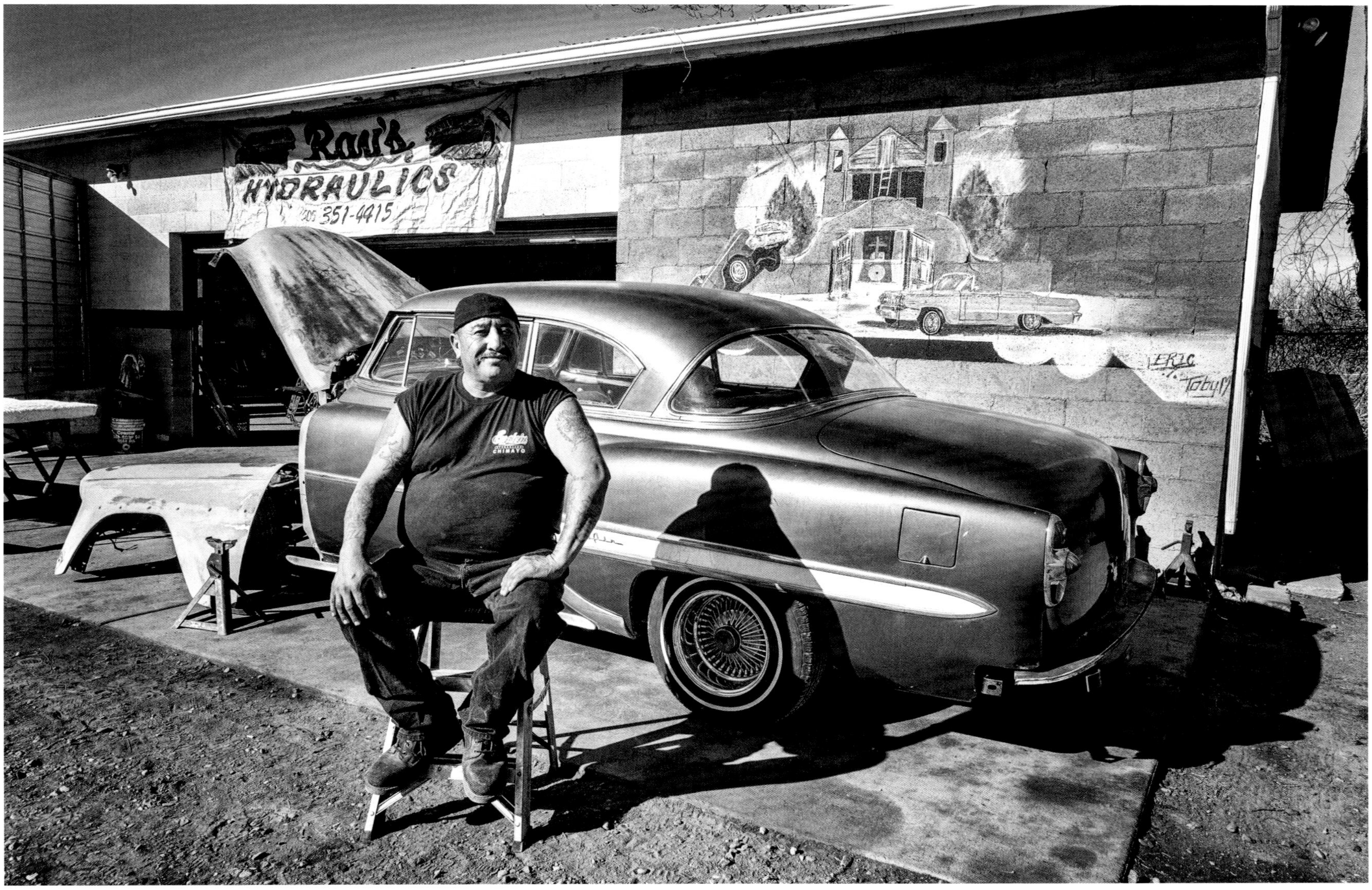

54. Don J. Usner, *Ernie López*, Chimayó, 2012

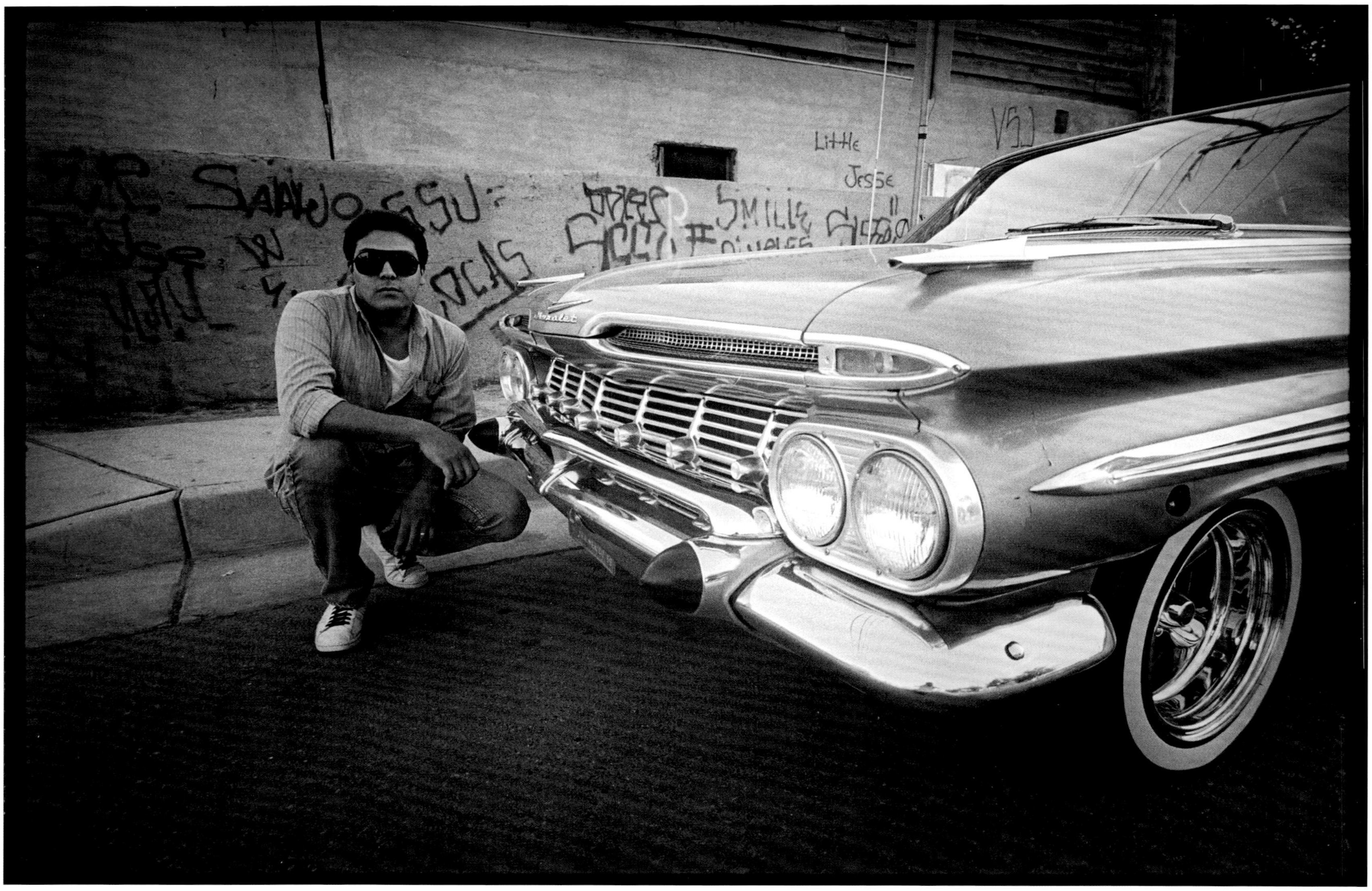

55. Miguel Gandert, *'59 Chevy*, Albuquerque, 1986

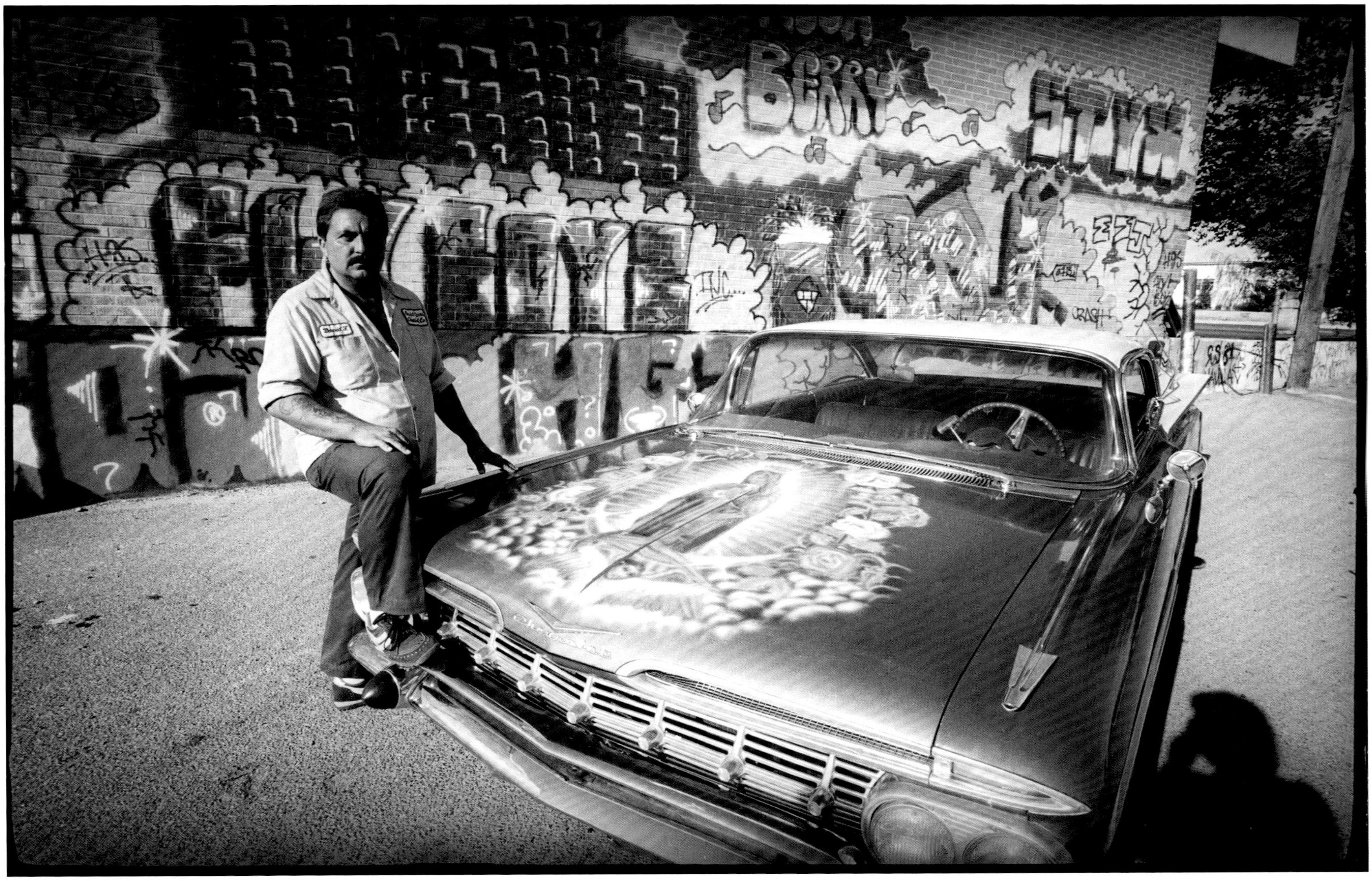

56. Miguel Gandert, *Frank Alderete,* Albuquerque, 1986

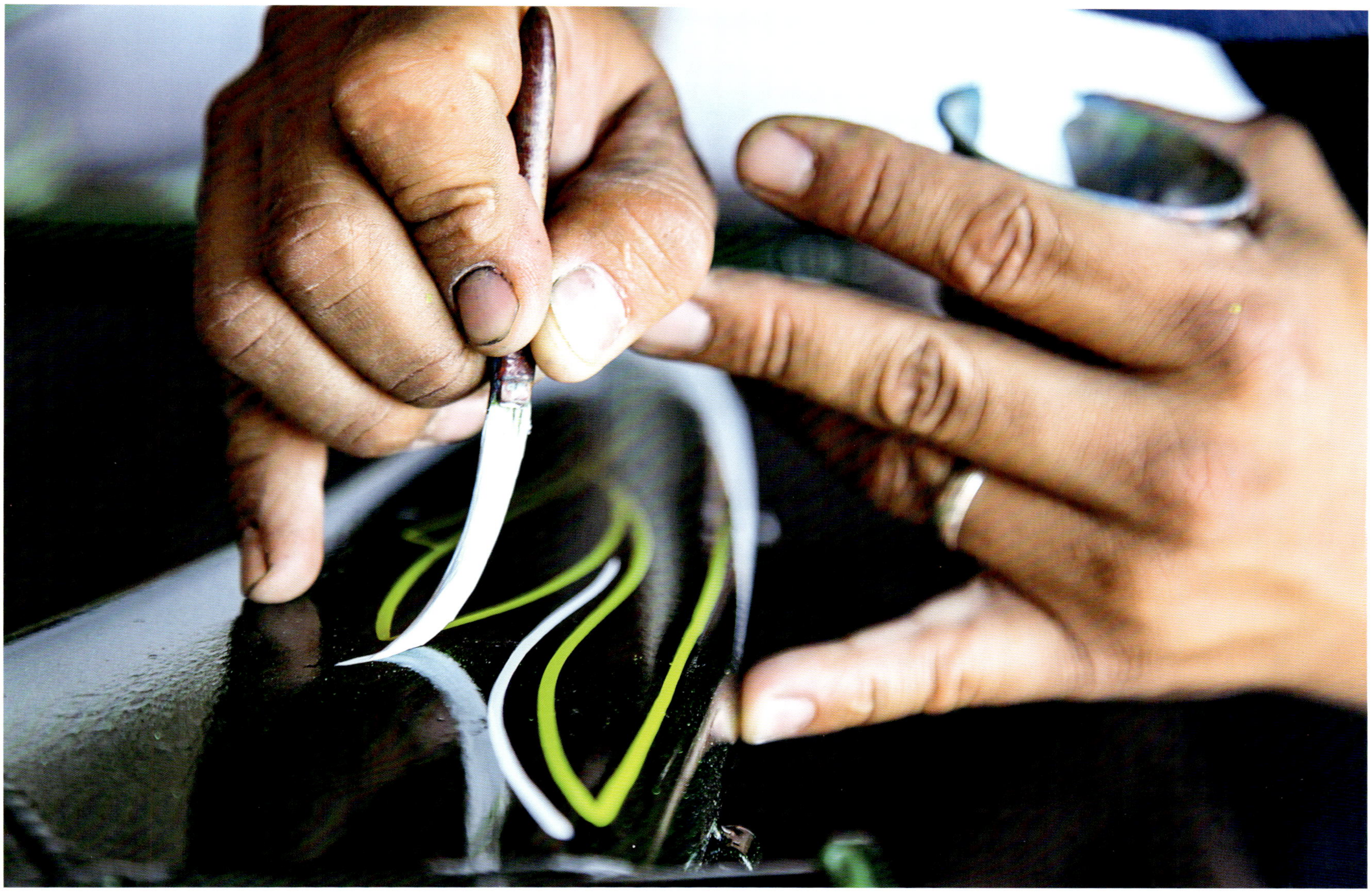

57. Gabriela E. Campos, *Pinstripe Precision*, 2014

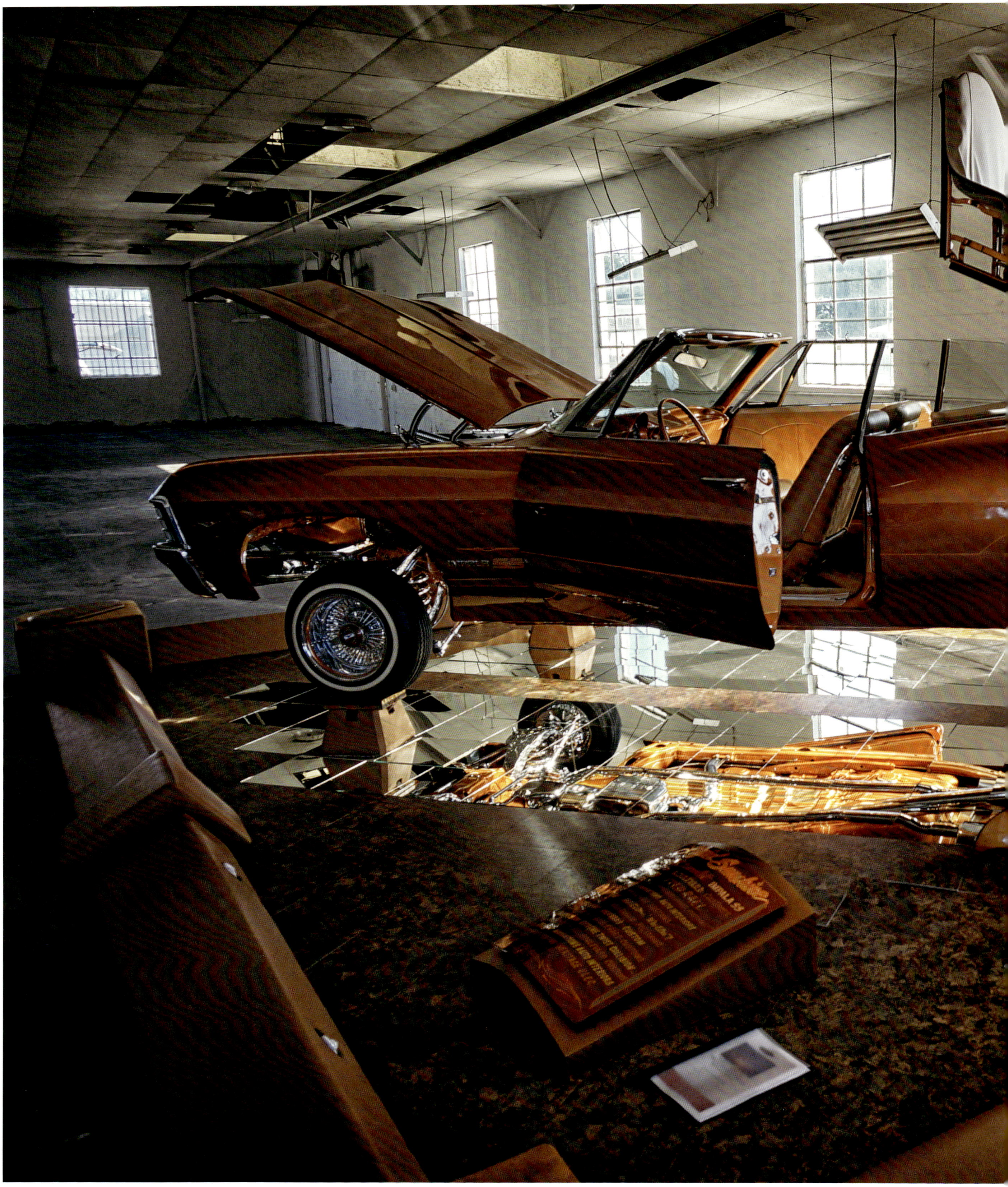

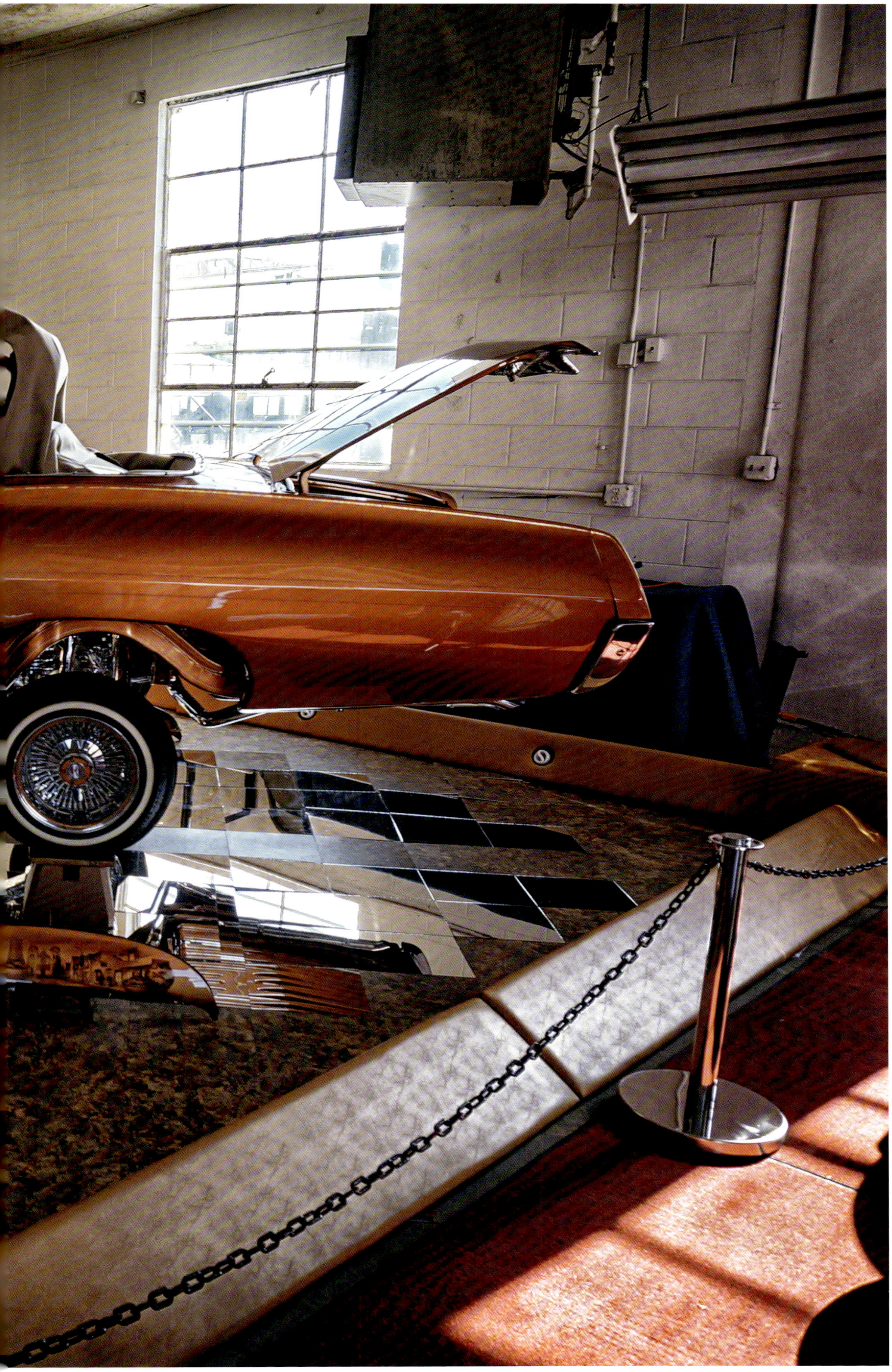

58. Bob Eckert, *Fred Rael's "Liquid Sunshine" 1967 Impala inside the Old Hunter Ford Building*, Española, 2014

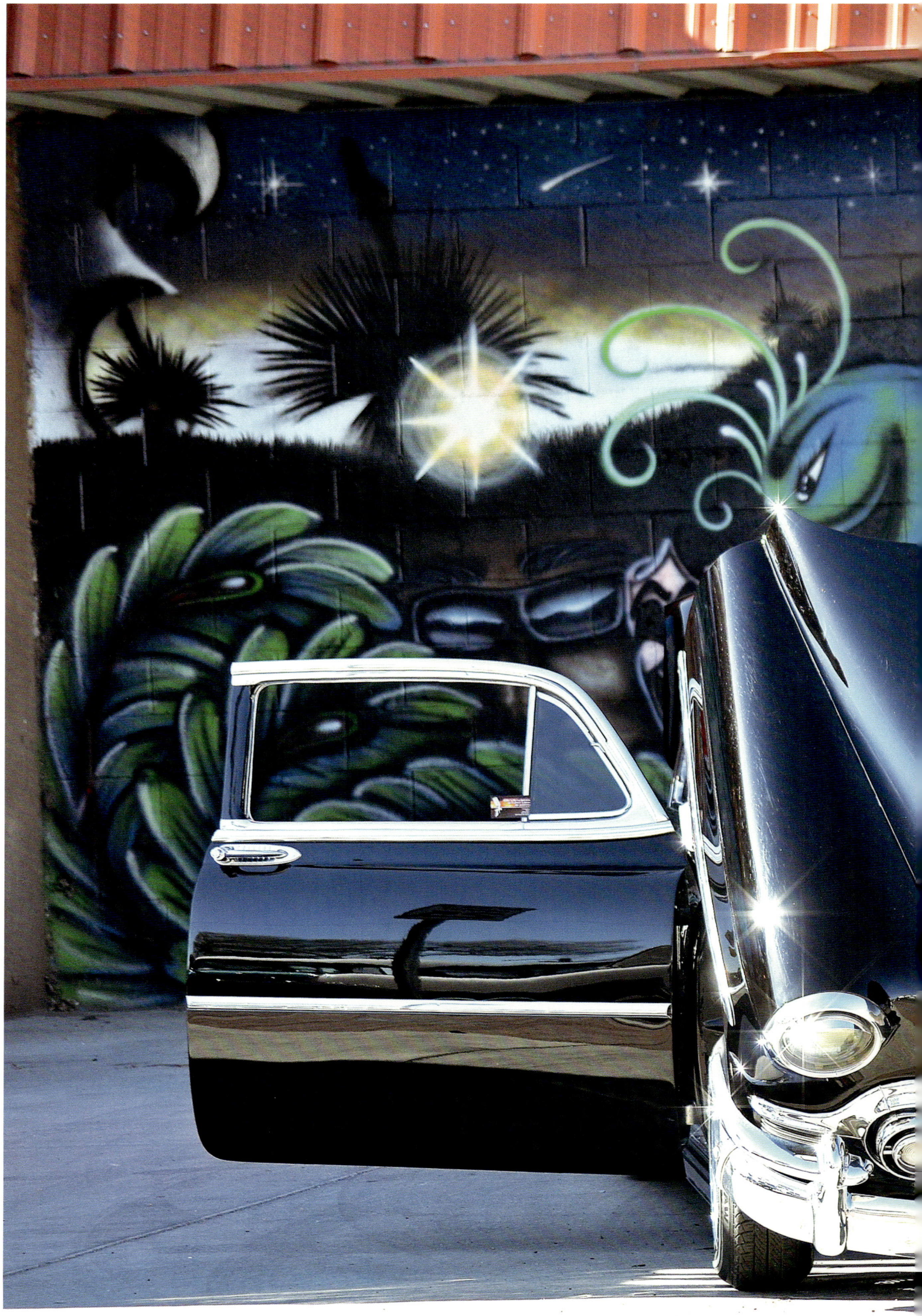

59. Bob Eckert, *Carmelito Martínez's 1953 Bel Air in front of Mural on Paseo de Oñate during Cinco de Mayo Car Show*, Española, 2014

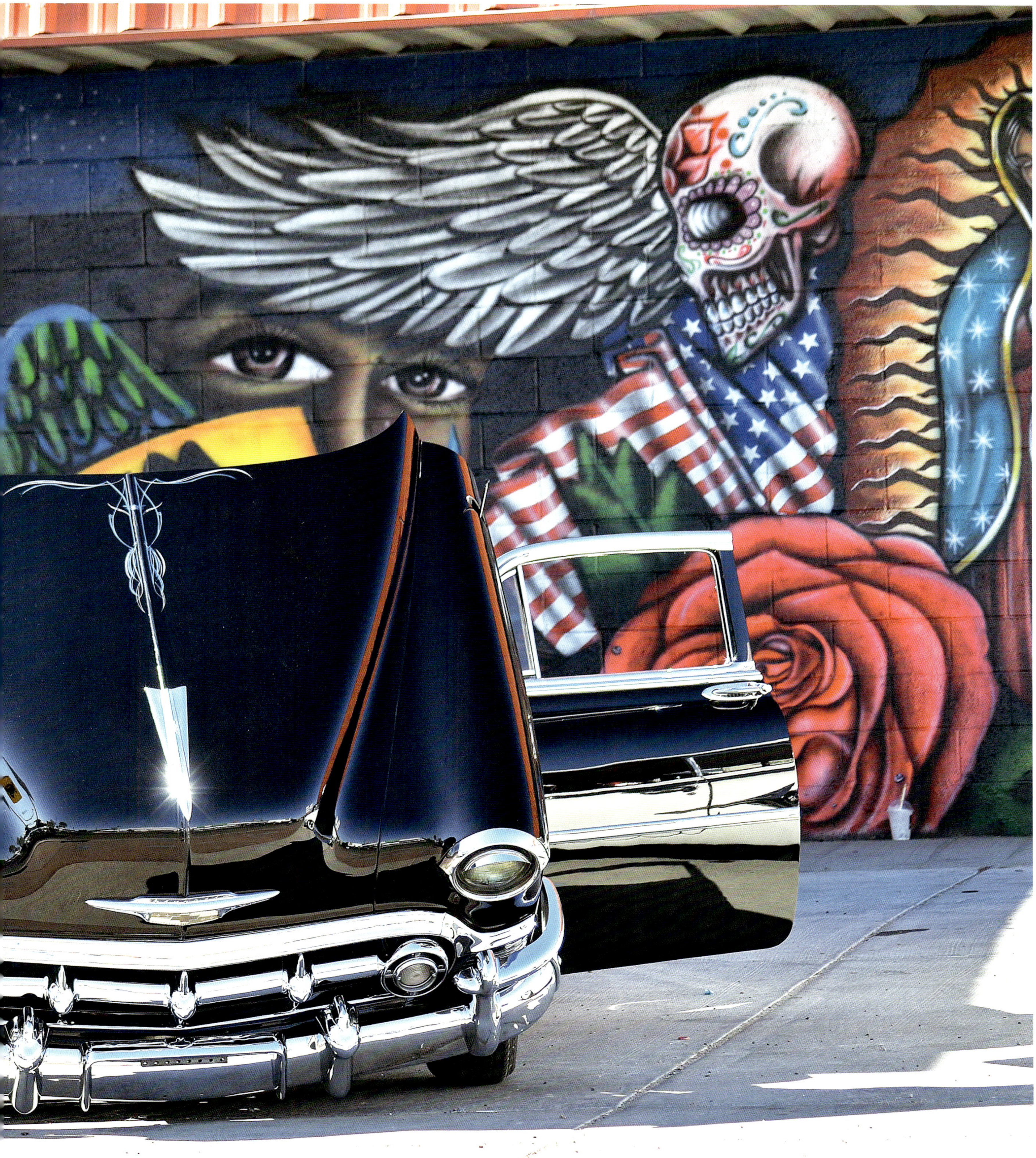

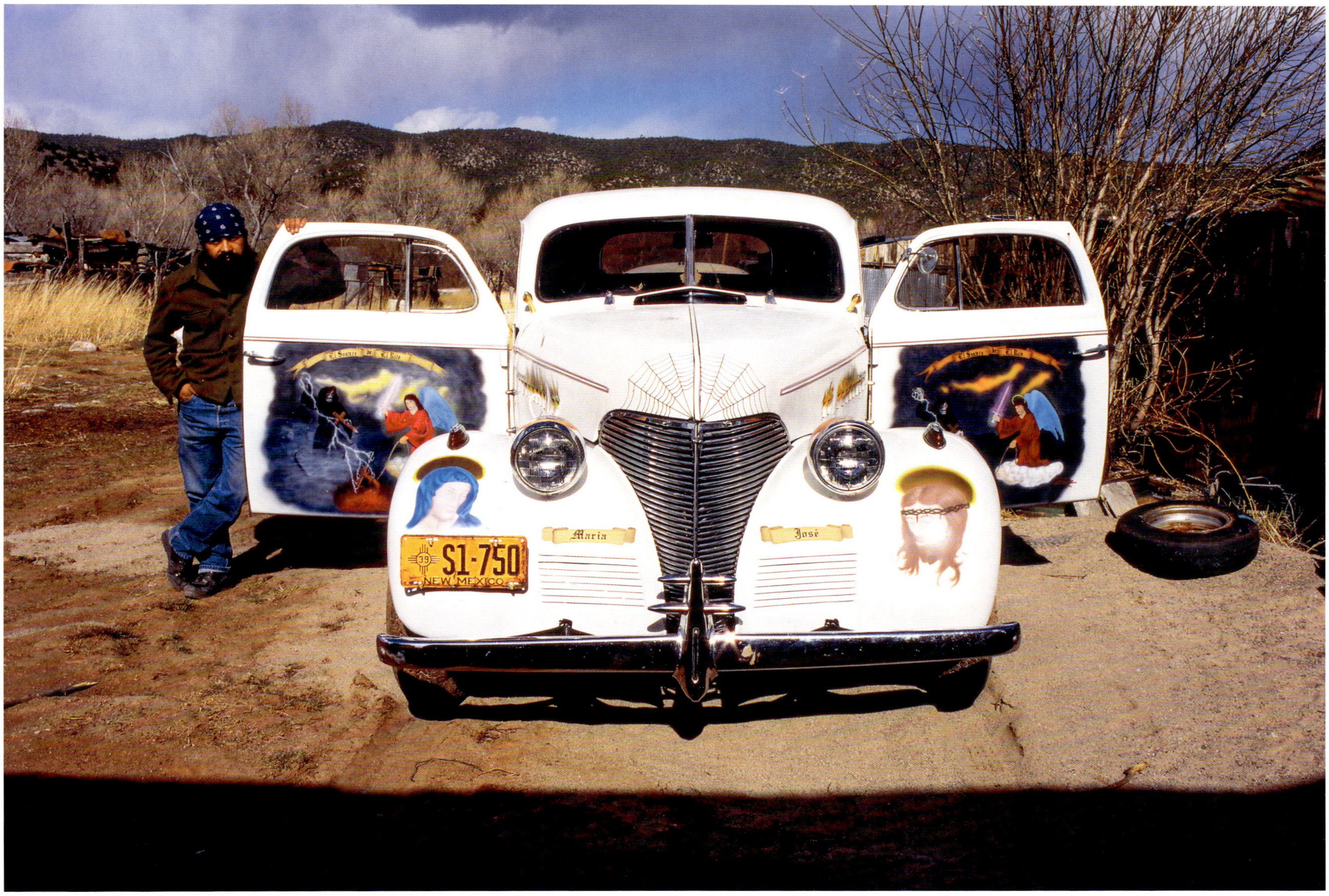

60. Siegfried Halus, *Nicolas Herrera, Lowrider Shrine*, El Rito, 1997

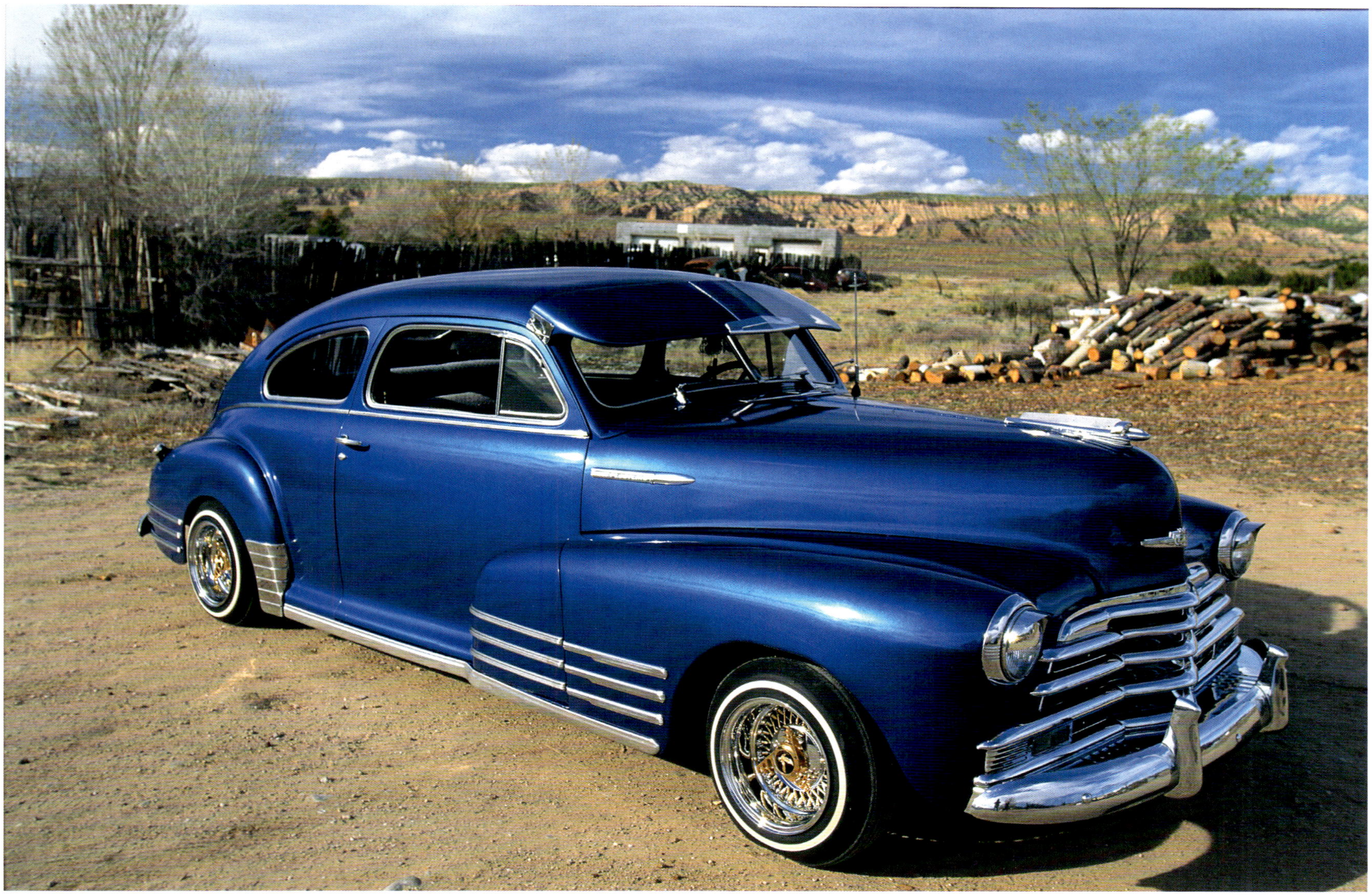

61. Jack Parsons, *'47 Chevrolet Fleetline, Owner Joseph Romero of Chimayó*, 1998

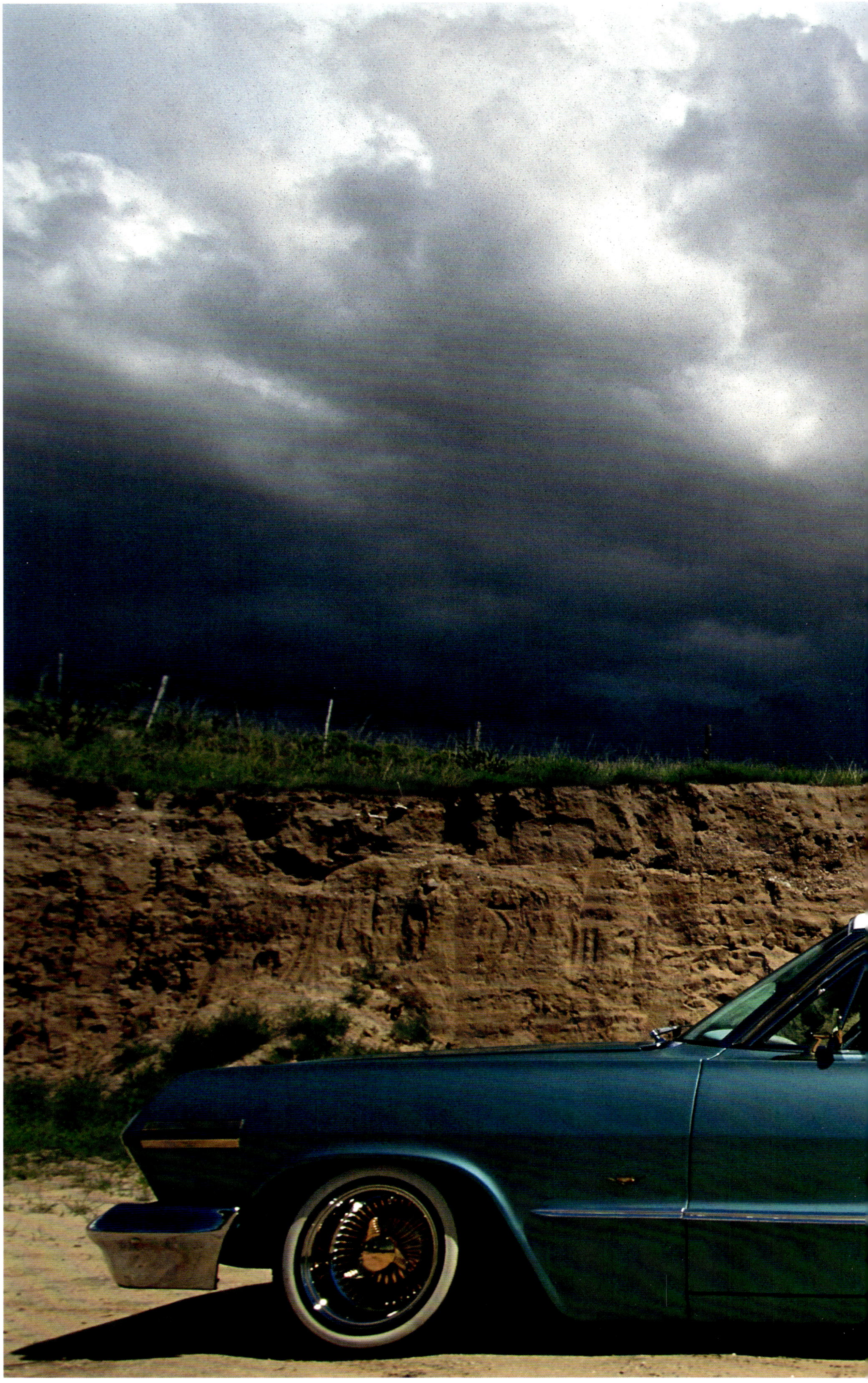

62. Jack Parsons, *'63 Chevrolet Impala, owner Lee Córdova of Alcalde*, 1998

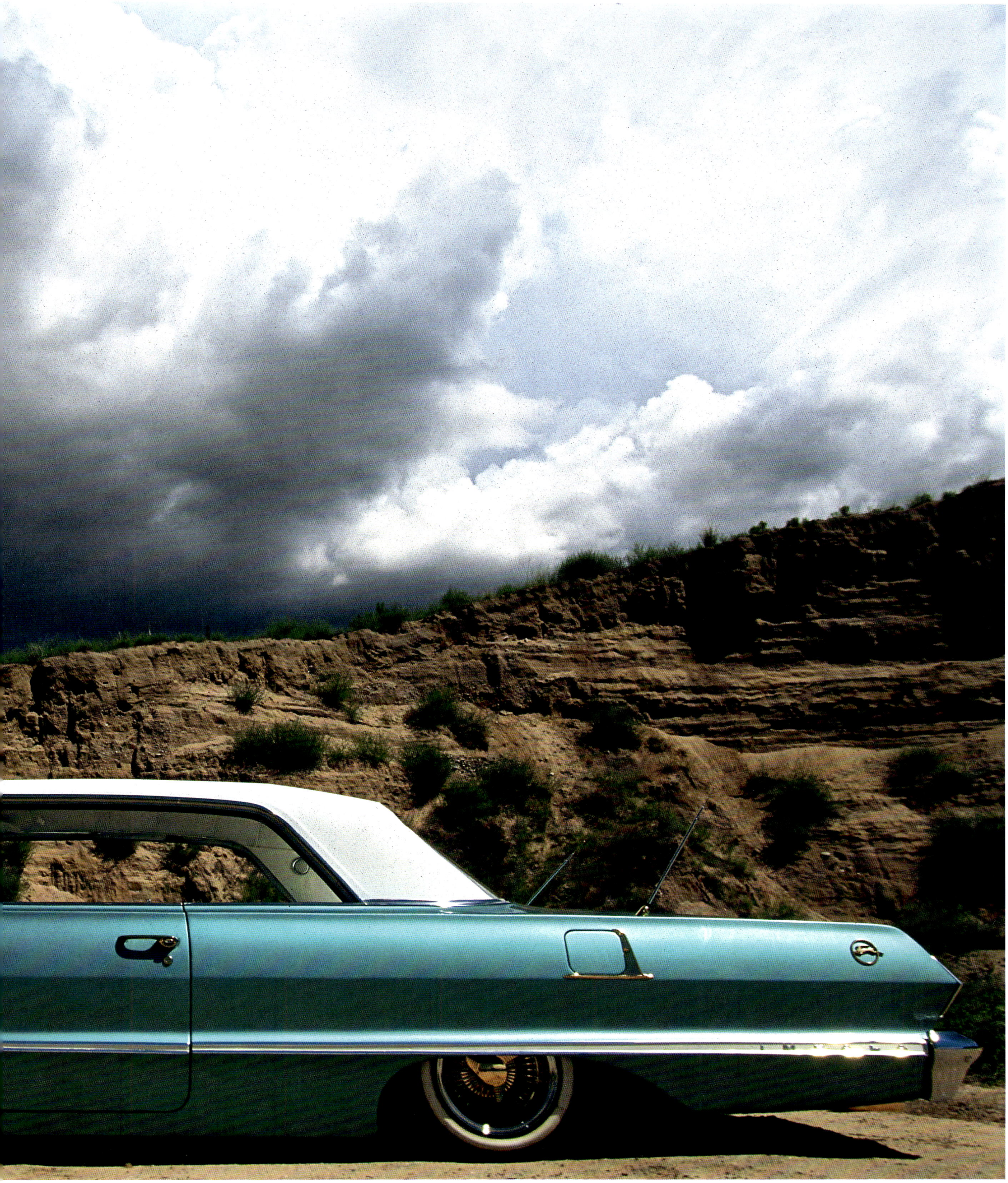

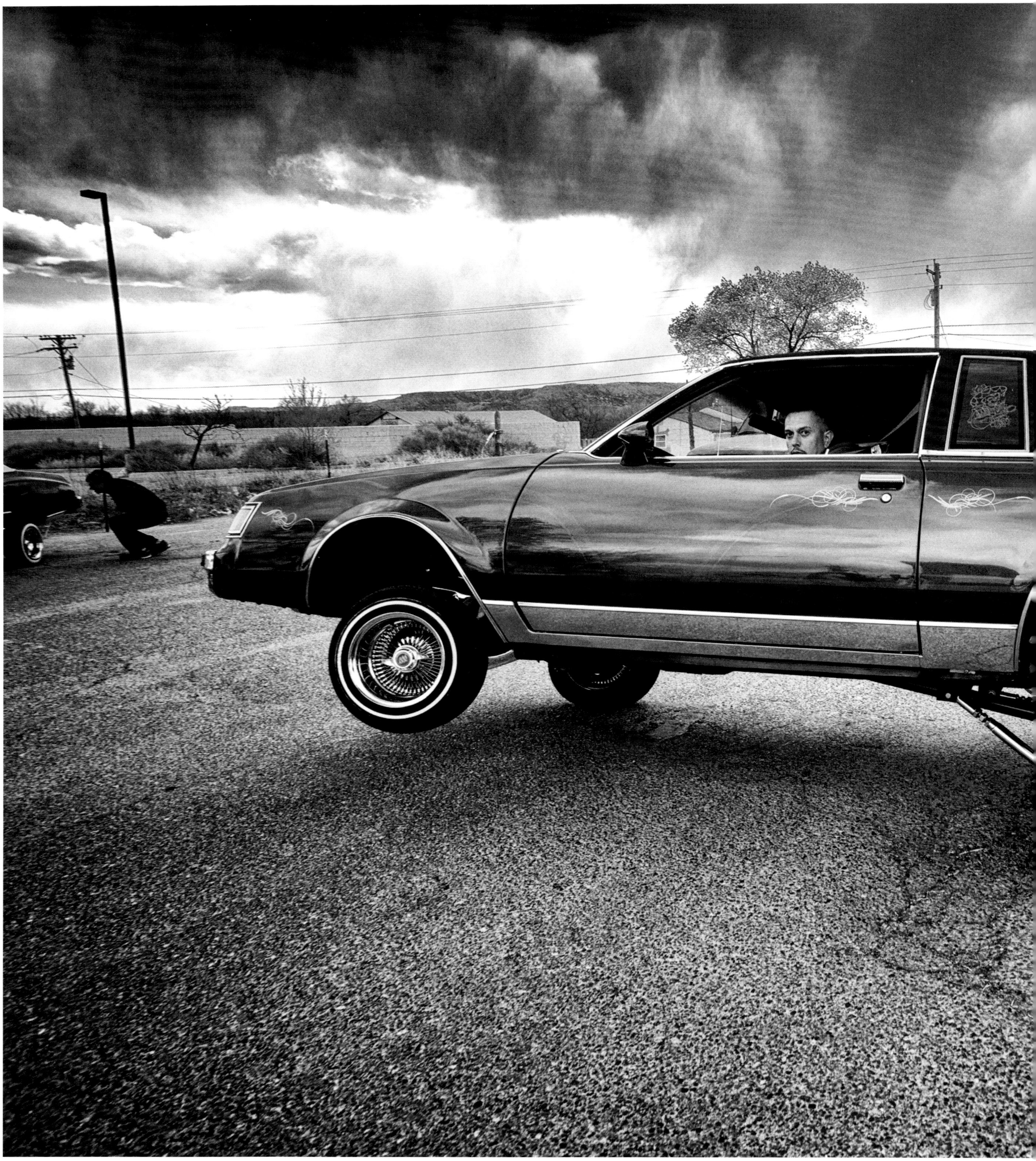

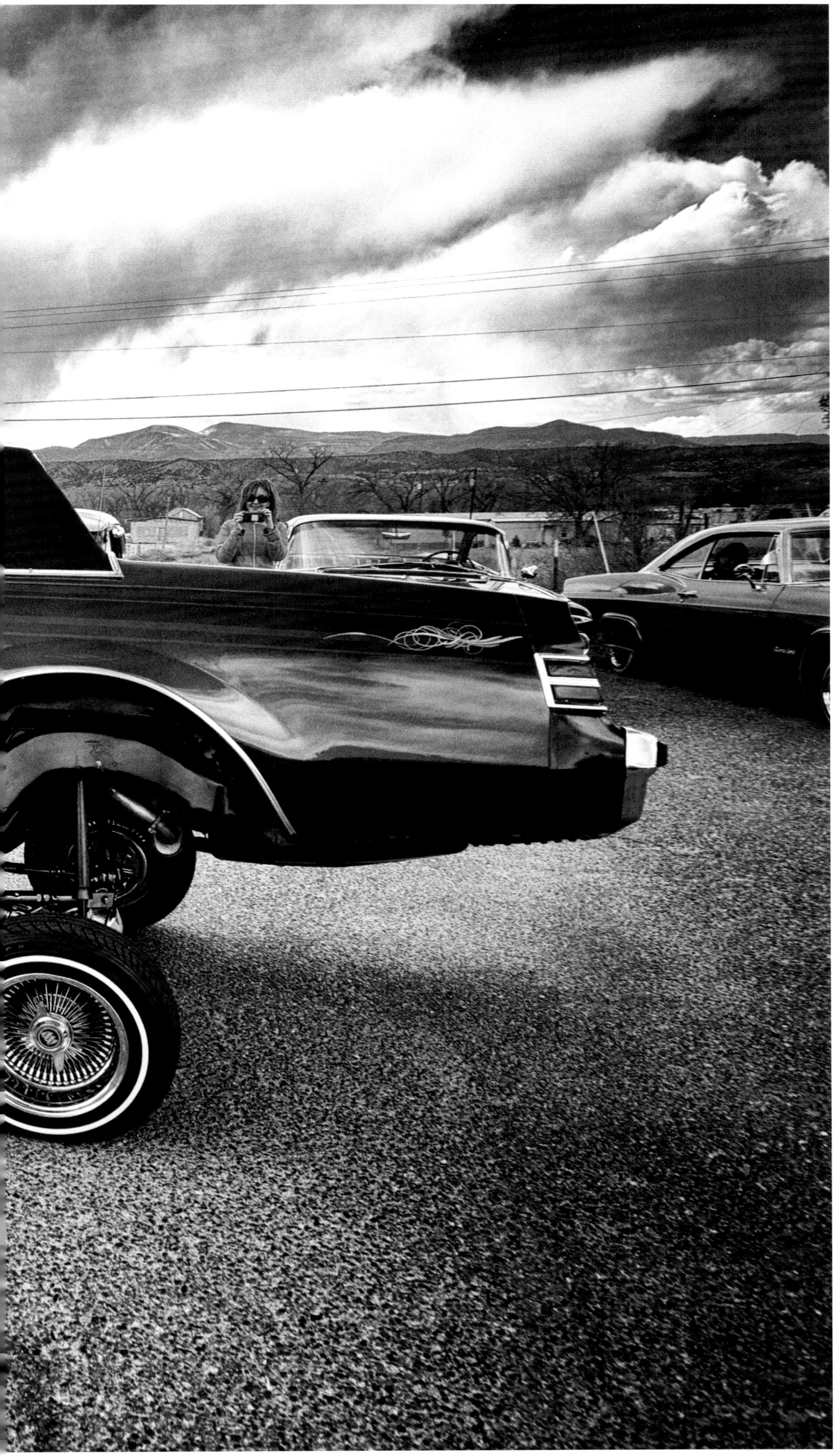

63. Don J. Usner, *Donald Manzanares Three-wheeling in His '85 Buick Regal*, Española, 2016

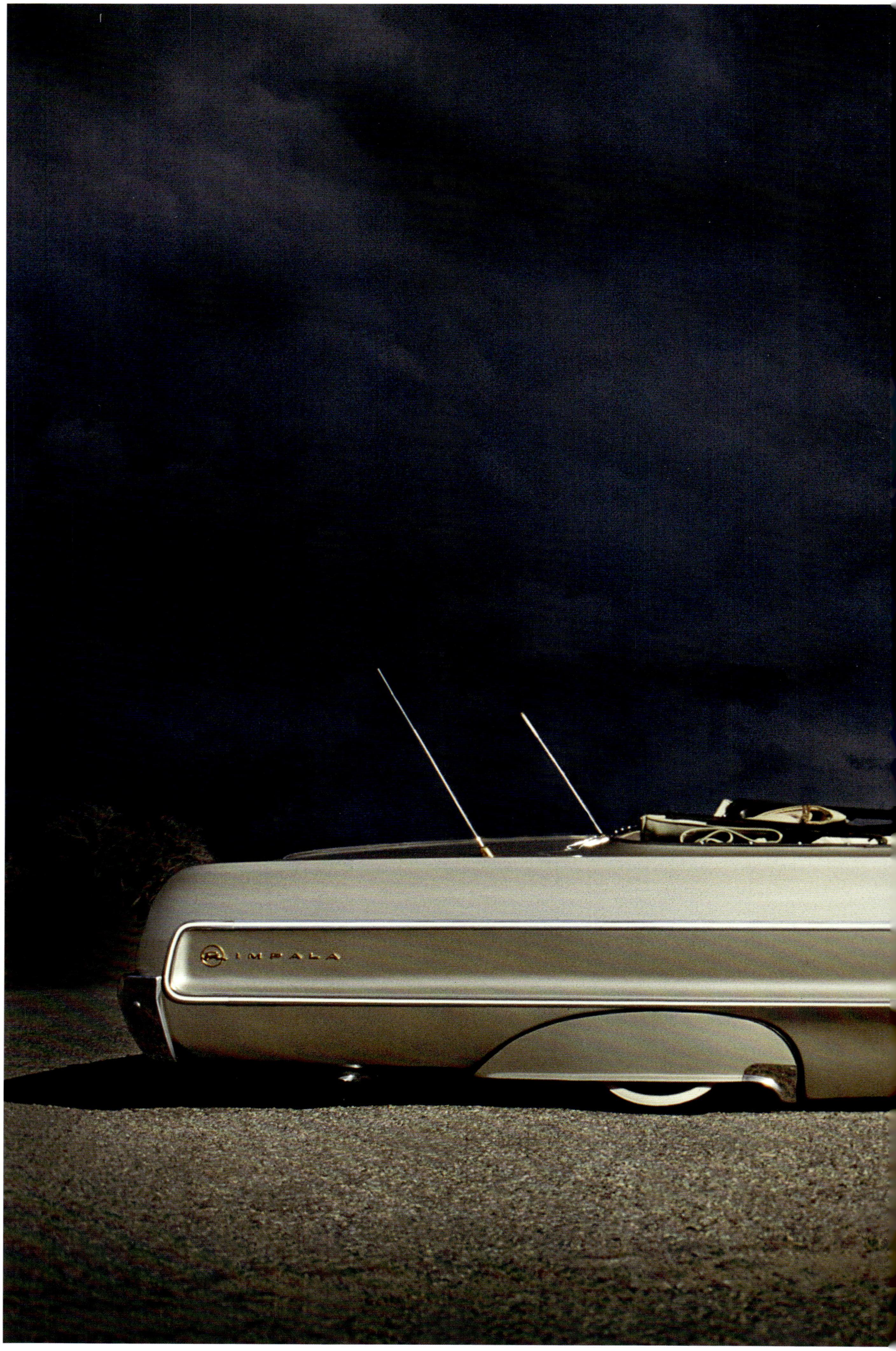

64. Jim Arndt, *Fred Rael in "Boulevard Legend," 1964 Chevrolet*, Española, 2003

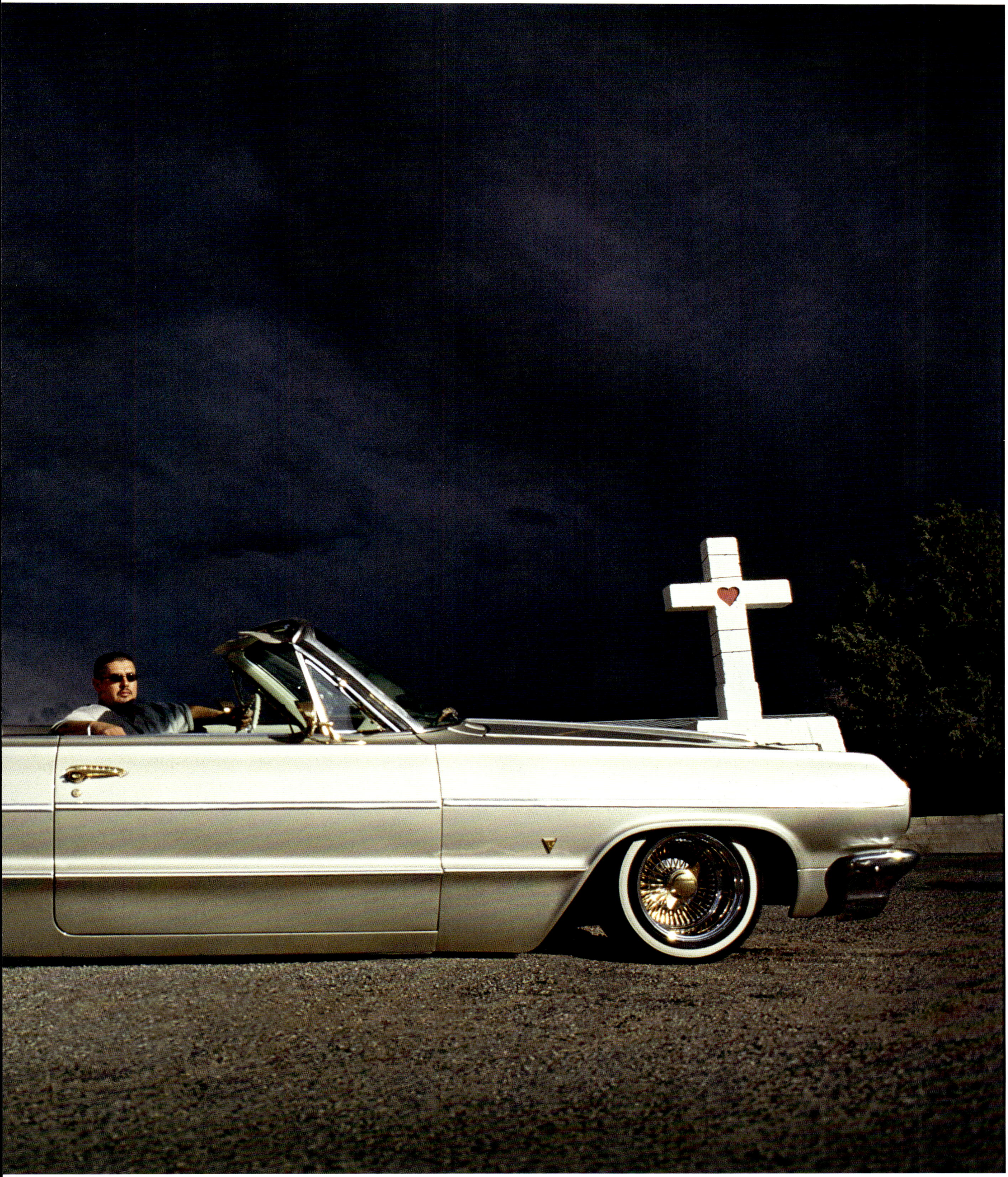

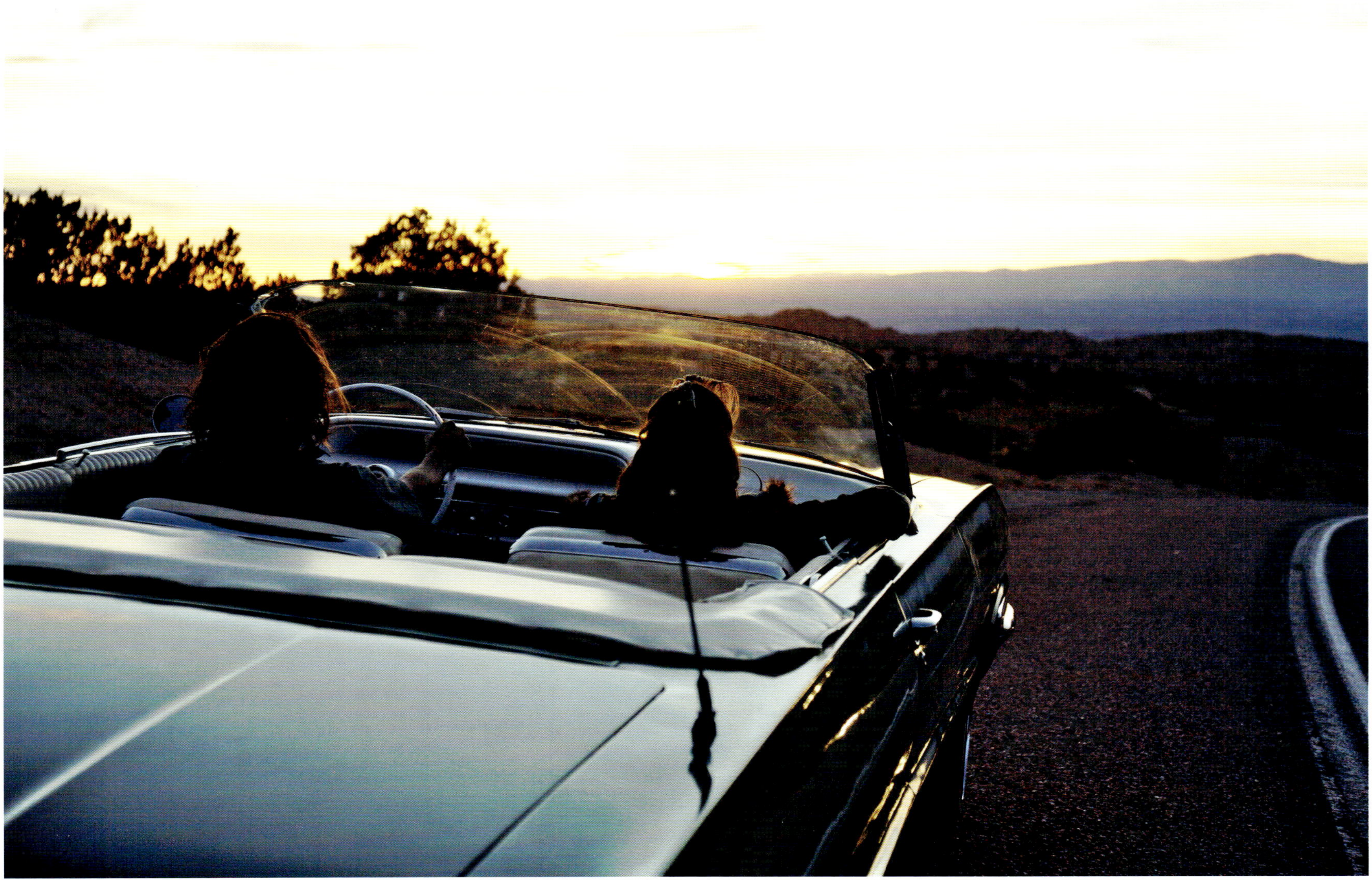

65. Gabriella Marks, *Low Riders in Chimayó*, 2010

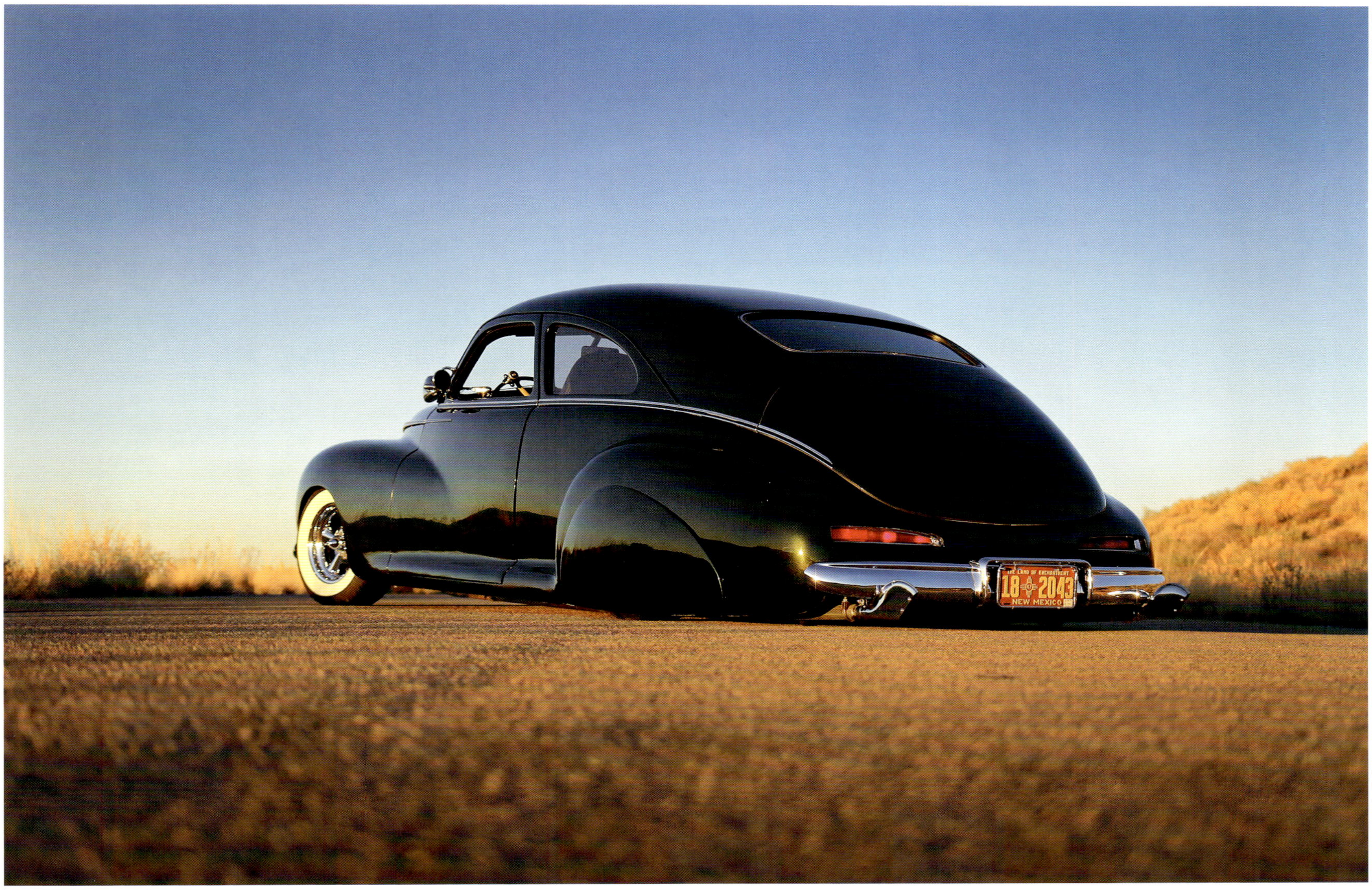

66. Corey Ringo, *Baby Got Back*, 2014

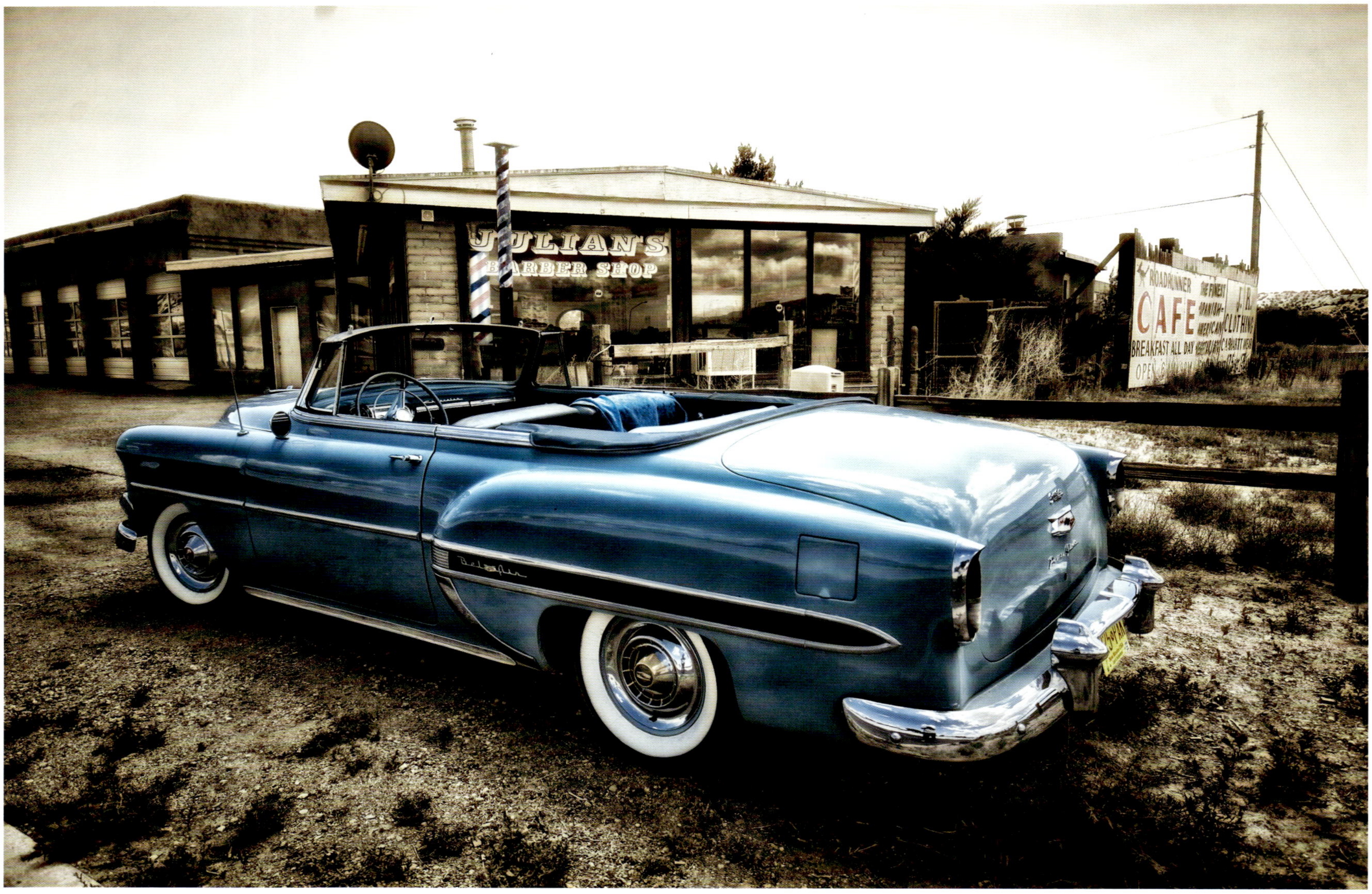

67. Bob Eckert, *Blue Bel Air at Julian's Barbers Shop*, Pojoaque, 2012

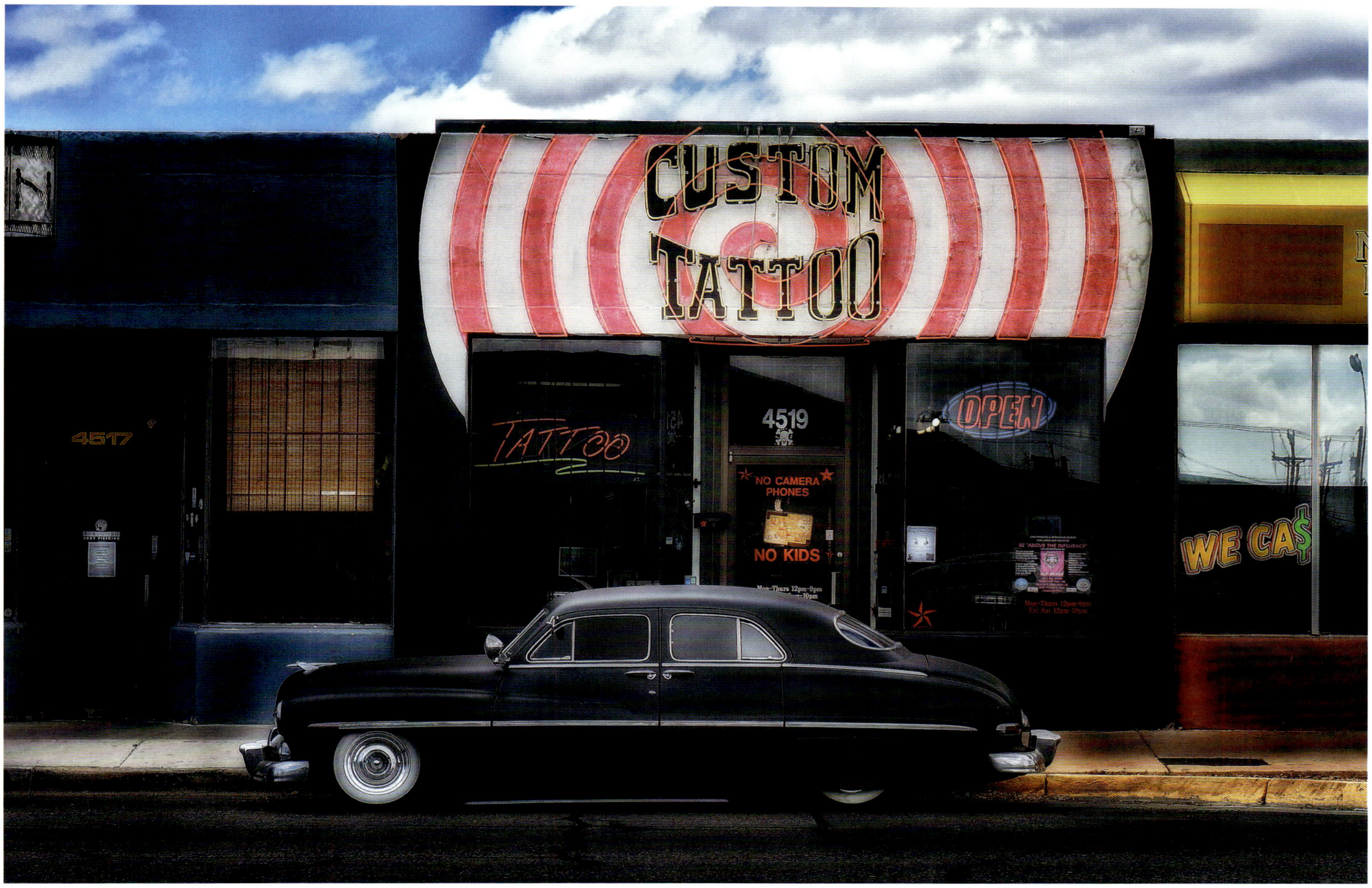

68. Bob Eckert, *Manuel Vega's 1950 Mercury outside Custom Tattoo on Central Avenue*, Albuquerque, 2014

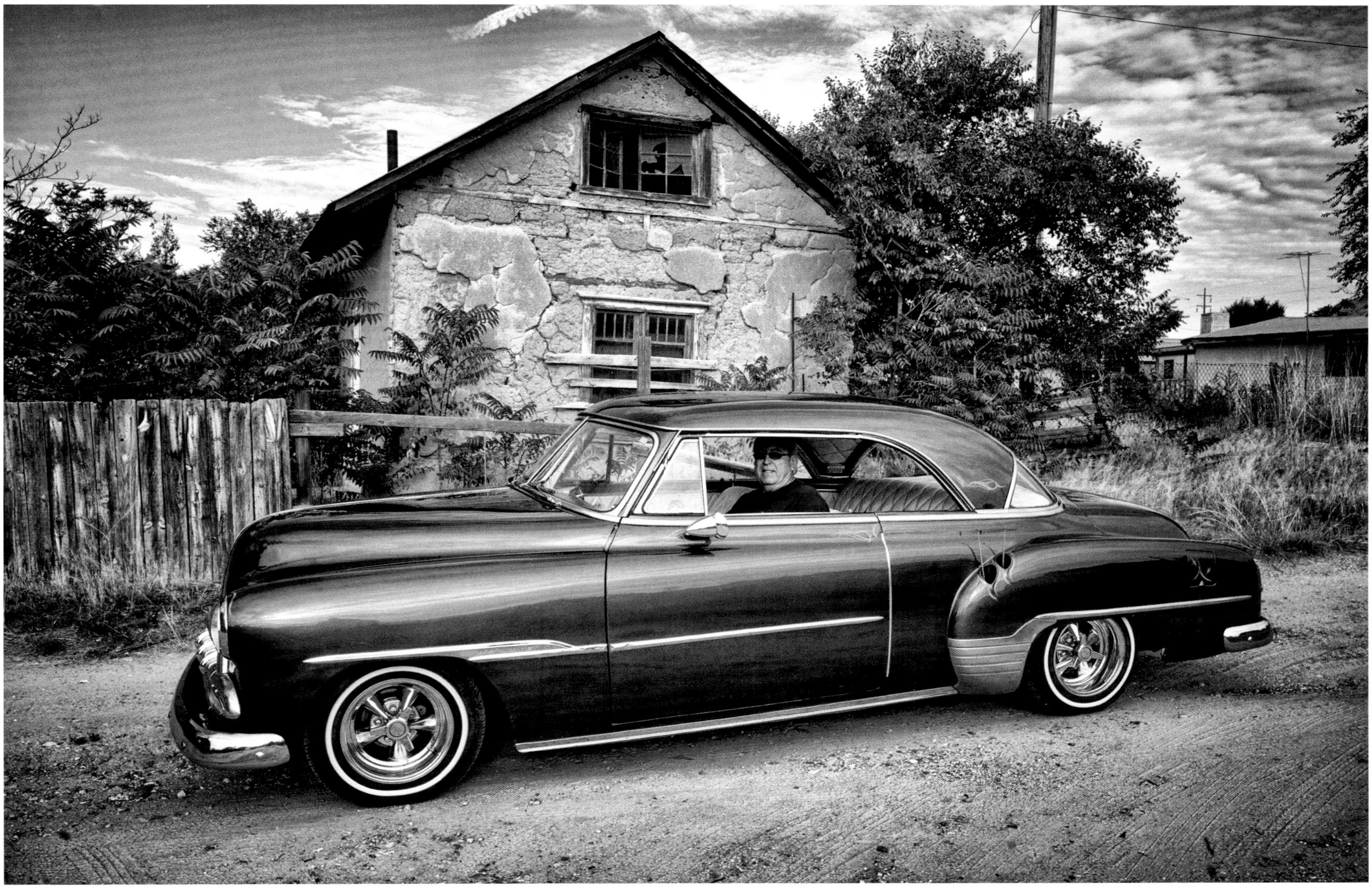

69. Don J. Usner, *Vince Trujillo*, Chimayó, 2015

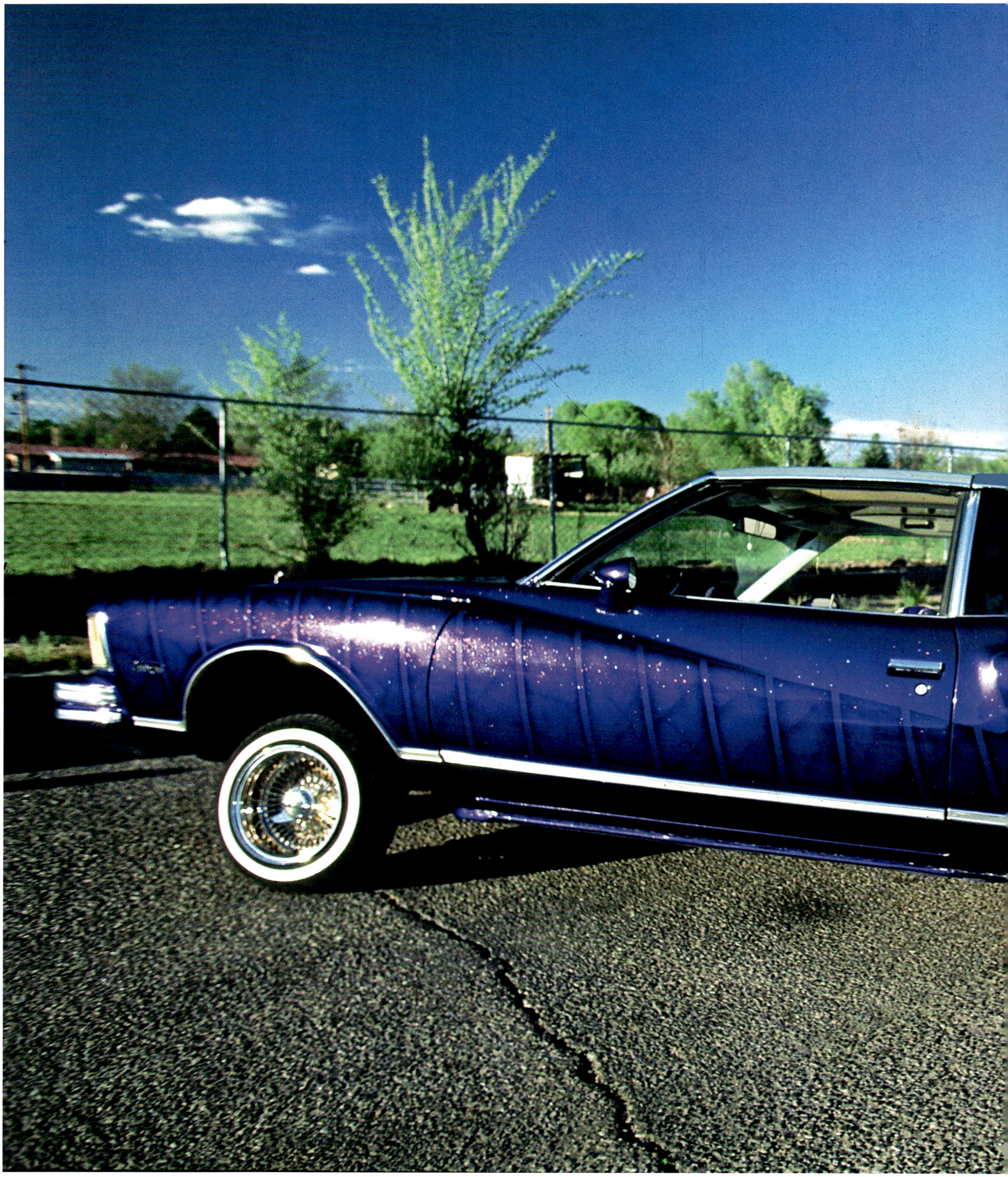

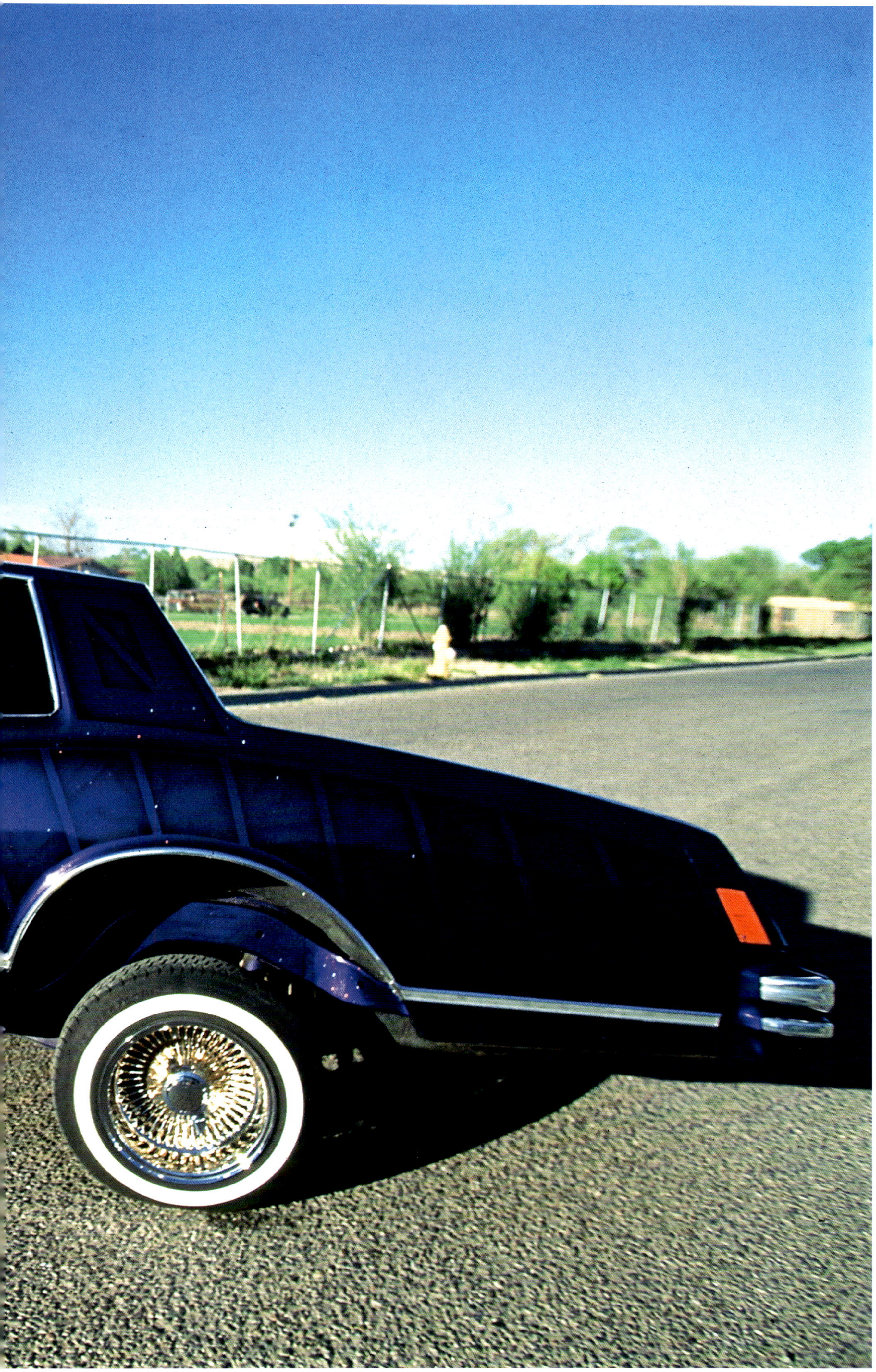

70. Jack Parsons, *'81 Chevrolet Monte Carlo, Owner Rhiannon Montoya of Española*, 1998

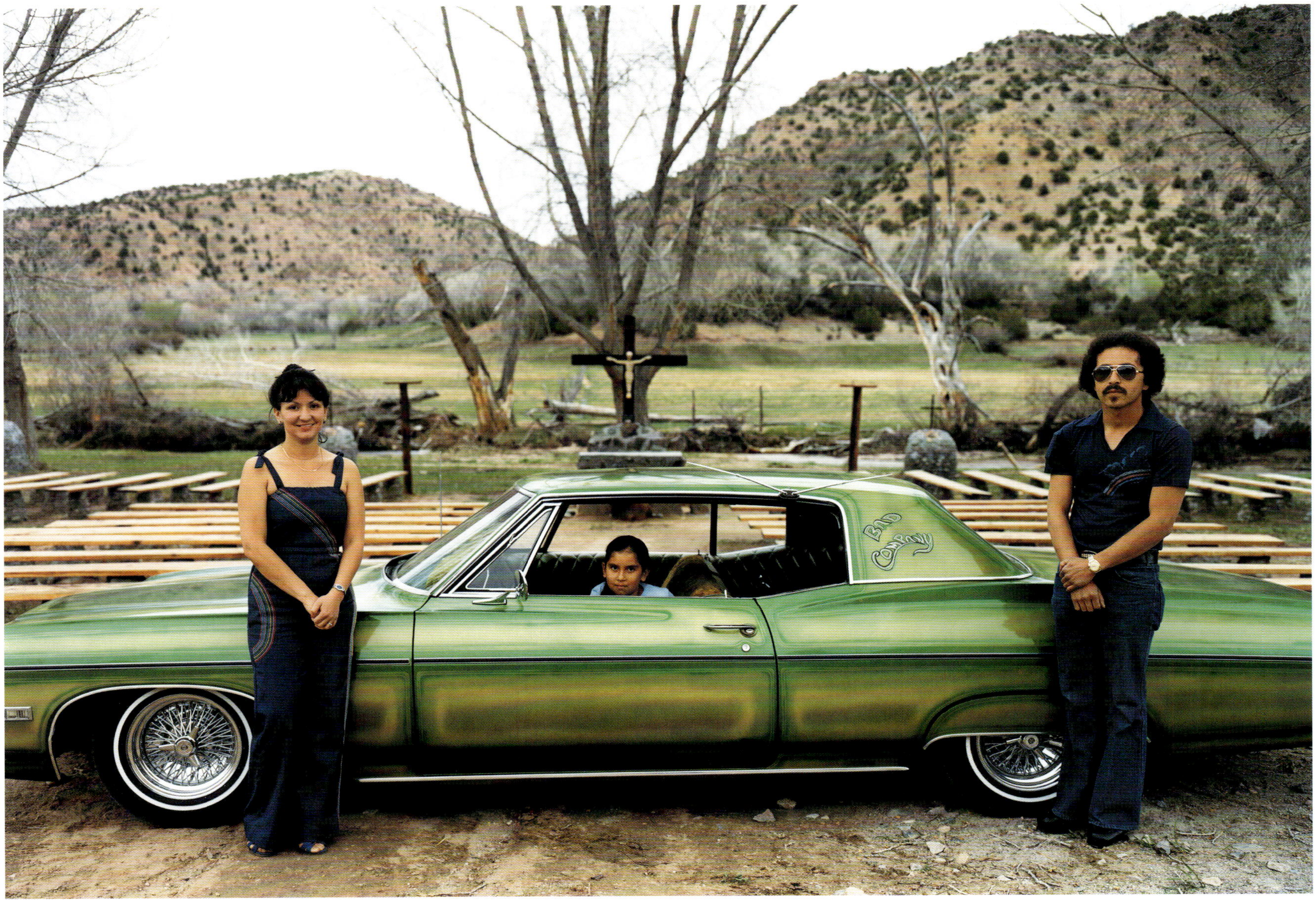

71. Meridel Rubenstein, *The Medina Family, Bad Company, '68 Chevy Impala*, Chimayó, 1992

72. Bob Eckert, *Benny Vigil's 1972 Buick Riviera with Mural in Rear Window*, 2015

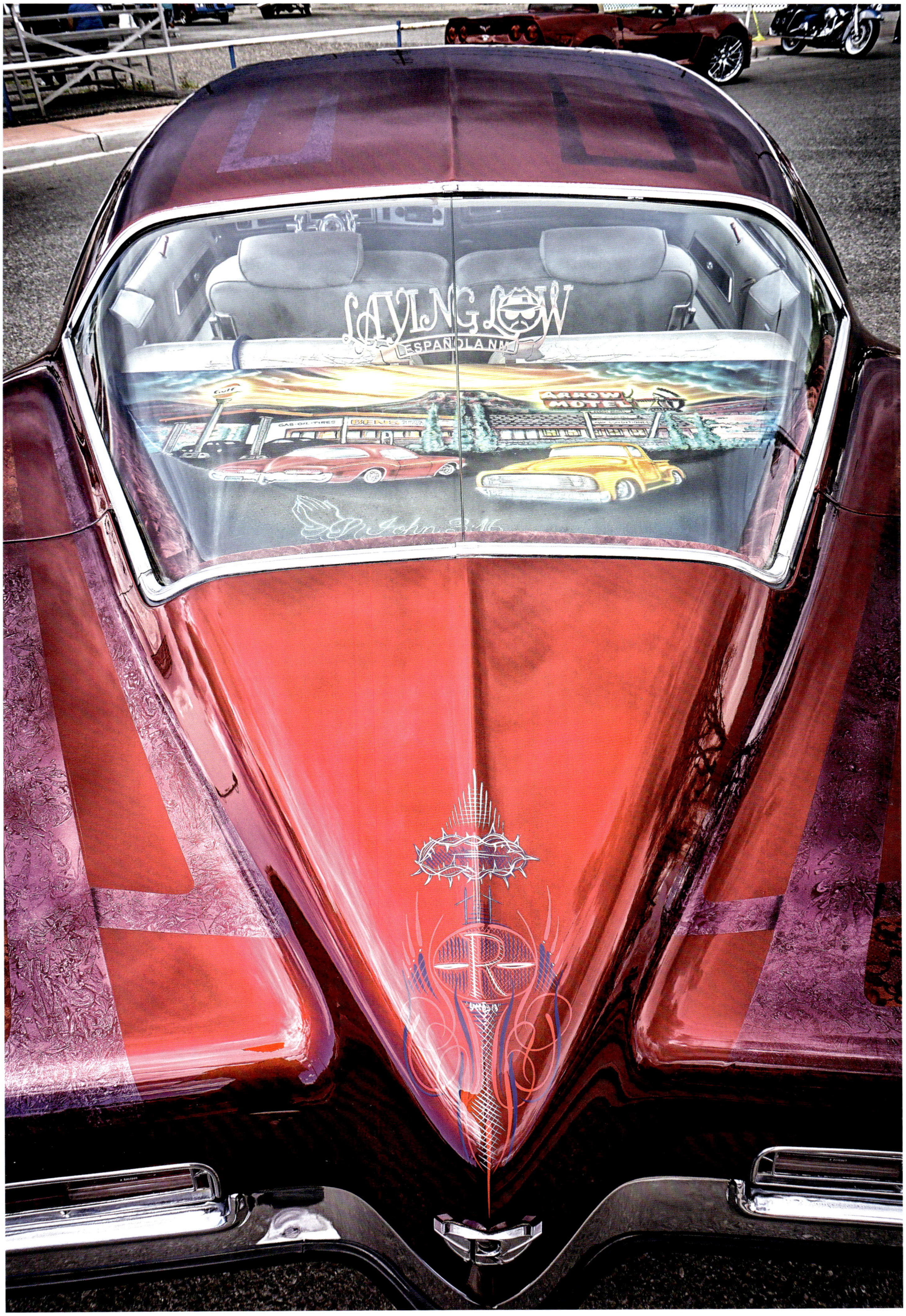
LAYING LOW
ESPAÑOLA NM
ARROW MOTEL

73. Corey Ringo, *The Calm Before the Storm*, 2010

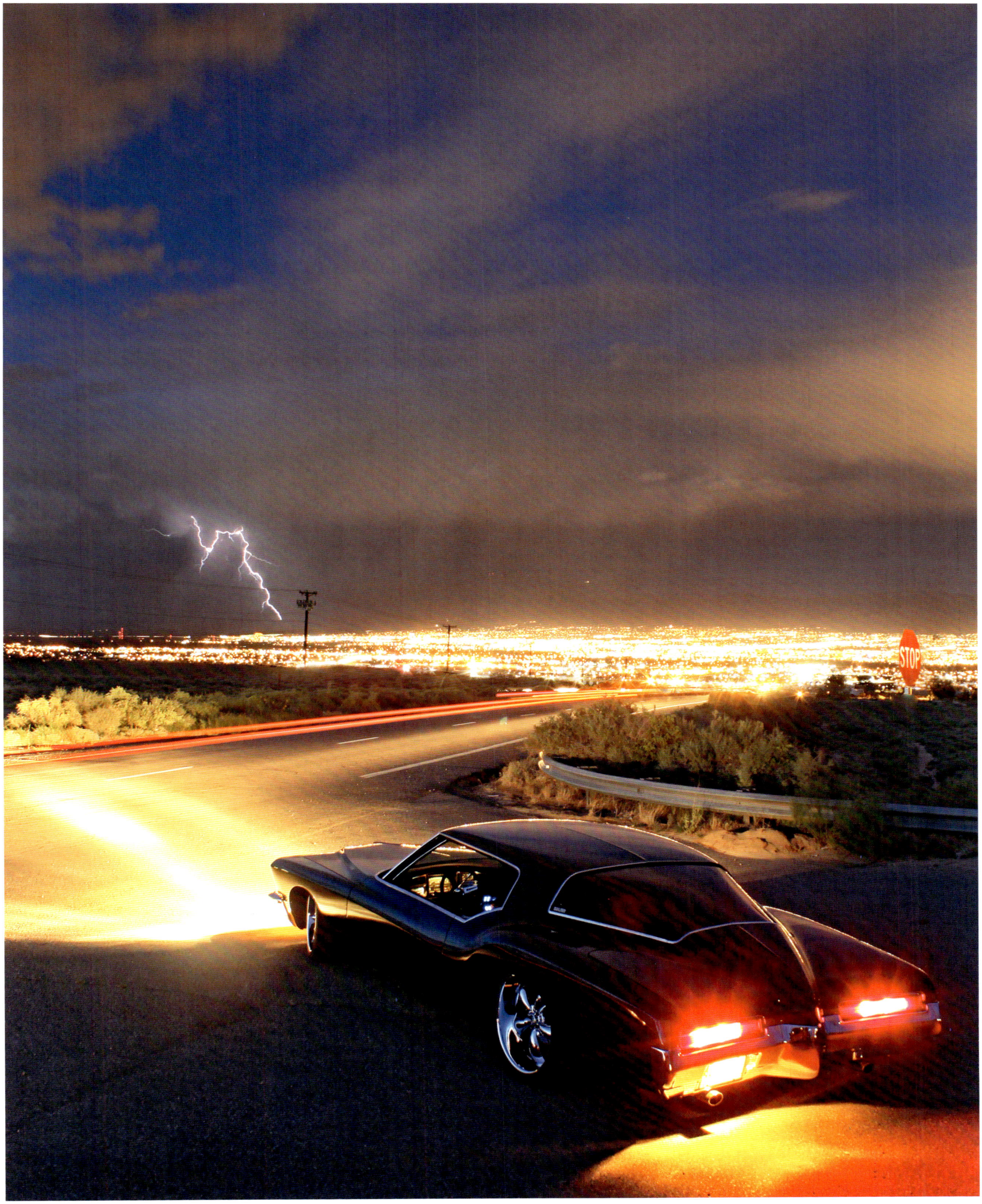
STOP

acknowledgments

It has been quite an experience spending time over the past few years with lowrider aficionados in northern New Mexico. Each one has opened up to share the passionate enthusiasm that is part and parcel of the art and craft of lowriding. I have had the opportunity to visit with lowriders in garages and homes, on the streets and at car shows, with remarkable individuals. They shared their stories and their rides generously, patiently bringing me "down to speed" with the jargon and technology of the lowrider world. This incredible cruise inspired in me a deep appreciation for the many facets of this distinctively New Mexican phenomenon. *Mil gracias* to Bobby Chacón and Pam Jaramillo, and their children Angel, Heaven, and Bobbie; Elmo Sánchez; Vince Trujillo; Eppie Martínez and his dad, Ray; Chris Martínez; Carmelito Martínez, his son Ricky, and his daughter Genevieve and her children Floyd and Vanessa; Fred Rael; David Vigil and his friend Ramón Esquibel; Robert Ortega; Pete Vigil; Johnny Martínez and his son, Johnny; Orlando Martínez Jr.; Ernie López; Leroy Martínez; John González and his wife; Mike Roybal; Andrés Valdez; Jeff Brock; Julian Quintana; Albert "Sonnie" Jaramillo; Robert Vanderslice; Travis Ruiz; Charles "Chuck" Montoya; and Sean Daly. I thank each and every one of these fine people—and others I may have forgotten to mention here—for the time they shared with me.

—Don J. Usner

In our accelerated, globalized, homogenized, and interconnected world, the lowrider is the one to know. Because lowriding is about a unique vision tied to family and place and culture. It's about the deferred gratification of creating a masterpiece that requires time and dedication and is never truly finished. It's about getting off life's merry-go-round and taking things low and slow for a change. Gracias and gratitude to my interview subject Meridel Rubenstein and to all the wonderful artists and mechanics who helped us with *Con Cariño: Artists Inspired by Lowriders.*

—Katherine Ware

My role as photo curator at the New Mexico History Museum has provided me with many interesting visual challenges. Nothing, however, quite prepared me for the experience of working on the *Lowriders, Hoppers, and Hot Rods* exhibit. In the course of putting together the book and exhibit on lowriders, my travels took me around northern New Mexico. I discovered at each stop yet another twist or unique expression for creating a distinctive ride. And the people creating these rolling works of art are the most passionate of artists. I thank the photographers who have documented this unique form of artistic expression and who share this passion for lowriders in New Mexico.

—Daniel Kosharek

about this book

¡Órale! Lowrider: Custom Made in New Mexico is a companion to two lowrider-themed exhibitions organized by the New Mexico History Museum and the New Mexico Museum of Art (Santa Fe, New Mexico) that launched in spring 2016. The book includes photography selected by curatorial staff from both museums' permanent collections in addition to new photography.

about the exhibitions

Lowriders, Hoppers, and Hot Rods: Car Culture of Northern New Mexico
Daniel Kosharek, Photo Curator, Palace of the Governors
New Mexico History Museum
May 1, 2016, to March 5, 2017

¡Orale! Take a ride into the creative reimaginings of American steel as captured in photographs, hubcaps, hood ornaments, car show banners, and, yes, actual cars. This exhibit focuses on mobile works of art and their makers—homegrown Nuevomexicanos who customize, detail, paint, and upholster these favorite symbols of Hispano culture.

Con Cariño: Artists Inspired by Lowriders
Katharine Ware, Curator of Photography
New Mexico Museum of Art
May 20, 2016, to October 10, 2016

It takes a special vision and a lot of hard work to transform an abandoned car into a one-of-a-kind sculpture on wheels, but that's exactly what makes New Mexico's lowriders so special. Though they are works of art in their own right, lowriders have also inspired artists working in other mediums. Responding to this unique cultural icon in photographs, paintings, sculptures, and videos, the artists in this exhibition explore issues of family, gender, religion, and status.

This book is made possible in part by a contribution from the McCune Charitable Foundation.

Director: Anna Gallegos
Editorial director: Lisa Pacheco
Art director and book designer: David Skolkin
Composition: Set in ITC New Baskervile and Eurostile
Manufactured in China
10 9 8 7 6 5 4 3 2 1

"Wheels" by Levi Romero originally appeared in his poetry collection *In the Gathering of Silence* (West End Press 1996). Reprinted courtesy the author.

Library of Congress Cataloging-in-Publication Data
Names: Usner, Donald J., writer of added commentary | Ware, Katherine, 1960- interviewer (expression) | Kosharek, Daniel, editor.
Title: ¡Órale! lowrider : custom made in New Mexico / essay by Don J. Usner ; interview by Katherine Ware ; photography selections by Daniel Kosharek and Katherine Ware.
Description: Santa Fe : Museum of New Mexico Press, 2016. | In English.
Identifiers: LCCN 2016017270 | ISBN 9780890136171 (hardcover : alk. paper)
Subjects: LCSH: Lowriders–New Mexico–Exhibitions. | Automobiles–Decoration–New Mexico–Exhibitions. | Automobile drivers–New Mexico–Interviews–Exhibitions.
Classification: LCC TL24.N6 O73 2016 | DDC 629.222–dc23 LC record available at https://lccn.loc.gov/2016017270

ISBN 978-0-89013-617-1 hardcover

Museum of New Mexico Press
PO Box 2087
Santa Fe, New Mexico 87504
mnmpress.org

Cover: Alex Harris, *Las Vegas, New Mexico, Looking East from Myles Sweeney's 1960 Chevrolet Impala,* 1987

Page 2: Dottie Lopez, *Precision,* 2014

Page 4: Meridel Rubenstein, *Los Unidos Car Club (burned negative),* Española, 1980

Pages 6–7: Jack Parsons, *Rim, Tire, and Pin-Striping Detail, Lowrider Car Show,* Las Vegas, New Mexico, 1993

Pages 38–39: Jack Parsons, *Rim Detail, 1978 Chevrolet Monte Carlo, Owner Annette Gonzales,* Española, 1996